# Against the Current

# AGAINST THE CURRENT

## How Albert Schweitzer
## Inspired a Young Man's Journey

Clarinda Higgins
with
William G. Armstrong Jr.

Westport, Connecticut

AGAINST THE CURRENT
How Albert Schweitzer Inspired a Young Man's Journey

ISBN-10: 069229953X
ISBN-13: 978-0692299531

Oakham Press
Westport, Connecticut

*Printed in the United States of America*
*Second printing December 2014*

*Printed by CreateSpace, an Amazon Company*

**For more information visit:**

**www.oakhampress-againstthecurrent.com**

# CONTENTS

*Slowly we crept upstream, laboriously feeling - it was the dry season - for the channels between the sandbanks. Lost in thought I sat on the deck of the barge, struggling to find the elementary and universal conception of the ethical which I had not discovered in any philosophy.*

*Sheet after sheet I covered with disconnected sentences, merely to keep myself concentrated on the problem. Late on the third day, at the very moment when, at sunset, we were making our way through a herd of hippopotamuses, there flashed upon my mind, unforeseen and unsought, the phrase, "Reverence for Life."*

Albert Schweitzer, 1915
Lambaréné, Gabon

*In recent months, I have been witness to many circumstances which have pointed out to me my own personal debt of gratitude, and I have become newly aware of another blessing: the chance to help,*

Mark Higgins, 1959
Lambaréné, Gabon

# Foreword

*SERVICE. Let this word accompany each of you throughout your life. Let it be before you as you seek your way and your duty in the world. May it be recalled to your minds if ever you are tempted to forget it or set it aside. It will not always be a comfortable companion but it will always be a faithful one. And it will be able to lead you to happiness, no matter what the experiences of your lives are. Never have this word on your lips, but keep it in your hearts. And may it be a confidant that will teach you not only to do good but to do it simply and humbly.*

*- Albert Schweitzer*

Albert Schweitzer was one of the most admired men of the Twentieth century. As a young scholar in Europe, he earned acclaim for his achievements in music, philosophy and theology. He set aside those careers to embark on a new profession as a medical missionary in Gabon, Africa. There, one hundred years ago, he developed an ethical credo called "Reverence for Life" that governed all of his subsequent actions and inspired the world. For that and for his humanitarian work, Schweitzer was awarded the Nobel Peace Prize in 1952.

Albert Schweitzer believed not only that reverence for life is the foundation of all true ethics but also that a life dedicated to experiencing and expressing that reverence in tangible ways is the source of the greatest human fulfillment and the basis for the better world for which we all long. Schweitzer summarized it by proclaiming, "My life is my argument."

Over five decades of work in Africa, as Clarinda Higgins shows in this book, Schweitzer attracted to his cause many supporters and medical personnel from around the world. His staff consisted of talented individuals willing to devote a year or two for the cause of better health among an underserved population.

One of the remarkable people Schweitzer accepted for employment at his hospital was Mark Higgins, a selfless young adult from Massachusetts who sought to make the world a better place. At age 18, Mark Higgins stepped into a demanding world of hospital maintenance and patient care amidst the heat and humidity of the equatorial jungle. Taking to heart Schweitzer's inspiring words about service, he accepted more assignments and ultimately went forth with a team of cardiologists deep into the jungles of Gabon, helping to discover the underlying causes of native heart disease and identifying solutions that extended and saved the lives of countless Africans, one patient and one gesture at a time. How he advanced in his work, how he grew as a result of his labors, and the inspiration his life gave to others, is the essence of this story.

Albert Schweitzer still inspires the journeys of young people across the world. Mark Higgins' spirit of good work foreshadows a story repeated over and over again today in the United States and Gabon by young people who are proud to call themselves Albert Schweitzer Fellows.

On a visit to the United States in 1940, Helene Bresslau Schweitzer, the wife of Albert Schweitzer, helped organize the Albert Schweitzer Fellowship (ASF) program. At that time, its purpose was to provide assistance and financial support to the jungle hospital that she and her husband had created. The work of the Albert Schweitzer Hospital and the Albert Schweitzer Fellowship continues to the present day.

The Fellowship goals are three-fold: Improving Health, Developing Leaders and Creating Change.

Each year ASF identifies and funds candidates from graduate schools who create programs that benefit sectors of their own communities as well as at the Schweitzer Hospital in Lambaréné, Gabon. Through mentored direct service and a multidisciplinary leadership development program, ASF builds community capacity and trains a professional workforce that is:

- skilled in addressing the underlying causes of health inequities,
- committed to improving the health outcomes of underserved communities and
- prepared for a life of continued service.

Albert Schweitzer's philosophy of reverence for life and his dedication to addressing the health needs of the underserved continue inspiring people across the globe. His work and philosophy is especially appealing to idealist young people who see that his legacy offers guidance on how to lead a fulfilled life through service to others.

Since 1991, more than 3,000 Schweitzer Fellows have delivered nearly 500,000 hours of service to nearly 300,000 people in need. Additionally, more than 150 Fellows have provided care at the 100-year-old hospital in Gabon.

During the Fellowship Year, their projects address the health and wellbeing needs of vulnerable people. Activities are directed towards intervention and prevention ranging from screening programs for acute health issues to mentoring programs for at-risk children. In the process of developing these projects, Fellows gain valuable experience and tools to help them learn how to work more effectively with communities to improve the health status of underserved people.

After completing their work, Fellows are welcomed into an elite network of alumni and become Fellows for Life. Our Fellows go on to lead in a variety of important and impactful ways; Fellows for Life are running city public health departments, running programs addressing health care for people experiencing homelessness, as well as filling gaps by creating new nonprofit organizations to address health inequities.

Because of the Fellows' devoted work and the commitment of generous benefactors, the Fellowship continues to grow to improve the health of vulnerable people now and for the future by developing this corps of Leaders in Service: professionals skilled in creating positive change with and in our communities, our health and human service systems, and our world.

As our organization prepares to celebrate 75 years of service, we invite support for the Schweitzer Fellowship program, and we honor the commitments made by our Fellows. They are the diamonds who make our Diamond Anniversary possible.

Sylvia Stevens-Edouard, MS
Executive Director
The Albert Schweitzer Fellowship
Boston, Massachusetts

Information about
The Albert Schweitzer Fellowship
may be found at
www.schweitzerfellowship.org

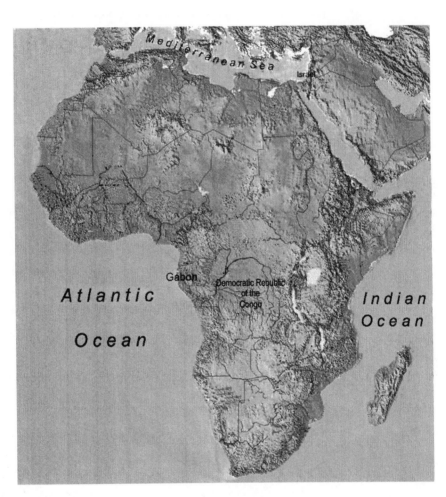

Mediterranean Sea

Israel

Gabon

Democratic Rebublic of the Congo

Atlantic

Ocean

Indian
Ocean

**AFRICA 1960**

One

# Welcome to Africa

On Wednesday afternoon, May 27, 1959, a 21-passenger Air France DC-3 Dakota makes a low pass over the famous hospital. It's something the pilots do as a favor for those who are beginning an assignment there. On this day, they bank the plane so their young American passenger can get a good look at the surroundings. In a few minutes they bring the plane down onto a small grass airstrip in Lambaréné, in the territory of Gabon, in the colony of French Equatorial Africa.

Mark Higgins, 18 years old, his lanky six-foot-five-inch frame cramped into a window seat, finds it hard to believe that the pilots have actually put the plane down here. After bouncing through cloudy mid-day turbulence and skimming over the treetops, they have found this landing site which is little more than a clearing in the jungle.

When the plane rolls to a stop, the co-pilot walks aft and cranks open a door on the left side of the aircraft, and a folding stairway deploys. Mark Higgins lowers his head slightly as he stands up in the cabin and walks to the rear luggage compartment. He retrieves his duffle bag and bounds down the four steps onto African soil.

Stepping away from the aircraft, he finds a staff member from the Albert Schweitzer Hospital reaching for his hand and then directing him into a waiting Land Rover. In a minute they are rumbling along a bumpy red dirt trail toward the Ogoué River.

At the river's edge, four natives, some of them missing fingers and bearing other disfigurements, greet Mark with a friendly smile. They load his duffle bag and rucksack into a 20-foot dugout canoe and tell him to sit in the middle. Shoving off, they keep the pirogue close to the shoreline and away from the swift current in the middle of the river. They row in unison, intoning a rhythmic chant.

Forty-five minutes later the pirogue rounds a bend and passes an island. There, the natives' incantation becomes louder and the tempo of their deep-throated chanting changes. This is their signal to the shore. Mark hears a distant bell chime. The narrow flat-bottom boat turns in the river, crosses to the opposite side and floats downstream before heading into a sandy semi-circle landing area where other pirogues have tied up.

Standing on the beach is a tall, slightly stooped-over 84-year-old man wearing a white pith helmet, white smock, black bow tie, white slacks and black shoes. It is Albert Schweitzer himself, the third most-admired man in the world, *le grand docteur*, the man Mark has come to work for.

As is his custom, Schweitzer personally greets the new arrival to his jungle clinic, asks a few questions, and then begins a quick orientation. Walking up the embankment and addressing Mark in French, his first instruction is to take a few days and observe the work of the clinic. It is important to understand the culture and the proscribed way of doing things.

Within a few minutes, Mark meets three women who are the de-facto gate-keepers and administrative managers of the hospital. Ali Silver of The Netherlands serves as Schweitzer's most trusted secretary and has been with him since 1947. Humorless, pale and loyal, Nurse Ali speaks English, and is Schweitzer's right hand in managing the place. Mathilde Kottman, a tall and stern German devotee has assisted Schweitzer with his correspondence since 1925. Mark has been warned that these two form the protective cocoon around Schweitzer and enforce the rules. There is also Hannah Obermann, the widow of a Dutch pastor publicly executed by the Nazis, who has been working with Schweitzer since 1948.

The taciturn Ali Silver duly records his arrival in the hospital's meticulously hand-written logbook. All important events are annotated here: comings and goings and places of origins of invited guests and staff, births, baptisms, marriages and deaths. Mark gives his address as 100 Barber Avenue, Worcester, Massachusetts, which is simultaneously the corporate office of Worcester Pressed Steel, the Higgins Armory Museum and the United World Federalists of New England.

Following a brief orientation covering the rules and expectations of an employee, Nurse Ali hands Mark a symbol of his permanence on the staff: a white safari-type helmet. This does not protect against falling coconuts, as a visitor once suspected, but prevents sunstroke, a much worse affliction in the equatorial heat. Schweitzer insists that all of his people wear them because he doesn't want to treat his staff as patients.

Schweitzer and Ali show Mark where he will live: the center room of a five-place wooden barracks-type building. At one end is a Dutch door, and at the other end is a latticework-and-wire-mesh window with curtains for

*Albert Schweitzer, standing to the right of the tree, greets an arriving pirogue as the business of his clinic continues around him.*

privacy. The room has a bed, a writing table and a few shelves. There is no electricity and no fresh water. There is a bucket for night waste, and two kerosene lamps, one for reading and one for carrying across the compound in darkness. A lock on the door is supposed to deter curious natives. Two other such buildings house the staff a short walk from the dining hall. Patients and their families live in longhouse huts fanning out from the center of the complex.

Mark's first impressions echo those of every other new arrival: this is clearly not a hospital in the Western sense of the word. Animals and their droppings are everywhere. Goats, sheep, wild pigs, chickens, ducks and pigeons roam about freely. Inside pens are red baby bongo antelopes with white stripes down their sides.

The smell of the lush vegetation is breathtaking: trees, ferns and papyrus. The jungle is alive with the sounds of insects. There are brightly colored birds: a blue fish catcher with a huge red bill; yellow birds, black and white birds, African red parrots, toucans and gorgeous butterflies. Some of the animals Mark sees are pets, such as a chimpanzee named Ooka and the pelican Parsifal, whom Schweitzer named after the Richard Wagner opera.

The old man has single-handedly put Lambaréné on the map. That the hospital exists at all is due entirely to his labors. Starting almost half a century earlier, he built or supervised construction of every structure on the island. It now comprises 72 buildings grouped around a central core: an operating theatre, an X-ray room, laboratory, dental clinic, delivery room, doctors' offices, and a pharmacy where drugs are issued and injections given and where, in the case of accidents, first aid is administered. Here doctors perform nearly 500 operations each year, ranging from hernias to urological, gynecological, abdominal, cardiologic and orthopedic surgeries. They deliver a baby almost every day, and treat a huge number of walk-in patients.

Most patients arrive at the clinic with their families, who serve as a built-in support structure. The doctor asks everyone if they can pay. Most cannot, but Schweitzer expects them to perform some physical work in return for the care their family member will receive. The patients live in areas according to their tribes of origin in order to minimize old rivalries between them, each having its own longhouse, essentially a village away from home.

Here they cook their own food and attend to their ailing family member.

The workday routine is firmly established. Operations are scheduled on Tuesday, Thursday and Saturday mornings. A noisy gasoline-fueled generator provides electricity to the surgical suite (donated by Prince Rainier of Monaco). It's the only place in the whole complex where power is available.

Monday, Wednesday and Friday are clinic days. Patients, some of whom have walked or paddled several hundred miles, line up outside of *la grande pharmacie* and await their turn to be examined. They carry a variety of tropical diseases such as malaria, filariasis and intestinal worms. Tuberculosis and venereal disease are common. They come for the treatment of a hernia, a skin infection, bacterial pneumonia, an enlarged liver or fluid on the lungs. Although Schweitzer no longer practices medicine himself, he occupies a desk in the center of *la pharmacie* on those days working on his correspondence and remaining available for consultation if any of his doctors have a question. He appears completely undisturbed by the noises all around him.

Sunday is a day of rest, and a time that Schweitzer keeps free to serve as the minister for his flock. He conducts an outdoor church service, reads a lesson from the Bible, delivers a carefully written sermon, and plays hymns for all those who assemble.

Lavatory facilities are basic. Africans go in the bush when they have to go. Two outhouses uphill from the garden, one for males, one for females, serve as the comfort stations for the European staff, except at night when chamber pots serve the purpose in each person's room. Mark is told that it is too dangerous to walk to the outhouse in the dark. He finds that Schweitzer economizes by re-using everything possible: the thin pages from the international edition of the *Reader's Digest* become toilet tissue.

Natives bathe in the river, and of course come down with all manner of waterborne infections. Staff members use a rainwater-filled shower just outside the main dining room. Mark's boyhood summers at Camp Pasquaney back in New Hampshire prepared him for such primitive trappings, and nobody hears a complaint. He is startled to see a small burial ground where a simple cross marks the final resting place for Helene Breslau Schweitzer, the doctor's wife, who died in Zurich two years ago. Schweitzer brought her ashes to Lambaréné.

Mark resolves to learn this operation from the bottom up. Without medical training, of course, he expects that much of his work will involve physical labor. Whatever he can learn along the way by associating with Albert Schweitzer and working among the natives will simply be an incredible bonus.

*One of Mark's first assignments is to hack away the overgrowth with his machete to create a new path to the leper village.*

Earlier in the spring, Schweitzer had directed a small group of leprosy patients and their families to start cutting a new trail half a mile through the jungle up to the leper village. This involves not just using a machete to cut away the overgrowth, but sometimes removing tall trees along the proposed path. Obviously, having lepers do this work with their crippled or missing limbs has slowed things down, but Schweitzer believes that patients and their families should be involved in maintaining their own village.

Schweitzer assigns Mark to a labor party working alongside those natives. Even some of the doctors have begun their orientation doing menial work. One of his team's first tasks is to hack away with a machete at the encroaching jungle growth that always threatens to choke the paths within the compound. Not only does Schweitzer physically resemble Samuel Clemens, Mark thinks, but he also seems to have a touch of the Tom Sawyer magic in him: everyone seems willing to pitch in to keep the clinic running smoothly.

Another of Mark's first jobs, using the same tool, is helping prepare the garden for a new growing season. Gabon will be dry during June and July. The growing season will begin in August and will continue for 10 months. The novelty of all of these experiences compels Mark to share what he has learned, and of course to tell his family of his safe arrival. In one of his first letters home, Mark describes his work: "This area, which is cleared every dry season for a garden, has grown about 12 feet high, and so thick that it took 12 men with machetes three and a half days of hard labor to level it, leaving for labor all stumps and roots." The 15-acre riverside garden, the source of all the vegetables that feeds the staff, volunteers and patients, will soon be filled with eggplants, beans, peppers, tomatoes, carrots, beets, lettuce, cabbage, turnips and kohlrabi.

Despite being 6,000 miles away, Mark holds his family in his thoughts and informs them about what he is doing. On one of his first days at the Schweitzer clinic, Mark writes a short letter to his nine-year-old cousin, describing to her an amazing scene. He has gone out to tend the garden and finds a hippopotamus standing there munching vegetables. "Imagine that!" he writes. What Mark doesn't know is that hippos are vegetarians; of course they love wallowing in the garden. A hippopotamus when threatened can be extremely dangerous. Male hippos actively defend their turf, which runs along the banks of the rivers and lakes.

Humans tend to get killed by hippos when they stand on a riverbank that a male hippo considers to be his territory. Females get extremely aggressive if they sense anyone coming near their young, who stay in the water while she feeds on the shore. Full-grown, these three-ton creatures can run at speeds up to 18 miles an hour and have enormous jaws which can squeeze the life out of smaller animals. Mark has a lot to learn about Africa.

In the most literal sense, he has his work cut out for him in this new life.

He is starting at the bottom, doing hard physical work in the intense tropical heat and humidity, 35 miles south of the equator. He is a long way from
prep school, from his life of privilege in Massachusetts, from the expectations of his family and from all of his troubles. He has brought his secrets
with him, but they are safe.

At long last, he is exactly where he wants to be.

# Two
# Le Grand Docteur

At the time Mark Higgins arrives in Africa to begin working for him, Schweitzer is one of the best known figures of the age. The Gallup public opinion poll throughout the 1950s has consistently ranked him among the top five most admired men in the world. The tall, broad-shouldered, darkly handsome, witty and charismatic character is already a Nobel Peace Prize laureate, a theologian, a musician and a humanitarian.

He is a Renaissance man. He wrote a provocative interpretation of the New Testament. He is a gifted organist and expert on the works of Johan Sebastian Bach; a best-selling author and philosopher, and a peace activist. Above all else, he is known as a medical missionary.

Nevertheless, Schweitzer has critics. Some people consider him a well-meaning but stubborn and patronizing old European bent on enlightening the Dark Continent and proselytizing through medicine. His paternalistic attitude toward the black people he serves leaves some people confused. "The African is my brother," Schweitzer once conceded, "but he is my younger brother by several centuries." Most people, however, view Schweitzer as a man whose work with men, women and children suffering from leprosy, malaria, elephantiasis, whooping cough, venereal disease, tropical dysentery; swamp fever; sleeping sickness; heart complaints; over-use of tobacco; strangulated hernias, many kinds of skin sores and other vile illnesses elevates him to something close to sainthood.

Over the months before arriving in Africa, Mark had been reading about why people thought the old man was so remarkable.

Schweitzer was raised along the Franco-German border in the Alsatian village of Gunsbach in the Muenster Valley. Because his father and grandfather were Lutheran pastors, music and theology were early interests and influences. When Schweitzer was five, his father gave him piano lessons; by eight he was playing the organ in his father's church. Schweitzer later studied music in France under notable tutors.

Schweitzer earned his diploma at Strasbourg, one of the leading universities in Europe. Besides being the political, economic, and cultural capital, Strasbourg was the largest city in Alsace.

He had a brilliant career as student, teacher and administrator in the fields of theology and philosophy. He earned his doctorate with a thesis on the religious philosophy of Immanuel Kant, the 18th century German scholar viewed as a central figure of modern philosophy. Schweitzer also studied the German philosopher and composer Friedrich Nietzsche and the Russian writer Leo Tolstoy, whose doctrine of love and compassion attracted him.

Having earned an advanced degree in theology from the University of Strasbourg, in 1901 he wrote his first religious book, *The Mystery of the Kingdom of God*. Schweitzer conducted major research on the life of Johann Sebastian Bach. His 1905 biography of Bach became an immediate success. In 1906 Schweitzer wrote *The Art of Organ-Building and Organ-Playing in Germany and France* in order to preserve the heritage of classical craftsmanship of the organ. He co-edited a five-volume series titled *Bach: Complete Organ Works*.

The definitive influence on Schweitzer, however, was the life of Jesus, to whose message he devoted years of research and reflection. His classic work *The Quest of the Historical Jesus* dealt with major scholarly writings on Jesus from the 17th century onward. Schweitzer argued that the life, words, and actions of Jesus were based on an expectation that He believed the end of world was near. Jesus willingly accepted His crucifixion, Schweitzer postulated, in the belief that the Kingdom of God would come soon after His death. That controversial and unconventional re-interpretation provoked debate among New Testament scholars and established Schweitzer as an eminent Christian scholar.

In 1904 Schweitzer read a pamphlet issued by the Paris Mission Society describing the need for Protestant missionaries in French Equatorial Africa. He experienced a "revelation" that at some point he would have to renounce his easy success and devote himself to the betterment of humankind. He took to heart the injunction in the Gospel of Saint Luke: "For unto whomsoever much is given, of him shall be much required." He wrote to the Society offering his services, but the search committee was not ready to accept his offer because they believed his theology to be "incorrect." He wanted to serve anyway, and decided to fulfill their need for a doctor at the mission.

At age thirty, near the height of his fame as a scholar, musician, theologian, and philosopher, he stunned his family and friends by enrolling in medical school with the intention of becoming a medical missionary in Africa. Seven years later, he graduated with a specialization in tropical medicine and surgery.

In 1913 a year after marrying his college sweetheart Helene Breslau, a nurse, Schweitzer journeyed to Gabon. There, after numerous setbacks, together they founded a hospital at Lambaréné "at the edge of the primeval forest." He hired a native assistant named Joseph who would remain with him for decades. Schweitzer was the architect, builder, director and chief medical doctor. Funds were scarce and equipment primitive, but native Africans in need of medical care thronged to the site.

He constructed an open-air patient dormitory and established one basic rule: patients who wanted to see the doctor had to bring their own food and the means to cook it.

Climatologically, the damp, low-lying ground along the Ogoué River is well-suited for growing coffee, cinnamon, vanilla and cocoa. But the product that most interested Europeans was timber: the forests that cover nearly 80 percent of Gabon contain more than 400 species of trees. Okoumé, the most valuable, was introduced to the international market in 1913 and found to make excellent plywood. There are also hardwoods such as mahogany, ebony, African walnut, Nigerian satinwood and zebrawood. Along the rivers, workers fell huge trees and drag them into the water where they float downstream to Port Gentil. The denseness of the jungle and the soft terrain preclude building roads or railroads, so extraction of felled timber takes place only near waterways, where the cut trees are floated down-stream. Cutting timber, of course, was dangerous work which resulted in many injuries requiring a doctor's services.

At Lambaréné, Schweitzer the philosopher ruminated over the value and meaning of existence. The most important moment in his life occurred in 1915, while he was on a barge on the Ogoué River:

> For months on end, I lived in a continual state of mental agitation. Without the least success I concentrated - even during my daily work at the hospital - on the real nature of the affirmation of life and of ethics, and on the question of what they have in common. I was wandering about in a thicket where no path was to be found. I was pushing against an iron door that would not yield.
>
> In that mental state, I had to take a long journey up the river . . . Lost in thought, I sat on deck of the barge, struggling to find the elementary and universal concept of the ethical that I had not discovered in any philosophy. I covered sheet after sheet with disconnected sentences merely to concentrate on the problem. Two days passed. Late on the third day, at the very moment when, at sunset, we were making our way through a herd of hippopotamuses, there flashed upon my mind, unforeseen and unsought, the phrase: "Reverence for Life."
>
> The iron door had yielded. The path in the thicket had become visible.

This great phrase became the basic tenet of an ethical philosophy which Schweitzer developed and put into practice. He expressed it in numerous books and publications, and applied it at his hospital in Lambaréné.

The First World War broke out a year after the Schweitzers went to Africa. As German citizens living in a French colony, Albert and Helene were arrested as enemy aliens, and sent to France as prisoners of war. When the war ended in 1918, they were set free. Their first and only child, Rhena, was born on his birthday in 1919, and they remained in Europe raising money to continue his work in Africa.

Schweitzer returned to Lambaréné in 1924 and rebuilt the hospital in a nearby location. He began writing again and in the years ahead published several memoirs of his life and activities in Africa, including *On the Edge of the Primeval Forest, More From the Primeval Forest, From My African Notebook*, and *The Story of My Pelican*.

Unfortunately, Helene's fragile health did not permit sustained exposure to the damp tropical climate of Africa. She stayed in Europe raising their daughter, whom Schweitzer would seldom see over the next three decades.

*Albert Schweitzer at his jungle clinic.*

His wife was in Europe in 1939 when the Second World War started. When Rhena married a French organ maker, Helene joined the couple in Paris. The three of them remained there during an uncertain, agonizing and difficult period. In 1941 she journeyed to Africa to remain with her husband through the war.

By the 1940s Schweitzer was a well-known figure. His lectures, organ playing and theological writings had made him famous in Europe even before his first mission to Africa. His reputation had only grown. He and Helene spent all of the Second World War in Gabon, often under house arrest. In 1947 *Life* magazine called Albert Schweitzer, "the greatest man in the world." Two years later, *Time Magazine* called him "one of the most extraordinary men of modern times." When in September of 1948 he returned to Europe, he met his four grandchildren for the first time. By then he was 73 years old.

Schweitzer made his only visit to the United States in 1949 to speak at an event in Aspen, Colorado, commemorating the bicentennial of the birth of the German philosopher Johann Wolfgang von Goethe. He invested his $6,100 honorarium in the leprosy clinic at Lambaréné. Schweitzer was acclaimed everywhere he went and spoke at dinners and assemblies in every city where he appeared. His travels took him by train from New York to Denver, and then to Chicago, where he received an honorary degree; to Cleveland, where he visited the Cleveland Museum of Art, and to New York, where he met representatives of pharmaceutical companies. In between meetings, he found time to inspect and play church organs in some of those cities.

He went to Boston for three days. At a press conference at the Unitarian Universalist Church on Beacon Street he was asked what impressed him most about his visit to America.

*The buildings are a little higher and the streets are a little longer, but the people are the same. My principle impression is of the very great kindness of the American people and the fact that my philosophy of reverence for life has spread among so many people as it has in this country.*

He sailed back to Lambaréné that fall where he would remain for a year and a half while Helene stayed at home in France.

The Nobel Foundation in Norway awarded the 1952 Nobel Peace Prize to Schweitzer for his selfless humanitarian efforts, and for his writings and teachings on Reverence for Life. He used the $33,000 cash award to construct a whole new village for his leprosy patients.

After seeing the destructive power of the atomic bombs that ended the Second World War, Schweitzer worried about the proliferation of such weapons. He addressed these concerns when he traveled to Europe in 1954 to deliver his Nobel acceptance speech, "The Problem of Peace in the World Today":

*In the course of the last two wars, we have been guilty of acts of inhumanity which make one shudder, and in any future war we would certainly be guilty of even worse. This must not happen! We are becoming inhuman to the extent that we become supermen. We have learned to tolerate the facts of war: that men are killed en masse -- some twenty million in the Second World War -- that whole cities and their inhabitants are annihilated by the atomic bomb, that men are turned into living torches by incendiary bombs. We learn of these things from the radio or newspapers and we judge them according to whether they signify suc-*

*cess for the group of peoples to which we belong, or for our enemies. When we do admit to ourselves that such acts are the results of inhuman conduct, our admission is accompanied by the thought that the very fact of war itself leaves us no option but to accept them. Whether peace comes or not depends on the direction in which the mentality of individuals develops and then, in turn, on that of their nations.*

Many people believe that Schweitzer's Nobel lecture was one of the best speeches ever given.

In America, Mark Higgins' father had become deeply involved in a movement called the United World Federalists, chaired by Norman Cousins, the prominent editor of *The Saturday Review of Literature*. The World Federalists promoted an ambitious agenda of strengthening the United Nations. Mark's father rose through the ranks to become head of the New England branch of the World Federalist movement and served on the national board of governors. Mark had signed up as a student member.

Cousins, a vigorous opponent of nuclear weapons, formed a subgroup called the National Committee for a Sane Nuclear Policy to advocate the cessation of atmospheric nuclear testing. Needing some high-level endorsements, Cousins visited Lambaréné in 1957. Schweitzer agreed to make a statement about nuclear weapons testing and wrote a series of three speeches to be read over Radio Oslo.

Thus on April 23, 1957, at the height of the Cold War, the first part of Schweitzer's Declaration of Conscience was made public. He called for the renunciation of all atmospheric tests. He explained in layman's terms the harmful medical effects of radiation in the bones and blood of newborns. He referred to the petition signed by 9,235 scientists throughout the world that the Nobel Prize-winning chemist Linus Pauling had presented to the Secretary General of the United Nations. He criticized the concept of "a permissible amount of radiation." He appealed to women to raise their voices against the nuclear tests that cause deformed babies. He cited the Soviet tests in Siberia and the American tests at Bikini Atoll that contaminated the Pacific Ocean and Japan. Humanity was imperiled by these tests, Schweitzer asserted. "Mankind insists that they stop, and has every right to do so."

His second broadcast discussed the danger of nuclear war:

*Those who conduct an atomic war for freedom will die, or end their lives miserably. Instead of freedom they will find destruction. Radioactive clouds resulting from a war between East and West would imperil humanity everywhere.*

*Missiles equipped with H-bombs have radically changed the situation. The United States and the Soviet Union threaten each other from a distance, and there is the danger of their war occurring on European soil. The United States is arming countries, which may use the weapons for defense against the Soviet Union, which in turn might defend itself. These countries include Turkey and key nations in the Middle East, where both the US and USSR seek alliances by giving financial and military aid. Conflicts between these smaller countries could endanger the peace of the world. The technology required and the short time intervals involved mean that war could originate from a mere incident or even an error.*

He criticized American policymakers for pressuring NATO countries to acquire weapons: "The theory of peace through terrifying an opponent by a greater armament can now only heighten the danger of war." He argued in favor of establishing a nuclear-free zone in Europe and insisted "that under no circumstances is Europe to become a battlefield for an atomic war between the Soviet Union and the United States."

In his final broadcast Schweitzer urged international negotiations at the highest level for complete nuclear disarmament with mechanisms for international verification. In his view, the health and very existence of mankind was threatened. He said America should promptly withdraw its military forces from Europe and let the Europeans, as well as Eastern and Western bloc nations, learn to get along with one other. Furthermore, the Soviet Union should also reduce its army and pledge not to attack Germany. "We must rid ourselves of the paralyzing mistrust of our adversaries and approach each other in the spirit that we are human beings, all of us." Schweitzer saw only two choices: either a mad atomic-arms race with the danger of an unavoidable atomic war; or a mutual renunciation of nuclear weapons in the hope that the world can learn to live in peace. Because the first is hopeless, he said, we must risk the second.

It was entirely consistent with his philosophy of reverence for life. The impact of his Declaration elevated Schweitzer to the world stage, and thrust him into a sometimes unwelcome spotlight.

# Three
# Lambaréné

On the afternoon of his first day, Mark sees that the schedule at Lambaréné is governed by the clanging of bells. Schweitzer has established a well-ordered daily routine to manage his little hospital. One gong calls attention to the arrival of a guest in a pirogue, another to the distribution of rice and bananas to patients' families. At seven p.m., Mark hears the bells calling the staff to supper. He lights his kerosene lamp and carries it through the darkness toward the dining room.

A small group of physicians, nurses and other volunteers greets him inside the dining hall. They have come from all over the world for the privilege of working here. Mark is the youngest among them and one of only two Americans.

By custom, no one takes a seat until Schweitzer enters the dining room, where he occupies a chair at the center of the table, flanked as always by Ali Silver and Mathilde Kottman. The rest of the staff sits wherever they find the napkin holder with their name written on it, a piece of political geography mysteriously regulated by someone very close to Schweitzer. The place of honor, directly across from *le grand docteur*, is reserved for the staff person most in favor at the time or for the principal guest or in this case, the newest arrival. It astonishes Mark that he – a young adult from Massachusetts whose father was involved in Schweitzer's peace movement – should sit across from Doctor Schweitzer on this first night. Mark finds a yellow anti-malarial quinine pill next to the placard with his name on it. Sitting to his right is an English physician named Frank Catchpool. Before the dinner begins, he learns that Schweitzer has assigned Catchpool as his mentor to ensure that he receives a proper orientation.

Schweitzer bows his head and leads the staff in a brief and simple prayer in German. Mark glances up at the white table cloth covering the massive solid wood table and the green shades covering kerosene lamps. He can see that the white medical professionals assembled in the screened-in *salle à manger* obviously look forward to this part of their day. Here they catch up on the hospital's activities or absorb the wit and wisdom of the doctor himself. Although he has been told that there is usually a great sense of *joie de vivre* at the end of the day, in fact Schweitzer's mood and conversation always sets the tone for the evening. It has a religious feeling. Mark had already heard people whisper that the scene over which Schweitzer presides each night reminds them of Leonardo da Vinci's painting *The Last Supper*, with Christ presiding at the center of a long table and the apostles strung out in a row, attentively leaning in to hear the Master's wisdom. But for now, this is all new. To him the prayer and procedures seem entirely fitting in a missionary clinic.

A tall, stern-looking African cook named Leo and two assistants enter the dining room and serve the food. Leo, who has been with Schweitzer more than 20 years, seldom speaks, but takes pride in organizing the dining room alone; he permits no one else to serve Schweitzer and his guests.

"Lambaréné is not a three-star restaurant," wrote Frederick Franck, a dentist who had enjoyed many a meal at that table, "but the cuisine is good and abundant. Schweitzer has tried to live as much as possible off the land. The vegetable gardens, one of the minor miracles he performed on the equator, abound with luscious vegetables.

"Meat is rarely served; the local fish, usually carp, consists mostly of skin and bones," he added. "Sometimes an excellent large fish similar to snapper is brought in, or a crocodile of which we whites eat only the tail. It tastes a little like a pork chop and I imagine a good French chef could make a series of masterpieces out of it. Crocodile cooked in the German manner is a little sauerbraten-ish or Wiener schnitzel-ish. It is hard to forget that you are eating a crocodile who would no doubt have preferred it the other way around."

Mark is impressed by the huge dishes of papayas, grapefruit, and other fruits, and the platter of vegetables, rice, beans and bits of fish that are passed around family style. Glancing up and down the long table, he takes his cues from Frank Catchpool.

Conversations take place in French, the official language, or German, Schweitzer's native tongue, but there is also a fair amount of English spoken. As the evening unfolds, Mark answers a few questions about where he is from and what he wants to do. Everyone around the table has a story and a personal reason for coming to work here.

It is a remarkably small staff, with a disproportionate ratio of women to men. Schweitzer, he hears, has kept the number of staff below 24 because that is the maximum number who can be seated in one place. Mark doesn't know whether to believe this or not.

After dinner Schweitzer picks up the Bible next to his place setting, reads a passage aloud in German, and discusses its meaning. This apparently is a ritual that he performs every night. He calls these little sermons the *Biblesse*, the German word for bible lesson. He then leads a 30-minute discussion about the excerpt. Looking up at the cuckoo clock, he stops abruptly, walks to a corner of the room and seats himself in front of an ancient and much-repaired upright piano.

It seems astonishing to Mark that any piano can be maintained in this heat and humidity. Mark knows what it takes to care for a piano, for at home his father relaxes by playing Rachmaninoff and Tchaikovsky and composing music on the family Steinway and is meticulous about keeping it in tune. Yet it seems so unlikely that one of the world's greatest interpreters of Johan Sebastian Bach will attempt to bring forth music from this decrepit keyboard. But play it Schweitzer does, and the staff and guests join in singing hymns in German. Mark loves using his deep bass voice, and he soon participates with everybody else, although he understands only some of the words. Singing around the piano brings him familial comfort reminiscent of some of his favorite boyhood memories when he and his sister and his brother sang as their father played.

In thirty minutes Schweitzer leaves the dining room and returns to his own cabin to plunge into the pile of correspondence and administrative paperwork stacked on his desk. Through his hand-written letters he maintains a remarkable network of influential friends and supporters such as the Jewish philosopher Martin Buber, the physicist Albert Einstein, the British philosopher and fellow Nobel laureate Bertrand Russell, the pre-eminent non-violence activist Mahatma Gandhi, the leader of the Indian independence movement Jawaharlal Nehru and with many other intellectuals and peace activists.

On the way back to his room, Mark notices that the night sky, full of fiery bright stars, contrasts with the few sounds he hears: a splash in the river or a bird crying in the forest. Falling asleep on that first night, he reflects on everything that he has seen that day. Then, very late into the evening, he hears a sound emanating from Schweitzer's cabin. He recognizes the magnificent haunting tones of Johan Sebastian Bach's *Toccata & Fugue*. Schweitzer is playing it on an  old zinc-lined piano equipped with foot pedals. It is a reminder that the doctor's first love had been music, and that his work on Bach had helped finance the missionary hospital in its early years.

The bells for breakfast chime at 7:30 a.m. Looking around the table again Mark knows that each of these people can be helpful to him while he lives in Lambaréné, and perhaps afterward. For the immediate future, they will be crucial to his plan for carving out a new and independent life. He resolves to learn as much as he can about their backgrounds.

He sits next to Frank Catchpool again, and as they talk, a natural friendship begins. The handsome 34-year-old physician from Great Britain had received his medical training in London, and is now serving his second tour at Lambaréné, having spent 14 months there before taking a break in 1958. He holds high expectations for a career at Lambaréné.

Catchpool has come by his Schweitzer affinity naturally, having been born into a Quaker family. That there seem to be a lot of pacifist leanings at the hospital is no surprise since Schweitzer attracts people who subscribe to his philosophy.

Catchpool suggests that Mark ought to learn the layout of the sprawling complex and they agree to meet after breakfast for a tour of the grounds.

On that first morning, as they walk the half-mile trail through a dense jungle paralleling the river, Catchpool introduces Mark to Isao Takahasi, a Japanese physician and expert in tropical diseases who specializes in treating the lepers. Takahasi has been at Lambaréné for two years. A happy man, he not only plays the guitar in an after-hours combo at staff gatherings, he also composes music. He has brought with him into the leper village his love for the international language of music, and encourages his patients to stage performances.

Patients and their families each occupy a small, comfortable hut and take pride in keeping the village clean and orderly. Their bamboo and thatch houses have concrete foundations, corrugated steel roofs and are large enough to allow each patient a separate room. It is called the *Village des Lumières* because it brings light into the lives of the long-suffering patients.

Takahasi had succeeded Catchpool's friend Omar Fareed, who had brought in medical equipment, put together a facility where lepers could be examined, made a survey of intestinal and blood parasites, and set up the bacteriological laboratory. The experience of working with Schweitzer made a deep and lasting impression on Fareed, who once said he "often had to struggle for self-control when I was working among the lepers. To be with them was a tremendously moving experience."

If he can handle the sight of the disfigured people in the leper village, Mark can become an asset to the whole clinic. Leprosy, one of the dreaded and chronic African diseases, causes permanent severe, disfiguring skin sores and nerve damage in the arms and legs, often resulting in the loss of fingers or toes. Since Biblical times, the disease has been associated with terrifying, negative stigmas; its victims have been shunned as outcasts and isolated. Untreated leprosy is progressive, but the disease can be managed with the oral administration of Dapsone, a form of sulfone. Most of those Schweitzer treats have chosen to remain in their self-supporting community within the compound; they would be shunned in their tribal villages. As a result, the leper village at Lambaréné is the permanent home for about 200 Africans. Considerable research is taking place here to eradicate this cursed affliction.

Neither Schweitzer nor his staff believes that leprosy is contagious by contact, and they work freely among the lepers.

Mark sees that caring for a leper means constantly draining, cleaning and re-bandaging putrid, pus-filled infections. Remarkably, Takahashi and Schweitzer enjoy the advantage of having attracted to their cause two vastly different and very prominent women.

One of them is Marion Mill Preminger, the tall, wealthy and vivacious former wife of the Hollywood film magnate Otto Preminger. The gregarious Hungarian has an outrageous sense of humor and a big heart. Depending on whose version of the truth one believes, Marion either had been raised in a Viennese castle with an aristocratic family surrounded by servants and holds a doctorate in philosophy, or she grew up in a modest house as an

*Marion Preminger*

impoverished middle-class Jewish girl who had changed her name and never finished high school. Whatever the real story, she is devoted to Schweitzer, whom she calls "the greatest man who ever lived," and actually does raise a lot of money for him during her winters in New York. Each summer she spends several months doing menial work at the clinic. She met Schweitzer in 1949, and decided to devote her free time to bandaging lepers in Gabon. A few years after she divorced Preminger, she received a trailing alimony payment of $48,000, which she turned over to Schweitzer so he could buy more medical supplies. In the leper village Mark finds wooden benches with plaques marking her consecutive summers there from 1951 through 1959.

The other woman helping Takahasi is a tall, pale 33-year old Englishwoman named Olga Deterding. Olga was educated at Oxford, but in 1956 she volunteered for duty in the kitchen at the leper village and has taken on a secondary duty as the staff photographer. She happens to be the heiress to the fortune of the Royal Dutch Shell Company, which her late father Sir Henri Deterding had

*Olga Deterding*

founded. Olga had once been a socialite featured regularly in the gossip columns of London. Worth an estimated $150 million, she was privately known as the Mad Millionairess, and developed a reputation as an infamously eccentric partygoer before she dropped from view of the society pages. Mark notices right away that she seems to have a fondness for Frank Catchpool.

Mark observes the selfless work of these doctors, volunteers and other assistants. He sees how the family members live with the patients and keep their part of the village spotlessly clean. He sees happy and friendly children everywhere. Takahasi invites Mark to come by whenever he has extra time.

———

Walking back from the leper village, Mark spots a sturdy English bicycle locked up next to one of the staff dorms. Catchpool says it belongs to Siegfried Neukirch, a 29-year-old German man who had arrived only a few months earlier.

In a few minutes, Catchpool introduces them. Siegfried was born in Freiburg, a city along the border with France at the gateway to Germany's Black Forest. The son of a bookseller, his early years had been spent like many German boys as a member of a Hitler youth group, and then enduring the hardships that ravaged post-war Europe. After early schooling in Germany, he attended school at the Sorbonne in Paris and then at the University of Toronto in Canada.

To earn his living, Siegfried has worked as a typist for a radio station in Germany, as a car washer in Toronto and as a waiter on the Canadian Pacific Railroad. While in Alaska, he hit upon the fantastic idea of traveling by bicycle to offer his services to Albert Schweitzer. Starting his two-wheeled journey in Vancouver, he pedaled across North America, entered Central and South America and then took a steamer across the South Atlantic to Africa.

Upon arriving at Lambaréné early in 1959 Siegfried proudly reminded the staff that his aunt, a schoolmate of the late Mrs. Schweitzer, had sent a letter of introduction to Schweitzer the previous year. Although nobody remembered that, Schweitzer admired his bicycle and his determination, and put Siegfried on the staff as the supervisor of maintenance and construction crews.

When the Daimler-Benz company donated to the hospital a five-ton Mercedes truck, Siegfried became its driver. Every week now, he drives to villages in the region buying produce. The most crucial of those, he explains to Mark, are plantains, the cooking bananas that are a staple of the native diet. The clinic needs four tons of these every week to feed the patients and staff.

Mark quickly concludes that this place is a haven for adventurers and world travelers. He likes that.

On the equator, the sun goes down about 6:00 p.m. As darkness closes in, the workday ends, the kerosene lamps are lit, and it is time for pre-dinner socializing. Affable and intelligent, Mark enjoys the evening discussions, and looks forward to learning more about the backgrounds of his new colleagues. Clearly, they enjoy one other's company. They play music on the old hand-cranked turntable, read aloud a poem, and socialize in other ways.

During his second dinner, now seated farther down the table, Mark notices that the dining room is full of attractive women.

One of them is the chief surgeon, Margrit van der Kreek, a lovely 33-year old woman from The Netherlands. It was her phrase he had seen in Norman Cousins' book *Dr. Schweitzer of Lambaréné*. She described the hospital as "a jungle village with a clinic." Mark remembers reading in Cousins' book the explanation that Margrit had given for coming to Lambaréné and leaving behind her life of middle-class comfort in Europe: "Here in Lambaréné, we do nicely without the frills. We have a purpose and apply ourselves to it. We never have to ask ourselves whether we are really needed. We are never at wit's end for what to do with our time. When our work is over for the day we can sit down and rest or we can make ourselves tea and we talk among ourselves or we can read and we can think. It is very good." Cousins had admired her work, and in the book he wrote about Schweitzer, he repeatedly noted the physical beauty of this physician whom everyone refers to as *la doctoresse*.

Next, a petite 34-year-old surgical nurse named Gertrud Raschke typi-fies the kind of devoted women that Schweitzer attracts. Gertrud had been born in East Prussia, Germany, the youngest of three daughters; she lost her lost her mother, father and sister in the Second World War. At the age of 20 in 1946, she had begun training as a nurse in Communist East Germany. The consequences of war became apparent as she tended to those in need, particularly the babies and children suffering from poverty and malnutrition. She was determined to have her freedom, and dreamed of escaping across the border into West Germany. Her first attempt failed, but in 1955, with the secret help of escorts she ran through fields carrying everything she owned and she crossed into West Germany. Gertrud was working at a hospital in Bern, Switzerland, in 1959, when she first heard of Albert Schweitzer and applied to work for him.

At the end of the table Mark hears three younger women chatting animatedly in French. He had seen Catherine Riedinger in the laundry room. He had seen Sonja Miller and her very pretty friend Adriana Calles Eller in the *pouponniere* taking care of newborns.

Mark can't help but notice that the man closest to Schweitzer tonight and speaking to him in German is a brooding, withdrawn Czechoslovakian doctor named Richard Friedman. A soft-spoken middle-aged man with a huge bushy black mustache, Friedman has a reputation of leading a reserved existence. Apparently, he seldom participates in social activities; his gruff manners sometimes intimidate people. Friedman took over treatment of the mentally ill when he arrived in 1956, and also works with the tuberculosis patients. In her book *Working with Doctor Schweitzer*, Louise Jilek-Aall said Friedman "could become so emotional that sweat pearls stood on his forehead. At times there was almost a fanatic intensity in his expression."

The sight of dark blue numbers tattooed on Friedman's left arm startles Mark. *Auschwitz!* It sends him into a moment of deep thought, as he recalls the nightmares recounted by Mary Bechhold Einstein, his stepmother and closest confidant.

Mary had told Mark the truth about her childhood in Bavaria, why she had gone to Holland before the Second World War broke out, what horrors she experienced during the war, and how that number got tattooed on her forearm. During Hitler's purge, Mary and her husband had been rounded up in Amsterdam and shipped to various concentration camps. Siegfried Einstein, scion of a successful banking family, had gone to the gas chambers at Auschwitz. After surviving the notorious camp at Auschwitz, Mary had been forced to march in wintertime to the Theresienstadt camp in Czecho-slovakia. Somewhere along that march, she found the courage to steal the boots of an SS officer, a theft which helped her survive. Theresienstadt was known on the outside as a "model" camp where visitors from the international Red Cross could watch the inmates perform concerts. But behind the scenes, Mary had told Mark, she and the others were brutally beaten. Finally Mary was sent to the so-called "holding camp" at Bergen-Belsen, where she was in the section known as the "star camp" for Dutch Jews. Working in the shoe factory, she became deathly ill from typhus, as had thousands of others. Weakened and suffering, she was admitted to a hospital ward where she met another young female patient from Holland: the not-yet-famous diarist Anne Frank. In the first few months of 1945, more than 35,000 prisoners died of typhus at Bergen-Belsen. Mary was fighting to stay alive when the 53,000 remaining prisoners were liberated by the British when the war ended. Mary survived; Anne Frank had died a few weeks earlier. When she emigrated to the U.S. in 1947 she was hoping to exorcise memories of the atrocities she had witnessed and endured. She married Mark's father two years later and wound up with three stepchildren.

Blinking, Mark now brings his attention back to the present and to the numbers on Dr. Friedman's forearm. Somehow this man had also survived Auschwitz. But the rest of his family had been exterminated. By the time he was set free, "I had lost everything," he told Jilek-Aall, "my people, my God, and my joy in life. Bitter and restless, I wandered from one place to the other not knowing what to do with my life, whether to live or to die. As a last straw I decided to visit Albert Schweitzer in Lambaréné. And here I have found some kind of peace, the only place on earth where I feel at home, so I have lived here ever since." Friedman said that helping patients "has been my daily task since I made my life here. When one of them improves, I feel my work is worthwhile; when I fail, I fall back into dark brooding."

It was eerily similar to the pathos Mark had heard from his stepmother, who alternated between being manic-depressive and overly charming.

To Mark's surprise, Friedman recruits him to help construct a new 24-bed isolation ward for tuberculosis patients. In the first few days on the job, he quickly realizes how much work there is to be done, and how all of this collective labor produces a satisfactory result.

But more than the physical work and the medical staff and the white Europeans, it is the natives and their families who draw Mark's attention. They are the reason the hospital exists. Long ago the people who lived in West Africa evolved into at least forty distinct ethnic groups. The Fang, Bongo, Kota and Baka and other tribes each have their own traditions and languages.

Mark wants to befriend these people, and learn about their ways of life. In a few weeks he meets a 36-year-old native named Joseph Ndolo whose parents had brought Joseph to the hospital as a boy because he had deformed knees and was unable to walk. The surgeons at the Schweitzer hospital repaired his legs and got him on his feet. In gratitude, Joseph's parents took jobs in the kitchen and have remained living in the area. Mark feels a kinship with Joseph because he, too, had endured several knee operations himself as a boy.

Mark occasionally has to remind himself that this is still old Africa, where the world of modern medicine often conflicts with old tribal customs. Out in the jungle, fetishers exacerbate fears, suspicions and suspicions. These witch doctors are jealous of Schweitzer. Occasionally one sneaks onto the grounds to track down a particular patient to extract revenge. Schweitzer hates having fetishers come into his clinic. Yet these village medicine men wield great powers over their tribes. They perpetuate myths about their power by ascribing some magical or curative power to a decorated statue or object. Fetishers add to carved wooded figures things like horns, shells, nails, feathers, mirrors, metal, twine, paint, cloth, raffia, fur, beads and herbs – any mysterious object they think will contribute to the appearance of magic. A fetish acquires power through ritualistic carving and consecration and the recurring activation of its spirit by offering sacrifices and secret words. Many patients come to Schweitzer after a tribal fetisher has failed to produce a cure.

One day while he is walking along the path toward the leper village Mark hears a sudden rustling in the bushes. He steps back a bit and stares at the frightening creature that emerges: a large middle-aged woman who is completely naked except for an old broad-brimmed hat, and a machete in her hand. She angrily shouts what sounded like curses in a language Mark has never heard.

He picks up his pace as he walks away. Later in the day, reporting what he has seen, other staff members laugh out loud. They tell him that the woman has been living in and around the Schweitzer clinic for years. No one knows where she came from or what language she speaks. She did not come with a family, and no one interacts with her. They have nicknamed the apparently deranged woman Madame-Sans-Nom, (woman without a name). It turns out that despite her threatening looks and gestures, she is in fact quite harmless. Everyone, however, gives her a wide berth. Madame Sans-Nom is part of the legend of Lambaréné.

———

As he works around the grounds, Mark enjoys being surrounded with the dozens of young children living in the leper village and in the tribal houses around the main clinic area. An idea occurs to him: he can read to the children. He comes up with the perfect story. One afternoon he carries an illustrated book into the leper village, holds it up and calls out in his deep voice: *"Venez ici, mes petits amis! Il est temps d'ecouter des histoires."* (Come here, my little friends! It's time to listen to some stories).

He opens *"L'enfant de l'éléphant"* by Rudyard Kipling. It has all the elements that can hold a child's interest. It asks lots of Why and How questions. It has a lot of lyrical repetition. Best of all, its characters come right from this neighborhood. Mark reads the story aloud in French, pausing so the youngsters can see the drawings. The snub-nosed Child of the Elephant lives in Africa and has an insatiable curiosity; he asks his relatives "ever so many questions." One day the little elephant asks what a crocodile eats for dinner. He asks his aunt the Ostrich, his uncle the Giraffe, his "broad aunt" the Hippopotamus, and his "hairy uncle" the Baboon. They all say "hush" and spank him. Then the Child of the Elephant asks a Kolokolo Bird, who tells him to go down to river and find out for himself. As the story evolves, the Crocodile lures the little elephant into the water, snatches and pulls its nose until it stretches way out. The elephant is saved by the Bi-Colored-Python-Rock-Snake and soon discovers many novel uses for its new long nose. Pretty soon all the other elephants go down to the river to have their noses stretched out, too.

Mark creates separate voices for each of these characters. The children giggle throughout the story, and ask to hear it again and again. Mark's story time for the little African children becomes a regular part of the week, and teaches the children that they can trust this tall white man. Soon, he is making up his own imaginative stories. The children and their parents return Mark's affection by bestowing on him an affectionate nickname that reflected his physical stature, Docteur Long-Long.

Elsewhere in the compound, when the children see Docteur Long-Long come striding along, they know it is story time, and the word spreads from tribal house to tribal house within the compound. Mark is earning the trust of the Africans, and he finds this hugely satisfying.

Early on the morning of Friday, June 26, before the breakfast gong sounds, Mark hears voices outside his door. Albert Schweitzer himself has led the rest of the staff to Mark's living quarters and they are all standing outside. With Schweitzer's high nasal voice leading the group, the two dozen people break into a rousing rendition of the German hymns *Harre meine Seele* and *Ach bleib mit Deiner Gnade*. Schweitzer then calls upon Mark to open the door, whereupon he and many other members of the staff enter his small room. This is Mark's introduction to one of the few personal traditions at the clinic. It's his 19th birthday, and his colleagues have come to celebrate.

Half an hour later at breakfast, Mark finds himself seated again at the traditional place of honor across from Schweitzer. Because it is his birthday, he learns, he is entitled to a ration of two eggs instead of just one. At the table, he receives a few handmade presents, opens some greeting cards and a telegram, and blows out the candles on a small German cake. Whenever they celebrate a staff member's birthday, Schweitzer presents a book or a box containing Gabonese wood carvings or other little treasures. During the evening meal, children of the clinic assemble outside the dining room and sing to Mark. The staff works exhausting days and this long-established ritual is a respite and a cause for a much-needed party.

On Thursday, July 2, with a twinkle in his eye, Schweitzer presides at the marriage of Nurse Sonja Miller and Robert Poteau. A native of Alsace,

Sonja has been working at Lambaréné as a midwife for five years delivering babies nearly every day. Months earlier, the paternalistic old Dr. Schweitzer had called Sonja into his office. In addition to the many other hats he wears, Schweitzer fancies himself a match-maker. He told Sonja directly that on Easter Sunday he was going to announce her engagement to Robert Poteau, a prosperous French logging entrepreneur who had been calling on her, and that he would officiate at their wedding.

The newlyweds are planning to leave Lambaréné and Schweitzer wants to give them a big send-off. Altogether 30 people attend the ceremony, each dressed in their Sunday best: suits, white shirts and tie for the men and below-the-knee white dresses for the women. The wedding party posed for a formal portrait on the steps outside the great dining hall. Mark poses for the photo wearing a tan suit and sporting a fashionable white pocket handkerchief.

*Wearing the tan suit on the right, Mark becomes part of the wedding party photo on the steps of the dining hall after Albert Schweitzer presides over the wedding of nurse Sonja Miller and Robert Poteau, a French logger.*

From time to time, Mark hears examples of Schweitzer's obsession with the phrase and philosophy of Reverence for Life. Apparently, the seeds of the notion had been planted in childhood. Thumbing through Schweitzer's *Memoirs of Childhood and Youth*, Mark finds a passage noting Schweitzer's earliest respect for living things:

> *I had an experience during my seventh or eighth year which made a deep impression on me. Heinrich Bräsch and I had made ourselves rubber band sling-shots with which we could shoot small pebbles. One spring Sunday during Lent he said to me, "Come on, let's go up the Rebberg and shoot birds." I hated this idea, but I did not contradict him for fear he might laugh at me. We approached a leafless tree in which birds, apparently unafraid of us, were singing sweetly in the morning air. Crouching like an Indian hunter, my friend put a pebble in his slingshot and took aim. Obeying his look of command, I did the same with terrible pangs of conscience and vowing to myself to miss.*
>
> *At that very moment the church bells began to ring out into the sunshine, mingling their chimes with the song of the birds. It was the warning bell, half an hour before the main bell ringing. For me, it was a voice from Heaven. I put the slingshot aside, shooed the birds away so that they were safe from my friend, and ran home. Ever since then, when the bells of Passiontide ring out into the sunshine and the naked trees, I remember, deeply moved and grateful, how on that day they rang into my heart the commandment "Thou shalt not kill."*

Mark sees firsthand how the old man applies the concept. In living his ethical philosophy, Schweitzer tries to be practical; he is not a vegetarian, but he opposes the unnecessary killing of any organism. He acknowledges that sometimes it is necessary to destroy other life in self-defense, for food, or simply because they cannot do anything about it, for example, when people crush microorganisms under their feet as they walk or when a physician kills dangerous microbes to save patients.

An oft-repeated example was the incident that occurred when the American statesman Adlai Stevenson was being escorted on a tour around the Hospital. The former presidential candidate noticed a large mosquito alighting on Schweitzer's arm and promptly swatted it. Schweitzer turned to him and said sharply, "You shouldn't have done that. That was *my mosquito*."

Siegfried Neukirch tells Mark about the time when he was driving the banana truck along a dirt road in Lambaréné. Schweitzer, who was riding in the front seat, suddenly called out: "Stop! Don't you see that ant trail?" He jumped down from the cab to look at a three-inch wide column of big dark ants crossing in front. Schweitzer retrieved two long wooden planks from the back of the truck and placed them in such a way that the ants could continue their journey without being crushed by the big truck tires.

But Mark's favorite story is about the timid first-time visitor whom Schweitzer was escorting along the path toward the leper village. Schweitzer looked down and said, "Be very careful on this path because serpents make their nest on it." The grateful visitor replied, "Oh, yes, doctor, I surely will." Schweitzer quickly added "... and I do not want you to step on the small snakes and harm them."

*Schweitzer with some of his pet antelopes, many of whom enjoy the run of the hospital grounds.*

In a more serious vein, Schweitzer explains to a visiting doctor that "to take any life unnecessarily, or even worse, purposely, such as killing an elephant for a trophy or a butterfly just to pin it to a board – even if it gives some people pleasure, which it obviously does – is *grievous*."

Schweitzer cares as much for the animals that roam freely through the grounds as he does for every other living thing. One day, Siegfried was sent to deliver a small antelope to the Catholic mission three miles upriver. It was a special animal that Schweitzer had named Cleopatra; at the mission, she was to be reunited with her five-month old cousin Cecile.

On July 16 Mark participates in a big welcome back reception. Dr. Frederick Franck has returned to Lambaréné with his wife Claske Berndes. Franck had worked there during the summer of 1958, spending half his time practicing dentistry and half pursuing his other passion, art. Now, Franck carries with him copies of a wonderfully descriptive and illustrated new book he had just published, entitled *Days with Albert Schweitzer: A Lambaréné Landscape*, based on his service there the previous summer.

Schweitzer had long wanted to offer dental care to his staff as well as to native patients. A mutual friend named Clara Urquhart several years earlier had called upon Franck at his office in New York. She persuaded him to take a leave from his practice and create a dental clinic at Lambaréné. When he accepted the offer, she helped arrange funding for all the equipment Franck would need through MEDICO, the newly created organization that Dr. Tom Dooley had co-founded.

A native of Holland, the 51-year-old dentist had migrated to the United States in 1945 and was doing very well. His bargain with Schweitzer was that he would go to Lambaréné as a dentist, but only if could allocate a portion of his time in pursuit of his hobby of sketching.

Franck had had a great time in Lambaréné. He drew the natives and the wildlife, as well as sculpting and writing. He had become a popular figure as he roamed through the clinic's grounds, stopping to pull out his sketch pad. Patients didn't seem to mind posing, and there were endlessly fascinating subjects to put into art form. Patients began suggesting things to draw, and soon he was running art classes for the Africans, even for the lepers missing fingers.

His return in the summer of 1959 is cause for a celebration, and the renewal of old friendships. He teaches more sketching classes to the natives, and even guides the budding new artist Mark Higgins.

Mark also becomes acquainted with another summer arrival, the 29-year-old American doctor Fergus Pope, who now spends most of his summers at the clinic. A few years earlier, after a brief stint as a U.S. Air Force pilot, Pope had driven a Land Rover across the Sahara Desert toward South Africa, stopping in Lambaréné to see the man whose work he had long admired. The first person ever to arrive over land at the hospital, Pope had been greatly inspired by the dedicated staff of professionals, as well as by the African villagers being treated there. But he had no skills of use to Schweitzer, who put him to work supervising the construction of housing and treatment facilities for the leprosy patients. This experience inspired him to study medicine; he became a physician, and he made a point of returning to work in the jungle clinic every summer. Secretly, Pope now harbors ambitions of succeeding Schweitzer.

Schweitzer and his daughter Rhena have had an arms-length relationship; for most of her life, he hardly knew her. When Rhena visited Lambaréné in 1958, it was only the second time in her life she had been there. The occasion was her father's 83rd birthday. She looked around, spoke with some of the doctors, and found that the hospital had no pathology laboratory. It should have been standard practice to examine body tissue for diagnostic or forensic purposes. Right then she determined – against her father's wishes – that she would become a pathologist and work there. Within two years she was well on her way and had set up a lab which Schweitzer reluctantly lets her operate.

Although she always defends him in public, privately she argues with him about some of his incongruous rules, such as wearing the safari hat (she rarely does) and his refusal to install electricity and modernize the hospital.

Mark watches Schweitzer and his assistant Ali Silver at the start of each day as they issue assignments to the African helpers who line up near the steps leading to the veranda of his cabin. The work assignments are clear and simple: clear a path, construct a bridge, offload supplies from this truck or fell a certain tree. Often the old man himself shows up to help with an assignment he has doled out. He supervises all of the construction, roadwork, planting and grounds maintenance. At age 84, he is as ready to push a loaded wheelbarrow or stack lumber as any muscled teenaged native. During a portion of every day Schweitzer will make a point of strolling around the grounds, sometimes deep in thought, with his hands clasped behind his back, observing every detail and stopping only to pay attention to his pets or to give an order. At the end of each workday, bells call the laborers back to this spot where they collect their reward in the form of food such as manioc, rice and plantains.

Daytime at Lambaréné sees a steady flow of tourists traipsing through, hoping for a snapshot or a word with the doctor. Visitors usually form quick opinions, but the people closest to Schweitzer maintain that the only way to get an accurate sense of life at the clinic is to spend a few days there and watch the interaction with native culture.

Such is the fame of *le grand docteur* that a news story or a new book triggers a flood of donations and offers. On Saturday, July 18, Mark joins a work party that was meeting a 13-year old black youth named Bobby Hill from Hempstead, Long Island. The boy, whose father was a U.S. Air Force tech sergeant stationed in Naples, Italy, had read Erica Anderson's richly illustrated book *The World of Albert Schweitzer*. The imaginative young man decided he wanted to raise money for medicine and supplies for the jungle clinic.

He wrote to his father's boss, Lt. Gen. Richard C. Lindsey, commander of NATO air forces in Europe. Starting with a radio campaign in Italy, Bobby Hill's personal appeal quickly gained momentum. Private citizens and pharmaceutical companies helped him collect more than $400,000 worth of medicines. To transport the 9,000 pounds of supplies to Gabon, the French and Italian air forces each donated an aircraft. Bobby and his father, along with General Lindsey, senior officers from the Italian and French military and 30 reporters and photographer, flew to Libreville, the capital city, where Gabonese officials joined the goodwill mission. When Schweitzer met Bobby, he kissed the boy on both cheeks and said, "I never thought a child could do so much for my hospital." He signed books for the Hill family while Mark and others offloaded the cargo. It became the stuff of newsreel footage, as well as a three-page photo story scheduled for *Ebony* magazine in November.

The media circus surrounding that remarkable humanitarian gesture, however, creates a big disruption in the routine at the hospital. Curious newsmen interrupt patient work. One diarist notes: "Very trying for everyone here. All the photographers, etc. Nurses and doctors incensed."

Among those descending on Lambaréné that day is a journalist with Hearst Newspapers named John J. Casserly. After a three-hour visit, he expresses shock at what he observes. He doesn't like the animals walking around, the lack of running water, the absence of a radio, the patients' families cooking out in the open, the "relatively primitive pagans" who "practice all kinds of sorcery and even witchcraft," or the poisonous snake he had heard about in one of the wards. He describes the facility as "filthy." Rhena Schweitzer tries to explain to him why the clinic is set up the way it is:

"The people come here *because* it is this way. Life here is like living in their villages and we feel that many would not otherwise be treated because they would not go to a regular hospital. Some natives come from as long a distance as 200 miles, rowing all the way by canoe to get here. They have told us that they feel right at home here, cooking and doing things just the way they would do where their tribe lives. This is an important consideration."

*In mid-summer, Mark changes his appearance by growing a neat goatee and chin curtain, shaving his soft blonde facial hair only above the lips. The new look gives him the air of a northern European artist. He fits right in and passes for a Frenchman, a Dutchman or even a Belgian.*

Casserly doesn't understand the African culture or the people who work there in the jungle. Assessing the staff of medical personnel and volunteers, he wonders in his story: "Why do they do it? Who are these people, really? Have some of them really fled the world - escapists?" Schweitzer, he writes, "is an unquestionably complex personality. So are the people who work for him. In fact, they are not at all easy to understand. Neither is Dr. Schweitzer."

The reporter spots Mark, obviously an American, and tries to get a few words out of him. Probably sensing Casserly's skepticism and realizing that this is not going to become a positive story, Mark gives Casserly nothing beyond acknowledging that he is from Massachusetts. Casserly mentions him in the story anyway.

As the youngest adult on the staff, Mark knows he is privileged to sit in the dining room and listen. Schweitzer's table has become a crossroads for serious and important people from around the world. VIP guests participate in high-level discussions about geopolitics, science, medicine, religion, philosophy and life. During lunch one day Schweitzer asks Frank Catchpool to meet a boat carrying a special guest. "Please come with me to the river's edge and greet this American who is coming," Schweitzer said. "His name is Linus Pauling."

Mark's ears perk up. This is the same Dr. Linus Pauling whose lecture he heard in a packed auditorium at Clark University in Worcester, Massachusetts, just seven months ago, and to whom his father had afterward introduced him.

Catchpool replies that he knows all about Pauling: "I read *Time* and *Newsweek* whenever I can and I see that he is saying the things that I want to hear. He is saying them loudly and clearly." Catchpool only has half an hour to clean up so he can meet his hero Pauling. When he does, Pauling is "standing on the banks of the Ogoué River with mud up to his ankles."

It is indeed an epic occasion. Pauling and his wife Ava have come for a nine-day visit that more closely resembles a summit meeting: two recipients of a Nobel Prize conferring in the jungle about strategies for world peace and nuclear disarmament. Each has shuddered with fear as they consider the stand-off between the United States and the Soviet Union. The madness and escalation must stop, they believe. To Mark, this is a familiar theme. His father expressed the same concerns while presiding over meetings of United World Federalist movement in New England. It was exactly what Pauling had been talking about in his lecture at Clark University.

Pauling is a scholar in the fields of chemistry, medicine and math. He received the Nobel Prize for Chemistry in 1954 and other awards from France, the United Kingdom, Italy the United States, the Soviet Union and Germany. Some people consider him one of the 20 greatest scientists of all time. Pauling and his wife have leveraged his fame in a campaign to free the world of nuclear weapons. In 1957 they started a petition calling for an end to nuclear-weapons testing and Pauling has become a very outspoken activist in the National Committee for a Sane Nuclear Policy, an off-shoot of the World Federalist movement, and that cause is the principal reason he has come to Lambaréné:

Catchpool is intrigued by the Paulings. They don't mind the heat or the dirt, or the squawking chickens and goats running around. They are genuinely interested in seeing the patients. Linus and Ava Pauling walk around hand-in-hand.

Pauling shares some of his advanced research on diseases afflicting Africans. When he gives an informal seminar on sickle-cell anemia, it dawns on Catchpool that he has been seeing sickle-cell anemia in his patients without recognizing that was the cause of the large ulcers on patients' legs.

Ava Pauling keeps a diary of this trip, as she does of all the travels with her husband. She notes that they have met Mark Higgins, and also that there are nurses from Holland, Switzerland, South Africa, "and one beautiful one from Mexico." Ava Pauling, like Mark Higgins and Frank Catchpool and almost everyone else in Lambaréné, has been noticing Adriana Calles Eller, the radiant young lady volunteering in the maternity section.

Adriana, 24 years old, is a strikingly beautiful woman of Mexican-American heritage. She was born and raised in New York City, but from the age of 10 attended boarding schools in Florida. Her grandfather Plutarco Elias Calles was a founder of the Partido Revolucionario Institutional, the single ruling party of Mexico, and a former president of Mexico. Adriana had studied at Wellesley College just outside of Boston and later had attended the Sorbonne in Paris.

She had met the ruggedly handsome Hollywood actor Hugh O'Brian, who made a career of portraying serious heroic characters. O'Brian had the title role in one of television's most popular westerns, *The Life and Times of Wyatt Earp*. Adriana had traveled with him in Europe where their names were linked by gossip columnists such as Walter Winchell. When "Wyatt Earp" went to Lambaréné to meet Schweitzer early in 1959, he brought along Adriana, ostensibly as his translator, but upon seeing the jungle hospital, she wanted to stay and found an assignment caring for infants in the nursery.

Fortunately for Mark, Frank Catchpool has already introduced Adriana to him. In the last few weeks, the three of them have been spending a lot of their precious leisure time together. In Adriana he finds a gentle woman with a great deal of empathy.

*Adriana, who worked in the nursery by daytime, became Mark's confidant.*

Mark and Adriana have been talking often, and becoming great friends. During their free moments they listen to music on the hand-cranked record player and read poetry to one other. They discover that they like the same authors. One of their favorites, who writes in English as well as in French, is Samuel Beckett, the Irish avant-garde novelist, playwright and poet whose bleak, tragicomic outlook on human nature is often coupled with black comedy and gallows humor. They sit together, read Beckett's *Watt* to each other and laugh out loud at the deadpan humor and wordplay.

Up until then, Mark has been introspective and reserved, and has revealed little about his own life. Now, far from home and in the company of these two trusted friends, he relaxes. It is time to share his own story about why he has come to Lambaréné. From the outset, Mark has been at ease in Catchpool's company and has been attracted to Adriana's intelligence, maturity and her physical beauty. He wants them to understand his story, and so for the next several nights after dinner, he pours his heart out.

He tells Adriana and Frank what he has been through in the last few years, and why it was necessary to step away from his upbringing, and to look for a deep purpose in life. He tells them how his parents' personal problems disrupted his life, how he had nearly died, and how he had been confined for almost a year. Much of what he tells them is still a painful memory. But he also talks about his aspirations for the future.

Adriana understands Mark's vulnerabilities, and she knows he is afraid of more emotional hurt. She settles back and listens as Mark unburdens himself.

# Four

# The Golden Boy

Working in Africa is his way of upholding a family's tradition of finding one's own way in the world, Mark tells Adriana and Frank. But convincing his parents of that had been a monumental struggle that almost cost him his life.

He lights the first of many cigarettes that night, and leans forward with his elbows on his knees to explain how he has arrived at this remote place.

His industrious family in Worcester, Massachusetts, is comprised of strong men, intelligent women, and solid New England stock. Their lineage dates back to the *Mayflower*.

His paternal grandfather John Woodman Higgins was one of two sons of Milton Prince Higgins who had formed a company ironically called the Plunger Elevator Company which they sold to Otis Elevator in 1902. The first brother, Aldus, invested his share of the proceeds in a business that became the Norton Abrasives Company which provides products to the steel industry. Mark's grandfather invested in a new venture named Worcester Pressed Steel. He built a factory, acquired patents, installed equipment and began stamping out products for industrial customers. During the First World War, Worcester Pressed Steel provided howitzer castings, tank parts, mess kits and helmets for American soldiers.

Mark's grandmother Clara Louise Carter was the daughter of a wealthy St. Louis, Missouri, grain executive. Her family roots had her somehow connected to Gen. Robert E. Lee, and she often refers to herself as "one of the Virginia Carters."

In 1914 John Woodman Higgins had given his wife a birthday present:

a classical revival-style house, an architectural masterpiece located at 80 William Street in Worcester. Even the plot of land where the house stood was famous. It had once been the site of the Worcester Agricultural Fairgrounds and a ballpark. Here on June 12, 1880, facing the Cleveland Blues, the pitcher for the Worcester Ruby Legs threw the first perfect game in professional baseball history. Somehow that striving for perfection would seem to imbue all of the family's pursuits.

John and Clara Higgins started their family in this house. Their first-born, a son they named Carter Chapin Higgins, was born there in 1915. Two years later came another son, Bradley Carter Higgins and then four years later a daughter named Mary Louise Higgins.

Times were good in the Roaring Twenties. Just about everyone was making money in the stock market, at least on paper. But Grandfather and a few other friends early in 1929 listened to a smart broker and liquidated their portfolios. When the market crashed and America entered the Great Depression, the Higgins family was sitting on a pile of cash.

Grandfather Higgins had always been enchanted by the tales of chivalrous knights. After all, knights wore pressed steel into battle. He bought a few suits of armor and delighted in recounting to his children the stories of King Arthur and the Knights of the Round Table. There was always a lesson about gallantry, courage and dignity: it was how a Higgins should live.

*The Higgins Armory Museum became a Worcester landmark as soon as it opened.*

He purchased more armor from European dealers and other serious collectors. He brought these treasures home and placed them around the house. But after a while, family lore holds, it became clear to his wife that these figures standing in the hallway and in her garden room were taking over the house. They would have to be displayed somewhere else. So he built a museum to house his collection.

Adjoining the steel plant, it was the first steel and glass building in the United States. The five-story structure resembled a medieval castle inside, with sheer walls and narrow stained-glass windows. When it was finished in 1931, his grandfather had spent $300,000 for a place to house his collection. Grandfather Higgins loved the artwork in steel craft. For his workers, the museum was an aesthetic tribute to their trade. For the public it showcased the beauty and history of the art of steel-making. It became the largest museum in the United States solely devoted to arms and armor, a major tourist attraction in Worcester, and a centerpiece for educational, civic and social occasions. It remained famous because every boy growing up in New England had been there, whether on a weekend with his parents, on a school field trip, or on an overnight visit as a Cub Scout.

*In the Great Hall of the Higgins Armory Museum, fantasies came alive.*

Mark's grandfather still kept a few suits of armor at home. Occasionally, he would place glow-in-the-dark eyes in the helmets of these knights. Neighbors sometimes spotted him walking in a full suit of armor right down William Street. His children often put on helmets and chased each other around the Higgins Armory Museum waving swords. No one seemed to mind.

Around the same time, Grandfather Higgins took advantage of Depression-era prices and bought two vacation properties. One was Breaknolle, an 18-room waterfront "summer cottage" in Little Boar's Head, New Hampshire that had once been owned by the Studebaker family of automotive fame.

But closer to home, just 12 miles west of Worcester in the little town of North Brookfield, there was a special property. Grandfather Higgins and several of his pals purchased about a thousand acres of undeveloped woodland surrounding a 172-acre private lake known as Brooks Pond. He built a sturdy rustic post-and-beam day cabin and boathouse right at the water's edge. Thirty acres of woods separated his cabin from the nearest paved road. This tranquil place became his favorite retreat. It had no electricity and water came from a well.

On this vast private playground his children could swim, read, build bonfires, race their sailing canoes, and generally let their hair down far from the view of any outsider. Grandmother Higgins' formal rules of etiquette didn't seem to apply at Brooks Pond; it was very casual. Carter, Bradley and Mary Louise couldn't get enough of the place.

***

Mark's father Carter Chapin Higgins attended private schools, studied economics at Yale, joined the Delta Kappa Epsilon fraternity, was inducted into The Aurelian Honor Society (one of Yale's famous secret societies), debated with the Yale Political Union, and toured as one of 14 members of the famed Whiffenpoofs singing troupe. He pulled for the Yale Rowing Club, played varsity tackle for the Bulldogs football team (7-1 in his senior year) alongside two of the first three Heisman Trophy winners, and was a champion of the Yale heavyweight boxing team, which famously fought Harvard to a 4-4 tie in 1935. He graduated *cum laude*.

At age 17, Carter had met Katharine Bigelow at Milton Academy, the boarding school she attended just outside of Boston. Kitsie, as she was known, was two years younger and hailed from a prosperous and artistic Manhattan family. Her father, Mason Huntington Bigelow, was the president of the New York Bar Association, and her mother, a professional woman named Elisabeth Macdonald, was the business manager for theatre companies in Manhattan and Cape Cod. Introduced to New York society in 1935, Kitsie studied English for two years at Barnard College. Mark's parents married in June 1937, just after Carter graduated. They immediately sailed for England, where Carter could study economics at Cambridge.

Kitsie became pregnant on the voyage to Europe. Nine months after their wedding, she delivered a son they named Richard Carter Higgins, after a family ancestor who landed at Plymouth Rock. During spring break, Carter and Kitsie toured France and Italy, carrying their baby in a basket. They sent back to Worcester treasures such as Italian and French furniture, tapestries and paintings by emerging artists and early French modernists. The storm clouds presaging the Second World War gathering over Europe had little impact on the couple. They could not have known how quickly the world was about to change as Hitler's army prepared to advance, about the atrocities being planned to exterminate the Jews, or how the war would change their happy lives.

When Carter finished at Cambridge, he and Kitsie sailed home. Grandfather made his firstborn son an offer he couldn't refuse and the young couple made Worcester their home.

Within a year and a half, Kitsie became pregnant again. On June 26, 1940, Mark Huntington Higgins came into the world.

War descended on the United States on December 7, 1941, when the Japanese attacked Pearl Harbor. Carter, a pacifist and a conscientious objector, was deferred from military service because of his dependents and because he worked in a critical industry: Worcester Pressed Steel was filling huge new military orders.

Mark's mother became pregnant again, and on December 1, 1942, she delivered his sister Elisabeth Lupton Higgins, to be known as Lisa. So in a short span of time, Kitsie had quit Barnard College, left unfulfilled her literary aspirations and had become a mother of three children under five years old. It was more than she had bargained for.

By age 25, she was struggling to balance her interests with the role of a wife and mother and still fit into the fast-paced business-and-civic-minded Higgins family. She wrote poems. She enrolled in a course at the Worcester Art Museum, where she studied with the Italian-American painter Umberto Romano. She even commissioned Romano to do individual portraits of herself and of Carter. The two paintings were exhibited in Boston and New York where a *New York Times* critic said the portraiture of Kitsie "sings with limpid joyousness." In her hand the artist placed a book of Kitsie's own poetry. In Carter's portrait, a cigarette dangles between his fingers.

Tensions were brewing within Mark's mother. Carter complained that she didn't understand the steel business and that she wouldn't play with the children. She hired a babysitter to stay with them and then began frequenting her old haunts in New York City and in Gloucester, the seaside art colony. She tried running an art gallery in Boston. She persuaded her husband to buy her a spacious summer house on Gloucester's Bass Rocks where she

*Mark's mother commissioned the artist Umberto Romano to do a romanticized oil painting of her and, separately, of her husband.*

could work by herself while he ran the business in Worcester during the week. Because she had become so obviously unhappy with domestic life, they began seeing a marriage counselor. Carter told Kitsie to think about whether she wanted to stay or leave. He needed her to be a business wife and a mother to Dick, Mark and Lisa.

Carter did what he could to entertain the children. Because he played the piano brilliantly, he loved gathering the children around to sing from *The Fireside Book of Folksongs*. He taught them ballads and old favorites; work songs; marching songs and songs of valor as well as old hymns; sometimes he mixed traditional folksongs with the pop music of his and Kitsie's childhood. Those moments were among the happiest of times, and made lasting impressions on each of the children.

Mark's father focused on the business opportunities presented by the post-war boom. Europe was rebuilding. Just after Mark's seventh birthday in 1947, he was sent away to summer camp in Maine and his father left for a six-week fact-finding tour of war-torn Europe where a group of his fellow industrialists met with business and political leaders in Helsinki, Stockholm, Warsaw, Krakow, Prague and Paris.

From Europe, Carter wrote to his depressed wife nearly every day. She occasionally wrote back, each time pleading with Carter to get away from Worcester and Worcester Pressed Steel and his family's intense social life.

One day, Mark's mother and Lisa were browsing through a Gloucester antique shop when a clerk struck up a conversation with the little girl and then with Kitsie. It was a moment that would change everyone's lives.

Ten years older than Mark's mother, that clerk Mary Bechhold Einstein moved easily among the artsy crowd in Gloucester. She listened to the young mother's frustration. Over the coming weeks she became a mentor and thought that Kitsie might benefit by taking some time off: she should go away for a while until she was ready to settle down. Kitsie liked the idea but hesitated because of the children. Mary solved that problem by offering to serve as their governess.

In a letter to her husband, Kitsie broached the idea. She told him that the children were well and that she had found someone to watch them: "There is a lovely person, Mary Einstein, who adores kids and might be good to take care of the children while I undergo a 're-education' process .... I'm not fit to be with them."

Carter agreed that his wife needed some perspective. Six months later, the new governess moved into the family's guest room, charged with running the household, providing discipline and managing the children. Dick, age nine, would be boarding at the Putney School in Vermont. Mary would care for Mark, age seven, and Lisa, age five.

A few days after Christmas 1947, seven-year-old Mark said a tearful goodbye to his mother. It was the second time within a year that one of his parents was going away. Fluent in French and longing to reconnect with the artistic and literary world, his mother was heading for Paris where she could meet prominent artists and indulge her passions for painting and literature and, in Mary's words, expunge the last bit of wildness from her system.

This new governess was a sophisticated, world-wise and attractive 38-year-old Bavarian woman. Her big Jewish family included lots of brothers and sisters, who had left Europe before the war to build careers in the U.S. as hoteliers, gold mine operators and businessmen. But Mary had not left

Europe in time. The Nazis captured her and her husband in Holland and held them in a series of concentration camps. The Germans had done terrible things to her and killed her husband at Auschwitz. She migrated to the United States after the war, but the memories haunted her. Late at night, Mark and Lisa sometimes heard Mary crying and screaming in her bedroom. Lisa would rush in to comfort her when she had these nightmares about the concentration camps.

In the daytime, Mary paid attention to Mark and Lisa. She became their confidante as well as their disciplinarian, despite the horrid flashbacks and her uncertain temperament.

Late into the evenings, Mary talked with Carter. The new arrangement with the attractive, intelligent and world-wise woman pleased him. They conversed in German to ensure their words remained private from the children. He took a liking to her. Within a few months he and Mary were sharing the same bedroom.

Mark and Lisa didn't know what to think.

By the time Mark's mother came home from France six months later, she was hoping to make a fresh start at the marriage. Instead, she found this shocking new domestic situation. Reconciliation failed. By the end of the summer, Mark's parents filed for divorce and agreed to split custody, separating the children: the boys would stay with their father. Lisa would go with her mother to New York. They would only see one another on vacations, holidays and at various times in the summer.

Mark was a very vulnerable eight year old. His parents' divorce profoundly affected him. His whole world was shattered. Now he would fall under the loving but iron hand of Mary. Not surprisingly, this started out as a contentious relationship. As a child Mark was often confused by Mary's erratic behavior. She usually displayed a good humor and happy nature, but was subject to chronic manic depression. She considered obedience the highest value, and imposed a strict Germanic code on Mark and his brother Dick. This had been a far different experience than they had with their mother. Mary showered the children with affection, but she could turn it off as quickly as she turned it on.

On May 27, 1949, just days after the divorce was finalized, Carter mar-

married the woman whom his wife had recruited as their children's governess. She was seven years older than Carter. Granddad served as best man for his son.

In the summers ahead, Mark finally spent some time with his mother. Once, she took all three children to Florida, where they enjoyed a typical family experience: attending minor league baseball games, fishing and swimming, and having a mother who was actually available and content. In the Deep South, the children observed extreme poverty in the black neighborhoods and became aware of the segregation laws still in force. The memory of that preyed on their social conscience.

Another time they traveled with her to Mexico and spent several weeks near Lake Chapala where her brother David Bigelow, a paleontologist, was excavating mammoth bones.

When he was 10, he was old enough to go to summer camp. He and his older brother Dick went to Pasquaney, their father's old camp in New Hampshire, and Lisa went to Onaway, a nearby camp for girls. But Pasquaney was not a good experience for Mark: campers teased him about his large, pop-out ears and his good looks. They called him "Pretty Boy" in the yearbook, a nickname he hated. His letters home pleaded with his father to write more often.

In 1951 Mark's mother married a man named Nicholas Doman, a Hungarian-American lawyer with an important book to his credit (*The Coming Age of World Control*). He had served in the U.S. Army and then attended the University of Colorado on a Fulbright Scholarship. Having worked as a staff prosecuting attorney at the Nuremberg Trials, he was obsessed by the Holocaust.

With her new husband and a lovely apartment in a tony Park Avenue neighborhood on Manhattan's Upper East Side, Mark's mother embraced domesticity and entertained an expanding social circle. Within a few years she bore two more sons, Daniel and Alexander, Mark's half-brothers.

To all outward appearances, Mark had become "a sociable, loving, smiling, dimpled and radiant child," as Lisa would say. No one seemed to notice the changes beginning to well up inside of him.

*The family gathered for a special occasion about 1954: Mark, his father Carter, grandfather John Woodman Higgins and his sister Lisa. The author is seated in front.*

Being separated from his new brothers, his mother and his sister depressed Mark. Back in Worcester, he attended elementary school at Bancroft, a well-established private institution not far from his grandparents' house. But learning didn't come easily. Mary discovered that he was dyslexic, and she devoted hours every day helping him to overcome the disability.

He also suffered from a congenital defect: a dislocating knee cap. Surgery corrected this, followed by six weeks in a full-leg plastic cast. This limited strenuous sports activity, but with some caution he could hike, walk, and use his legs in normal activity. His brother Dick was away at boarding school, Lisa was living with her mother, and his father was focused on work and civic pursuits. Mark's upbringing depended on Mary. They became very close, and Mark appreciated the attention and support of his stepmother. He learned from her. And he empathized with her. He could identify with the dislocations and hardships she had experienced.

He began seventh grade at St. Paul's School in Concord, New Hampshire, which his brother Dick already attended. All-male and highly selective, the boarding school stands amidst 2,000 acres of woodlands, fields, and ponds. Mark's father had gone there himself, played guard on the football team, rowed on the Halcyon crew team, become a student supervisor in one of the residence halls and won academic scholarships. Surely, his sons could do as well or better.

"Paulies" led a regimented and highly disciplined life. The four full days each week begin with a mandatory interfaith chapel session involving reading, speech or music presentation, and announcements. Most classes were taught using the Harkness method, with students and the teacher facing one another around a big oval table. The average class size was 12. St. Paul's required that all students play at least one sport, ranging from internationally competitive crew to intramural hockey. Students could join one of two boat clubs, but a legacy was automatically assigned to the same club as his forebear.

Mark's experience at St. Paul's, however, did not replicate that of his father. Sure, he joined the choir (Dad had sung with the Whiffenpoofs at Yale!) and was assigned to the Halcyon boat club (Dad rowed for Yale!). But by the beginning of eighth grade, Mark had become the victim of intense bullying by upper classmen. They went right for Mark's big floppy ears, which they pulled as they taunted him with epithets such as "Dumbo" and "Bat Ears." Eventually, the ear-pulling caused physical damage and pain that accompanied the psychological trauma. By the end of his first semester of eighth

*Mark, prior to his otoplasty, with his stepmother Mary at a big Thanksgiving party at the Higgins Armory Museum.*

grade, Mark couldn't stand the place. He felt belittled by classmates. Moreover, at home he found it hard to relate to his father who was frequently away on business. He began keeping an emotional distance from people.

Over Christmas break, Mark's mother arranged for him to see Dr. Benjamin H. Balser, an adolescent psychotherapist in New York. The doctor summarized in a letter to both parents: "Mark does not want to return to

St. Paul's, and I think it is understandable in view of his past experiences there." Adding a hopeful note, Balser added, "Mark pointed out to me that on his last visit home at Thanksgiving, he had come to accept Mary on a much healthier basis." For the immediate future, however, Mark would stay with his mother and her new husband and Lisa. First, Mark was taken to an ear doctor, who performed an otoplasty, a relatively common pediatric plastic surgery that pinned back his big ears so they wouldn't stick out so much.

To finish eighth grade, he was enrolled at The Buckley School in New York. Mark's leadership skills began emerging: he was elected secretary of the student government, and led the committee that wrote a play for the annual Athletic Banquet. He was excelling at math and in such crafts as wood carving. The headmaster wrote that Mark had "responded exceedingly well here to the kind of close contact and friendly relationship that exists in a school of this size," adding that "a few more years of this kind of socialization would be good for Mark to build up his self-confidence and his relationship with his fellow students." On the surface, this seemed like a good environment.

But life at home with his mother was the opposite. Although Mark loved being reunited with Lisa, he saw that his mother's relationship with Nick Doman was stormy most of the time. To complicate things, Mark saw his stepfather as a temperamental, demanding and authoritarian figure. Mark and Lisa watched how Nick managed their mother, opened her mail, controlled her finances, and acted diffidently toward her children.

He had to find a respite from all this confusion and tension.

He couldn't stay in New York.

# Five

# Tranquility at the Pond

In 1949 Mark's grandfather John Woodman Higgins suffered a heart attack. Doctors warned him that he had to slow down. Mindful of the threat to his longevity, he established two trusts. Much of that consisted of stock in the Norton Abrasives Company, of which his brother Aldus was president. All the children and grandchildren would be well provided for. The trusts and life insurance proceeds eventually provided about $7 million in benefits to Carter, Bradley, Mary Louise and their children.

Mark's 36-year-old father became president of Worcester Pressed Steel and head of the Higgins Armory Museum, pushing himself hard to keep the company profitable and the Museum presentable. He replaced outmoded equipment, dealt with the unions, and kept winning new business contracts. He managed both organizations, sat on the boards of several others in which the family had investments, and emerged as a civic activist. As one of the most prominent employers in Worcester, he became the Red Cross chapter chairman and raised millions for dis-

*Mark's father became president of the Higgins Armory Museum after Grandfather Higgins suffered a heart attack.*

aster relief. He welcomed to the city national figures such as Ellsworth Bunker, the national Red Cross President. He joined the highly networked Young Presidents Organization, and addressed their national convention in Phoenix.

His pacifist inclination ran strong amidst the global tensions lingering after the Korean conflict, with the threat of Soviet domination and the fear of nuclear war. Carter put his beliefs into action. A Yale colleague, Cord Meyer, the wealthy son of a career diplomat, had been a delegate to the conference that founded the United Nations. But Meyer didn't see the U.N. as strong enough, so he founded an organization called the United World Federalists. One of its most important goals was to establish controls on the use of atomic weapons. Carter called him up and said he wanted to be part of this new movement.

The United Nations, Carter agreed, was too weak to manage the world's problems; a more powerful entity was needed. Carter began hosting meetings of the United World Federalists. When Norman Cousins, the organization's new national chairman and editor of the widely respected magazine *The Saturday Review*, spoke at a meeting Carter hosted, the two men, one whose strength was industry and one whose strength was journalism, began a long and close friendship.

At the height of the Communist menace, Carter and a lot of other serious people saw threats everywhere. The World Federalists enrolled more than 50,000 members, including such notables as Albert Einstein, Kurt Vonnegut, Senator Alan Cranston, Mortimer Adler, E.B. White, Oscar Hammerstein and others. They were adamant about creating a structure for peace more powerful than the United Nations.

Carter became president of the New England chapter. Cold War tensions pervaded every aspect of daily life. It was just after the era of Sen. Joe McCarthy, when Communists were suspected of infiltrating the American government, and when nuclear war was being held off only by the frightening theory of "mutually assured destruction."

The fear of nuclear war was real in the 1950s, and intensified after the Soviet Union launched Sputnik, the world's first satellite, in 1957. Suddenly, America's geographical security was gone: the Communists could deliver nuclear bombs anywhere. Municipalities across the country built

Civil Defense Shelters where citizens could hide in the event of a nuclear attack. School children were drilled in how to hide under the desks in their classrooms to protect themselves from the blast. Families built bomb shelters in their backyards or basements and equipped them with cots, bottled water and food. Even the Higgins family summer home in New Hampshire had a fully equipped bomb shelter deep underground.

Carter's fast-paced and intense life was taking a toll on him, and was taking time away from his kids. Privately he knew, as his father before him had known, that he should slow down.

Seeking tranquility in his life, Mark's father bought a 40-acre lot at Brooks Pond and constructed a year-round house on a bluff overlooking the water. He and Mary moved to the rural community of North Brookfield. Within his spacious one-floor house was a large office and huge round living room with floor-to-ceiling windows. There, amidst the pines, oaks and birches, he could relax and study in absolute peace and quiet. He became a lay reader at Christ Memorial Church, became involved in the little town's civic life, and donated $50,000 toward construction of the town hall.

Carter built a separate three-bedroom house on the property for Dick, Mark and Lisa. On weekends and long holidays, he invited whichever of his kids was there for long walks on the trails around the pond. In the evenings, Carter read aloud to his young boys. He read them Rudyard Kipling's *Just So* stories. He read them *Treasure Island*. He read them *The Story of a Bad Boy*, the Thomas Bailey Aldrich semi-autobiographical novel that celebrates a misbehaving boy as a protagonist rather than an antagonist. Despite these occasional interactions, the children found it hard to establish a relationship with their father when he lived in a separate house. Nevertheless, Mark and his siblings loved Brooks Pond.

Most of the time, Mark had that little house all to himself. He could go fishing and he could paddle his foldable kayak around the pond, slipping into its numerous inlets and coves. He mastered the Old Town sailing canoe and raced it every Sunday. He could also do a little shooting, first with a B-B gun and then with the .22 rifle he received for his 14th birthday. In the woods he could spot moose, deer, fox and other wildlife. In the evenings Brooks Pond was a quiet place to read, write or sing.

Early each morning and at predictable intervals during the day, Mark would hear the bells of St. Joseph's Abbey, the new Trappist monastery in Spencer, calling the monks to prayer, to work or to meals.

Mark converted the spacious top floor of his grandparents' boathouse into a secret "boys-only club." Sometimes Mark and a few of his younger cousins would camp on the big island in the middle of the pond. They snuggled in their sleeping bags as Mark sang his favorites lyrical ditties such as "Abdul Abulbul Amir," "Sam Hall," "Dink's Sing (Had I the Wings of Noah's Dove)" or "The Chivalrous Man-Eating Shark." On weekends and summer days he and his friends simply lost themselves in laughter and play.

*Brooks Pond became a tranquil refuge for the Higgins family. Mark loved exploring its inlets in his kayak.*

Although Mark had been shy and reserved around girls his age, there was one with whom he was very close and comfortable. Patricia Getz, his stepmother's niece, was a frequent visitor to Brooks Pond. She and Mark were about the same age and they spent a lot of time together. Mark had genuine affection for her. They became great pals, spending lazy summer days together in a canoe paddling around the pond, picking blueberries off the bushes and popping the fruit into one another's mouth, and trying to catch the painted turtles that somehow always eluded them. It was idyllic.

By the time Mark was ready to enter high school, his towering physique, gentle sense of humor and good looks attracted attention wherever he went, but he remained reserved. His parents made the decision to enroll him at Milton Academy, the boarding school where he already had a few friends. His cousin Prentiss Higgins and Barry Morgan, his neighbor across Brooks Pond, were going there. So was Phil Kinnicutt, who had lived a few doors away in Worcester.

One of the most expensive and elite prep schools in the east, Milton was a feeder school for Harvard and other Ivy League institutions. Its alumni roster includes captains of industry and luminaries ranging from the architect Buckminster Fuller to the playwright T.S. Elliott and to future Senators Robert F. Kennedy and Edward M. Kennedy, Nixon Cabinet member Eliot Richardson and other prominent men.

Mark found himself assigned to Robbins House, one of four residence halls. Living together for four years built camaraderie, friendship, and life-long networking. At Milton, his classmates gave him the affectionate nickname "Higgs." He lent his strong bass voice to the Glee Club and loved the performances.

Unable to play aggressive contact sports because of his knee problems, "Higgs" instead became manager of the soccer team, which in his junior year won six games and lost two. Occasionally, Mark's kneecap became dislodged when he turned the wrong way. His roommate John Scholz found him on the floor one afternoon writhing in pain: Mark instructed John to pull his leg as he pushed the knee cap back into place. Mark knew it was horrible for John to watch this, but the experience only served to deepen their friendship.

Mark and John considered themselves oddballs with a lot in common. They figured out how to get a pass to leave campus on Sunday mornings on the pretense of attending local church services, but more often wound up at the drug store soda fountain, a considerably livelier place for boys on Sunday mornings.

Mark provided John with companionship and a second home to go to on the weekends they were allowed to leave Milton. They stayed in his guest house at Brooks Pond, interacting with Mark's parents only for meals.

In the summer after his freshman year, Mark got a job picking apples at Brookfield Orchards in North Brookfield. The next summer, he went to work for the Evansville Art and History Museum in Indiana where his mother's brother David Bigelow was the education director.

After his junior year, he signed on as a summer intern at a division of Norton Abrasives, the company owned by his uncle Aldus. It was located in Fullerton, California, an industrial suburb of Los Angeles. Mark made a little money as he explored the West Coast. He loved the scenery, the weather and the people of Southern California, but he found the work boring and not worth writing home about. What excited him most was a cash birthday gift from his grandparents that, as he said in his thank-you note, would help him pay for "a custom-built rifle, two and a half months in the making, the very best that money can buy."

Life back at Milton Academy was full of irresistible temptations. Mark and John Scholz conspired on a few memorable hijinks that reflected their sense of rebellion. Each night their housemaster, a man named Bob Daley, would prowl the house to see if they were asleep. He would start at the top floor and work down to the ground floor where Mark and John lived. To do so, Daley had to walk down a tight little staircase, and then open a door leading to the hallway. With flashlight in hand he would do bed-checks to ensure every boy was tucked in. He always thought he was doing this without waking anyone. Usually the boys would be reading books with their flashlights under the covers, or talking.

The boys hated these nightly inspections. One day Scholz devised a way to stop this. An amateur electronics whiz, he decided to give Mr. Daley what they called "a little tweak." The door to their room had a metal door knob. Scholz electrified the knob by attaching wires which he plugged into the wall outlet. That night when the housemaster crept down the stairs and grabbed the doorknob, the circuit was completed. They had never heard Bob Daley swear before, but just then he did, and he shouted, "Who did this? Both of you are really in trouble here!" Fortunately, he didn't throw them out of school. Nor did he report the incident to the boys' parents. Their prank ended the nightly inspections. And the housemaster never checked on them again.

Another otherwise brilliant classmate, Randal Whitman, joined Mark and John in what became the most memorable stunt of their entire high school career. In science class they were exposed to the chemical principles of dry ice and the pressure that evaporating dry ice produces. Mark, John and Randal decided to test this concept one weekend. Mark brought in a big cider jug with a small neck, and someone else got hold of some dry ice, which they chopped into pieces. They went into the third floor bathroom, opened the window, crawled out onto the fire escape and shoved pieces of dry ice into the bottle. With the top screwed on tightly, they lowered the jug over the side by a rope, and then dove back though the bathroom window. All of a sudden there was a horrendous explosion.

The force of the blast shattered a dozen windows. The top of the jug projected over the roof and landed in the garden of a nearby residence hall, where a faculty member was planting flowers. It didn't take long for the three culprits to be apprehended. Given the damage, they thought they might face arrest, expulsion, fines or some serious punishment. Instead,

*At Milton Academy, Mark studied French for four years, but his passion was chess.*

upon reviewing the facts, Robbins housemaster Bob Daley directed each of the "bombers" to write a long essay on the properties and proper uses of dry ice. Again, their parents were never notified.

Another of the trio's adventures involved exploring the steam pipe tunnel that linked their dorm with the Forbes House next door and ran beneath the kitchen that served both houses. The area was strictly off-limits, but the boys found a way down and penetrated the depths quite often and, remarkably, were never caught. They called themselves The Moles, with their motto being *semper sub terra*. The Democratic candidate for president in the 1956 election was Adlai Stevenson. Since Randal's mother had an acquaintance with him, they sent him an honorary membership in The Moles. Stevenson wrote back: "As

I have always been considered an underground movement, I will feel very comfortable *semper sub terra.*"

Mark sometimes invited John and Randal home to Brooks Pond. They could reach there by trolley and bus in less than two hours. Randal liked going to Brooks Pond for a different reason: he had taken an interest in Mark's sister Lisa, who in addition to her literary and vocal talents had blossomed into a curvy, vivacious blonde. Soon, Randal was calling on her fairly regularly at Brooks Pond or in New York, with or without Mark. Their relationship endured for years.

———

Mark became a reasonably good student although not an academic stand-out. He had inherited an appreciation of language and the written word and was doing well in his mandatory two years of Latin. He earned better than average grades and his four years of French at Milton gave him a conversational proficiency that would serve him well in the years ahead.

Expressive in writing and possessing a precocious vocabulary, he contributed prose and poetry to the student magazine, *The Orange and Blue*, during his junior and senior years. One poem stood out:

### The Cleansing

*Tension . . .*
  *Spark . . .*
*Hysteria, holocaust, havoc,*
*Rubble, fear, death,*
*And peace midst the swirling dust . . .*

*Fear is gone, for there are none to hate;*
*Ideals do not exist.*
  *Science, which taught men to kill, is dead;*
*Religion, which told men they were right, is dead,*
  *And so is God . . .*

*The World, after forever, is clean.*

- Mark Higgins '58

But more than any other activity, Mark's passion was chess. He played mail-order chess. He joined the Milton chess club. His teammates elected him President of the Chess Club and he led their practices in the beautiful Strauss Library on campus. He played chess incessantly with John Scholz and with Randal Whitman.

They all idolized Bobby Fischer, the teenaged prodigy who was three years younger than them but who became an American chess grandmaster and eventually World Chess Champion.

Mark and his buddies devoured the daily newspaper reports about Bobby Fischer's strategies and moves. In 1956 at age 13 Fischer had won a match in New York that became known as The Game of the Century. The next year, 1957, when Fischer was 14, he played in the first of his eight United States Championships, winning each by at least a point. By 1958 Fischer was on the verge of becoming both the youngest grandmaster and the youngest candidate for the World Championship up to that time. Mark

*Mark was president of the Milton Chess Club, and led regular practices in the Strauss Library.*

spent hours in quiet contemplation, perfecting his game and devising winning strategies. Scholz was astonished by Mark's ability to always think about 15 moves ahead. Each year the club made a respectable showing against other prep schools. In the *Milton Measure*, the school newspaper, Mark declared loftily after an important victory, "The high plane of both our recent intra-mural interest and interscholastic achievement prognosticates nothing but our continuing success." But something else was brewing beneath that confident veneer.

John Scholz noticed during junior year that Mark went into some kind of deep funk. There was no anger or outburst; he just showed some irritability. He was in and out of the housemaster's apartment a lot. Not everyone noticed the change, but John made note of it. Mark just wasn't himself.

Mark had quietly continued seeing his adolescent psychotherapist, Benjamin Balser in New York, who prescribed anti-depressant medication that he hoped would enable his young patient to see a brighter side of life, and a path forward.

Mark tried to conceal his depression and the fact that he had been taking prescription antidepressant medication from his friend John Scholz. Robert Daley was in the loop and communicating with Mark's father regularly, even though no one talked about it. But John knew.

Scholz became a more frequent weekend guest at Brooks Pond, where he and Mark ice skated in winter and hiked through the woods in autumn. Those weekends allowed Scholz to observe how Mark and his father interacted: "On my weekends in North Brookfield his father would sternly bark at Mark like a drill sergeant. The man could be scary at times. He was imposing and dictatorial, and he treated Mark harshly. I could feel the stress: Carter Higgins used his size to intimidate both passively and aggressively. When you walked into their house and saw him, it was a bit like you'd expect a monarch to act when you came into the room. Mark's overbearing father played a big part in Mark's emotional and psychological problems as we went through Milton. The message he gave off was that you had better grow up and be something. You'd better do it because you are from a privileged background, and we have lots of expectations."

Mark had been hearing that "be-something" injunction all his life. To him, having a privileged background was an accident of birth, not something he had chosen or earned. All the trappings of wealth: the world-class artwork, the famous museum bearing the family name, the big house in Worcester, the private pond, the summer mansion in New Hampshire, the chauffeur, private schools, his mother's chic New York address, his father's civic influence, the steel company . . . it was all too much. Mark wasn't eager to embrace that. Sometimes he felt like he was going to burst.

Mark's senior yearbook portrait shows a confident, focused face alongside the other future masters of the universe. Most of his classmates were declaring their college choices. "Higgs" wrote "undecided." Yearbook editors asked seniors to name their preferred and most probable occupations. Mark said his probable future occupation would be "President of Worcester Pressed Steel." For his preferred future occupation, he wrote "Wild Game Hunter in Africa."

Mark confided in his roommates that he was under increasing pressure from his father to do well on his College Board exams so he could apply to Yale. That's where his father had gone. That's where Dick had gone. That's where Mark was destined to go, too. But Mark was troubled by all this pressure.

Mark was about to turn 18 years old. He had won the respect, admiration and friendship of his classmates at Milton Academy. But behind the mask of the calculating chess player, the dutiful equipment manager and the thoughtful essayist, only Mark knew the extent to which he was wracked with self-doubt. The fact was that he didn't know what he wanted to do with himself. Soon he would

*Mark listed his preferred future occupation as Wild Game Hunter in Africa.*

have to sit for the college entrance exams. Although he had been an underachiever, he had always tested well. But what was ahead?

Many in the Milton Class of 1958 were headed to an Ivy League campus. About half of them would go to Harvard and a handful would go to Yale. If Mark did well on the exams, he knew that the next steps would be to get those scores into the hands of the right admission committees.

His classmates were deep into their studies. These boys of privilege were planning ahead for university life and plotting their careers. It was understood as a birthright that they would become leaders in business, medicine or law. Mark held back. He wouldn't rush into college or stay home and await his turn running the family business. He had seen what that was doing to his father. It had caused his grandfather a heart attack.

Furthermore, Mark felt confused by what he perceived as an ethical conflict: his father the conscientious objector and world peace activist was running a business producing military hardware.

Mark gradually withdrew. He didn't feel ready to be slotted into that groove. But there was no resisting the pressure from home. His father expected decisive thinking. Ultimately, Mark and his father just couldn't talk. There wasn't a way to say "no" to his father.

Before long he would be told to step right into the family business. His pre-ordained destiny was to work his way up through a series of positions until he became president of Worcester Pressed Steel. Then the burden for maintaining the business would fall on him, just as it had fallen on his ever-busier and increasingly aloof father.

That was all mapped out, but it was not all he wanted. He knew that if he started down that track, his adventurous, exploratory spirit would never be satisfied. Instead, one day, the whole family would all depend on him. He wouldn't be able to live out his dreams because he'd be working his tail off stamping out military hardware at Worcester Pressed Steel.

Obviously, his brother Dick wasn't going to run that company. Dick had a nervous breakdown at Yale, forcing him to drop out. He spent several months at Silver Hill, the Connecticut psychiatric sanitarium. Dick was now living in Greenwich Village writing sonatas and poems and pursuing his preferred life as an avant-garde artist.

Mark thought a compromise might be possible. He thought about a college curriculum where he could spend three years in a liberal arts program, then maybe transfer to the Massachusetts Institute of Technology to earn a combined bachelor and masters degree in two more years.

Meanwhile, economic events that would have repercussions for the steel industry were being felt. Across the country, the early signs of what became the Recession of 1957-1958 were beginning to show up. There was under-utilized production capacity, excess inventory, fewer government orders and tight money. Carter felt the squeeze. Worcester Pressed Steel business was suffering; Carter proposed reductions in salary and hours for workers. It was going to be a difficult year.

Carter was almost frantic looking for a way to save his business.

Mark was almost frantic looking for a way to find meaning in his life.

Saturday, February 23, 1958, was a typical cold winter day in eastern Massachusetts, 24 degrees and overcast. Without telling anyone, Mark left the Milton campus and caught the trolley into Boston. He took the bus to North Brookfield. He walked the two miles along Oakham Road to the mailbox marking the Higgins property, and then a half mile down the gravel driveway to the children's house overlooking Brooks Pond. He arrived quietly, and stayed up late thinking.

If he succeeded in what he planned to do, he wouldn't have to face the final few months at Milton and watch everyone else celebrate their college acceptances.

He wouldn't have to take any more pressure from his father.

He wouldn't be channeled into a stifling and demanding business career.

He wouldn't continue on the treadmill of no choices.

In anticipation of this evening, Mark for months had been removing one or two sleeping pills from his stepmother's medicine cabinet, and hiding them away.

He opened the secret stash of almost 100 pills and methodically began swallowing one after another.

He lay down on his bed and drifted into an incoherent stupor.

# Six

# A Gap Year

In the cold haze of dawn, Mark felt drowsy and limp. He was nauseous, breathing slowly and had trouble speaking. Through his blurred vision he could barely make out the horrified look on his father's face.

Carter had been rushing off to Christ Memorial Church in North Brookfield on Sunday morning when he sensed something was amiss in the other house. He found his son unresponsive and called out for Mary. They rushed him to St. Vincent's Hospital in Worcester, where emergency room doctors pumped out his stomach.

Once their patient was stabilized, the doctors and his family wanted to learn what had prompted this behavior.

In a few days, Mark found himself waking up at the Payne Whitney psychiatric clinic of New York Hospital. He was locked in a fifth floor room of the 120-bed hospital where the security precautions included barred windows and glass panes in the door through which nurses could peer inside. The average length of stay for a patient was seven months.

Mark was in trouble.

Carter made two snap decisions. First, he concocted a cover story that Mark had contracted "a stomach illness." Second, Mark would not be returning to Milton Academy, and what really happened would not be disclosed.

John Scholz and Randal Whitman never saw him again. Even when Randal visited North Brookfield the following weekend for a date with Lisa, she couldn't tell him where her brother was.

Five long days after Mark's encounter with the sleeping pills, Carter sat down and wrote a letter to his father and mother who were at their Palm Beach winter home. He began by reviewing the state of business at Worcester Pressed Steel; there were issues related to salary cutbacks. He shared news about Lisa's and Dick's social lives before getting to the point about Mark.

> *His thinking is seriously off, with no apparent single cause. Apparently he has had this in mind for a long time, and he fooled everyone. He sees no pleasure or purpose in living at present, and is his charming self. Superficially Dick stood it ok; Dr. Balser told him. He will miss College Board exams. I shall take Lisa and Dick to the Caribbean as planned. I really don't see anything more we can do right now.*

> *We have told those few who know anything about it that Mark has some sort of poisoning in his system and that he has been taken to the New York Hospital for a further effort to get at the base of it; that we do not understand the cause - all of which is true.*

> *This letter would be most seriously incomplete if I didn't tell you how wonderful Mary has been through all this with understanding and help in many, many ways. Mark tells her things he tells no one else.*

In a hint that Mark had begun rejecting some of the trappings of materialism, Carter suggested that if they wrote to Mark, they should exercise caution about what they discussed: "Incline toward outlining and suggesting there is pleasure for you in some of the things that you two enjoy, generally simpler and less material things - nature, health, relationships, each other, grandchildren etc. No presents please, though Dad might mail a leaf or two, or talk about lobsters." Mary added a handwritten postscript: "We are very blessed that we found him and saved him. All we can do now is to try and be very strong and hopeful. It was a great trial."

Benjamin Balser must have wondered what had happened to the young man he had been seeing for the past five years. Up until that time, he had been treating Mark's depression only with medicine. Now he had to recommend a much more radical treatment regime. After his initial evaluation at the Payne Whitney psychiatric clinic, Balser ordered Mark's transfer to the Hartford Center for Living in Connecticut, a sprawling 35-acre campus.

On May 1, ten weeks after the onset of his "stomach ailment," Mark wrote to his grandparents from Hartford telling them the good news: he had earned enough credits to graduate from Milton on June 7, despite having missed almost a semester. He said "there is a good chance they will let me leave here for the day, and that I may graduate with my class." He invited them to attend his graduation. Mark seemed to be in on the cover story his father had concocted, but apparently had not been told that his grandparents knew the truth about why he had been hospitalized, as indicated by the misleading but affectionate way he finished his letter to them: "I've just gotten over a bad cold but am completely well now. I hope you are well too. Keep smiling, and stand straight like the knight and maiden you are. Love, Mark."

June 7 was indeed graduation day at Milton Academy, but Mark Higgins was nowhere to be seen on campus. He remained confined at Hartford. Doctors were still in the early stages of treating him, and they didn't consider their patient well enough mentally or emotionally to go anywhere.

Mark wrote another letter. He pleaded with Mary to send him the radio that he had left in his room at Brooks Pond. Nobody knew why he wanted that particular radio, but after several requests, she packed it up and sent it to him. The hospital staff was wise to all kinds of tricks from patients, and was cautious about uncensored packages. The screeners thought the package felt too heavy for a mere radio. They opened it and discovered a false back in the radio where Mark had hidden a gun. The staff removed the weapon and gave him the radio.

Family members and friends were discouraged from contacting him. Patricia Getz, Mary's niece who had been a frequent visitor and his favorite playmate at Brooks Pond, was hoping to take Mark some books when she learned that he had been hospitalized. She was prohibited from doing so, and was never told why.

The Hartford Institute for Living, although it had a long history for treating people with mental disturbances, could be a place of great intensity. When it opened in 1824 it was known as the Connecticut Retreat for the Insane. The old hospital housed up to 40 mostly affluent patients at a time. While it was often called simply the Hartford Retreat and the fenced-in campus was lovely, the treatment there was no retreat for patients.

The famous and beautiful but troubled Hollywood actress Gene Tierney had been admitted there in 1957, just the year before. While at Hartford she was subjected to 27 electric shock treatments that she claimed erased significant portions of her memory.

*The actress Gene Tierney endured the same electric shock treatment as Mark received.*

If Gene Tierney's experience provides any insight into Mark's treatment, it would be an ordeal for anyone. Each patient was kept in a tiny room, with the door locked and the window barred. The first six weeks of confinement consisted of isolation from the outside world coupled with psychotherapy and electric shock treatments. No contact with family was permitted. Patients were not permitted to use the telephone. After a certain period of time, depending on a patient's progress, family members could visit once a week.

In 1958 the typical treatment for depression or "lack of interest in most things" was electro-convulsive treatment. The procedure was performed by a psychiatrist and an anesthesiologist assisted by nurses and other medical staff. It involved injecting an anesthetic and then a muscle relaxant. With the patient sedated, technicians strap an oxygen mask on his face. The doctor wedged a rubber stick in the patient's mouth to bite on, placed paddles on each temple, and administered a jolt of electricity until the patient's feet moved. The current caused a brief seizure in the brain. The patient was awakened after five or ten minutes, then was encouraged to walk around and "join the hospital's daily activities." Patients received multiple treatments over a period of months.

Gene Tierney endured eight months of such shock therapy. She found out the hard way that any misbehavior, such as trying to escape, would result in her being placed into a large locked room with other patients who were "rocking back and forth on the floor ... pacing and twitching uncontrollably ... shaking, talking and screaming, all of them fearing their own demons, all of them having slipped far beyond the realm of sanity," according to Tierney's biography. A second offense meant the isolation unit, a solitary locked room without a window, toilet or running water.

Shock treatments often produced an immediate but temporary feeling of elation, followed by a period of depression. Doctors prescribed drugs between the shock therapy sessions and nurses inspected every cavity of the patient's mouth to be sure the pills were swallowed. Patients were expected and encouraged to have long talks with the doctors on the theory that they might eventually talk themselves out of their own problems.

Francis J. Braceland had served since 1951 as the facility's chief psychiatrist. He was regarded as one of the country's most influential leaders in the new field of mental health, but he had some unorthodox ideas. Braceland was a proselytizer on morality and culture who characterized rock and roll music as a "communicable disease," and championed creation of a federal agency to deal with a postwar society that he viewed as a cauldron of psychic ills. "The numbers of sick and suffering people are legion," he wrote in his official history of the Hartford Institute. Braceland estimated that there were more than five million alcoholics in the United States, that the population also contained countless drug addicts, and that beyond the million or so citizens languishing in psychiatric wards were millions more who suffered from "crippling emotional disorders." He asserted that psychiatrists constituted the nation's front line against a crisis that was becoming pandemic. He was so well regarded that he was elected president of the American Psychiatric Association in 1956 and 1957.

Electro-convulsive treatment seemed barbaric. However, even the well-respected Mayo Clinic called it "one of the fastest ways to relieve symptoms in severely depressed or suicidal patients . . . when severe depression is unresponsive to other forms of therapy. Or it might be used when patients pose a severe threat to themselves or others and it is too dangerous to wait until medications take effect."

A Duke University analyst contended that electric shock treatments "often quickly resolve the symptoms of major depression, including depressed mood, lack of interest, appetite and weight disturbance, sleep disturbance, feelings of hopelessness and helplessness, loss of self esteem, and thoughts of suicide."

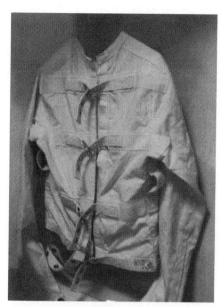

*Patients at the Hartford Center for Living were sometimes confined to a straight-jacket, similar to this one on display at its "Myths, Minds and Medicine" Museum.*

His doctors asked probing questions and let Mark delve deeply into his own psyche. He argued back by quoting existential philosophers such as Jean Paul Sartre, Soren Kierkegaard and Friedrich Nietzsche. It took many months before Mark finally showed signs of progress, and stopped his talk of self-destruction.

The whole family still worried about him. Mark had survived his overdose of sleeping pills. He had received treatment for his depression. Now he had to build up self-esteem and find a purpose for living. He had to answer the question: What should he do with his life?

Mark's mother made numerous trips to Hartford to see him and listen to him. She said over and over again that the family would do anything Mark asked. He had to get well enough to attend college. This would take time and maybe more counseling. Mark pushed back. Instead of going to college right away, he began talking about an interim step.

Mark's stepmother Mary visited often, too, and discussed some options. She encouraged Mark to think beyond himself, to think about service to others. Mary reviewed the inner strength she had called upon to survive the Holocaust, and the desperation and deprivation faced by so many Jewish people in Europe. Mark began to accept the idea that he might have an obligation to help others rather than dwelling on his own problems.

There was another influence besides his mother and his stepmother. Hollywood had just produced an 80-minute documentary on the life of Albert Schweitzer. In the style of newsreel footage, the film by Jerome Hill and Erica Anderson traced the career of the jungle doctor. The film showed the elderly Schweitzer working at his hospital at Lambaréné. The film conveyed a strong Christian influence as it depicted day-to-day activity at the hospital. The critically acclaimed film won the Academy Award for the Documentary Feature of the year on March 26, 1958. Bob Hope and David Niven hosted the nationally televised ceremony.

*The film's promoters, Jerome Hill and Erica Anderson, unabashedly called Schweitzer "The Greatest Man of the 20<sup>th</sup> Century."*

Across the United States, Schweitzer was already a household name. Books and magazine articles about Schweitzer sold well. People talked as reverentially about the African jungle doctor as they talked about the popular young American Navy officer-doctor-and-best-selling-author Tom Dooley in Southeast Asia. Schweitzer's name was in the news a lot and he had heard his father's World Federalist friends mention it.

The idea formed in Mark's head that he should go to Africa and work for Schweitzer. He bargained and argued. Finally, in exasperation, his parents gave in. The trade was that if he promised not to harm himself again, he could go work for Schweitzer for one year. Mark's mother went along with the plan, suppressing her doubts about his going overseas alone. In her mind, it was the best opportunity for helping Mark to discover a purpose in life.

His vision of going to Africa gained momentum. Upon being released from Hartford, Mark became a student member of the United World Federalists in the Worcester chapter and attended meetings of the World Federalist Association with his father, gaining insight into the movement.

In order to support himself independently during the year ahead, Mark planned to draw some of the funds from the Higgins Grandchildren Trust that John Woodman Higgins had created.

Mark began collecting information and reading books about Schweitzer. He inquired whether the Higgins family had any contacts who could get him an assignment with Schweitzer. In fact, there were several connections. Linus Pauling, a friend of Schweitzer and a fellow Nobel laureate, was allied with his father's friend Norman Cousins in the Committee for a Sane Nuclear Policy. He was surprised to learn that Pauling would be delivering a lecture about nuclear policy at Clark University in Worcester on November 15, 1958. Here was another opportunity to meet people who were close to Schweitzer. Mark learned that there was always a need for non-medical, handyman workers over there.

Mark's father knew that Schweitzer's circle included people involved in the World Federalists movement and the campaign to end atmospheric weapons testing. Among the most prominent of these was Norman Cousins, the editor of the *Saturday Review of Literature*. Cousins, the president of the United World Federalists, had just written a series of articles and a popular book about Schweitzer. Carter knew his friend could help.

Cousins endorsed the idea. When the arrangements were made, he exclaimed in a letter to Carter: "I'm delighted to hear that Mark is going to Lambaréné. What a magnificent investment in the development of his spiritual and social resources."

In many ways, letting Mark go to Africa appeared to be an ideal compromise. Working for the great Doctor Albert Schweitzer was a noble cause of which the family could be proud. It could help Mark in his quest for a purpose in life, and give him time to find himself. It would certainly be one step closer to the wish he had expressed in his high school yearbook: becoming a wild game hunter in Africa.

Not insignificantly, it would also put some distance between Mark and his overbearing father.

All in all, it is quite a story that Mark shares with his trusted friends Adriana and Frank. He feels relieved after telling them his problems. In return, they congratulate him on his courage, stamina and remarkable spirit of self-determination.

Mark was on the road to becoming his own man.

Seven

# Secrets in the Jungle

Schweitzer might be an octogenarian stuck in his ways, but his hospital is staffed by vigorous young adults. They have to be intelligent, ambitious, and physically fit to live and work in the tropical heat. Nearly all of them have arrived without a spouse. Not surprisingly, testosterone levels run high among these young professionals; similarly, the Schweitzer operation appeals to adventurous, wealthy, attractive women. As a result Lambaréné sometimes seems like a cross between an Olympic village and an African Garden of Eden, albeit without any real opportunity for privacy. The open truss ceilings and thin walls separating the barracks rooms do little to mask sounds made in the middle of the night.

During his first tour at Lambaréné a few years earlier, Frank Catchpool had been drawn into a highly charged relationship with the Royal Dutch Shell heiress Olga Deterding. The British woman had arrived at Lambaréné in 1956 almost by accident: she was crossing Africa in a large jeep with some friends but the vehicle broke down one too many times. The expedition disbanded. On a whim, Olga boarded a supply flight to Lambaréné, where she discovered Schweitzer. Abruptly she volunteered for duty in the kitchen at the leper village. It was her way of stepping back from the limelight and her fast-paced, sometimes reckless social life in Europe, where she was known for hard drinking and outrageous eccentricities.

Olga had taken an instant liking to Catchpool, and they quickly paired up. When he left for a break, Olga followed him to the United States, publicly linked herself with Catchpool in newspaper interviews, and began suggesting that they should get married. Catchpool demurred, asking for more time to determine their suitability for one another and to establish his career. He had been hoping that Schweitzer would regard him as a doctor with such unique professional skill that he could one day take over the hospital. After he left Lambaréné, Catchpool received several letters from Schweitzer urging him to come back.

After considerable correspondence, the persistent Schweitzer convinced the vainglorious Catchpool to rejoin the staff. At that point, Catchpool then believed that Lambaréné would become his life's work, and that Schweitzer might consider him an heir to the whole operation. Catchpool was under the impression that Schweitzer bought into this line of thinking. Olga followed him back to Africa.

But since his return, Catchpool has found that Schweitzer had put no further thought into choosing and grooming a successor than he ever had. Once again Catchpool is just one of several doctors, not even the first among equals.

"Since my return in April I have been bitterly disappointed," Catchpool wrote to a friend. "Dr. Schweitzer obviously considers me to be just one of the four doctors. I think he respects my clinical judgment, but he certainly does not want my help in any other field. He does not intend to let one detail of the organization and administration of the hospital out of his hands." Catchpool frets over the physical condition of the hospital, the fact that repairs are not being made, drugs not being ordered on time, and that critical decisions are being postponed, adding, "I feel that the hospital is not worthy of his great name, yet I seem to be powerless to help." Others have pointed out that the x-ray machines are next to the room where babies are born, but Schweitzer refuses to install lead walls. Another person notes that the open pit outhouse is just uphill from the hospital garden, resulting in occasional hepatitis outbreaks.

Catchpool shares his concerns with Mark, upon whom they make quite an impression. Mark also notices something else about Catchpool: Adriana Calles Eller has clearly caught his eye.

◆━━◆

Schweitzer encourages his hard-working staff to detach from Lambaréné once in a while to regain perspective on their work. He knows that a person without an occasional vacation exhausts all energy and enthusiasm. But he could never really enjoy any personal vacation time. There are continuous demands on his time; stacks of mail on serious topics always awaiting his hand-written responses. Periodically he persuades himself to return home to Gunsbach, France, do a little fundraising, perform an organ recital and re-charge his batteries. In the late summer of 1959, Schweitzer is planning a trip that will take him away from Lambaréné for many months.

First he makes certain that everyone knows who will be in charge of what. He requires that weekly reports be sent to him, although he will only communicate with some of the senior staff. He has great respect for the people who handle the daily work, especially the women who loyally serve him. He places special trust in his long-time assistant Ali Silver, who even makes a practice of reading the staff's outgoing correspondence before it gets mailed; Schweitzer thus knows who is being critical of his hospital. On the day before he is to leave on his European tour, Schweitzer conducts a small ceremony, baptizing his chief surgeon, the 33-year old Dutch woman Margrit Van der Kreek.

On Monday August 3, 1959, Schweitzer and his assistant Mathilde Kottman leave Lambaréné enroute to France. As always, he spends the night at the Protestant mission in Port Gentil in Gabon before boarding the cruise ship *General Leclerc*.

* * *

The hospital accepts summer interns every year. In mid-July, a young American medical student named Eugene Schoenfeld from the University of Miami arrives at Lambaréné for a two-week project assisting Catchpool. Assigned to an adjacent cubicle in the staff dormitory, Gene and Mark become fast friends.

Schweitzer has always discouraged his people from wandering off to explore tribal villages and virtually forbade them from eating meals outside of the clinic. Years of experience had taught the old doctor that because villagers didn't boil their water or cook the impurities out of their food, it was easy to come down with food-borne illnesses. But of course that doesn't prevent the most adventuresome among them from embarking on some after-hours expeditions. When Schweitzer leaves for Europe, the rules seem to relax a bit.

Mark longs to slip away from the clinic at night, watch the native dancers and observe their rites. He knows that the dentist Fred Franck and some others have done this. Some secret rituals are intended to be observed by males only; some require an invitation from one of the tribesmen.

Like most of the staff, Mark and Gene have heard stories about late-night sacred dances and voodoo ceremonies in surrounding villages. "Schweitzer doesn't like people going to these village dances," Schoenfeld tells Mark. "The old nurses, here Ali Silver in particular, look down on this. They are very conservative and by-the-book."

But the young men find the attraction too tempting. Often, while out on a pirogue in the Ogoué River at night, they hear the drumbeats in villages calling dancers to a ceremony. Every Saturday night the natives in each village celebrate the return of their men who have been away all week working for the logging companies. Sometimes festivities are more elaborate.

A *Bwiti ceremony, one of whose objectives can be to enhance female fertility, was augmented by ingesting a hallucinogenic drug derived from the locally grown iboga shrub.*

One particular ritual, a healing ceremony, takes place in total darkness during the new moon. Late on Tuesday night, August 4, Mark, Gene and a few others slip away from the clinic in a motorized pirogue heading for the small Galoa tribal village of Azo, about 15 miles away. There, a two-day event is coming to a climax at midnight with a dance performed by the tribal priest and the medicine man. Inside a grass hut is a young man who has ingested a massive dose of iboga, the psychotic drug derived from the indigenous plant ibogaine. This hallucinogenic drug is central to the ritual of the Bwiti religion. The ordinary-looking iboga shrub, with its white and pink flowers and tasteless orange-colored citrus fruit, grows plentifully only in West Africa. It usually stands about eight feet tall but can grow as high as 35 feet.

Its root bark, when scraped off, pounded into powder and ingested, produces a mysterious high that stimulates the central nervous system and induces visions that sometimes last for days. The masters who lead Bwiti ceremonies believe it gives them the power to see the future, to heal the sick, to drive off harmful spirits, and to speak with ancestors. Women who want to conceive children, or who believe they had not yet had enough children, participate in a Bwiti ceremony. Natives also chew the bark of the root while hunting to enable them to stay motionless and alert for days.

Gabonese consider the plant a principal source of spiritual knowledge, and a cult of secret societies has grown up around its use. Because Mark speaks French and has befriended some of the natives who have been treated at the hospital, he and his colleagues are allowed to observe. To add to the authenticity, Mark has acquired a colorful African sarong which he wears at night to such events. The Africans begin the ceremony by imitating the sounds of jungle animals: crocodiles, lions, elephants. In a narrow, long hut at the end of a field, torches are lit. The medicine man appears wearing a bird-like costume. Suddenly there are people leaping over the fires, carrying torches. There are people playing instruments that sound like an Indian sitar. The 'patient' remains inside the lodge with 10 or 15 other people.

At the end of the ceremony, Mark and Gene find their way back to the clinic. But their appetite for native African culture has been stimulated. They promise one another that they will go out into the bush more often and absorb as much of this as possible.

In the weeks ahead, the adventuresome American duo attends several other Bwiti ceremonies. The Bwiti ritual is controlled by an *nganga*, a tribal official who serves as the Bantu herbalist and healer. Music is an essential element in these colorful and mystical ceremonies which play out in the jungle to the percussion of rapid drumbeats and the melody of expertly crafted African harps. It all makes a lasting impression on the young Americans.

Mark's friendship with the native population leads to an extraordinary gesture of goodwill on his part. He has been limiting his spending to essentials, but now he finds a worthy cause and embraces it. Mark has befriended an African co-worker named Obianga M'Koma. He learns that the man's dream is to send his two sons to school in Libreville, the capital of Gabon. The cost would be $75 per year per student. Mark tells his friend that he will cover the cost of the boys' education. The results are quick and rewarding as Mark writes in a letter back home:

> The younger, frightfully intelligent at 16, will learn to read and write, and the elder who can already write, will learn typing and some accounting in hopes of a good job. In a country of perhaps five percent native literacy, this is a tremendous asset, and Obianga's proud face when I read him the first letter he had ever received, his son's, has already repaid me. Unfortunately, when news of this got around, I got a reputation as a soft touch, and now every starving man in the hospital comes to me to buy him a fish.

As Mark works with Frank Catchpool, he develops a deeper relationship with him and with his friend Adriana. He hears more about Catchpool's concerns over Schweitzer's management style and unwillingness to accept new ideas. In many late-night talks, the three of them bond. They become allies in the maneuvering for position within the Schweitzer camp. Catchpool still fervently hopes to succeed Schweitzer one day and become the medical director. So does Fergus Pope, and so does Richard Friedman, the abrupt Czechoslovakian Holocaust survivor.

Frank Catchpool has determined that Mark is not only a hard worker, but also that he is capable of a lot more than cutting paths through the jungle, tending the garden and working in construction. The overworked English physician places Mark in *la pharmacie* and teaches him in how to administer daily inoculations and injections to lepers and diabetics. The language difficulty and the patients' general level of understanding make it impossible to teach them self-administration of insulin. Schweitzer has long rejected the idea of giving native patients an oral agent because of the risk that they might take all the tablets in one day or share them with friends.

This opportunity gives Mark daily physical contact with the patients who represent tribes and cultures from across central Africa. Every day as he approaches these patients for their inoculations, Mark talks and jokes with them. He asks where they are from, learns about their families, life in their villages and about their tribal customs. He puts them at ease. He develops a deep respect for the people who need the services of the hospital, and in turn the patients respect Mark. He feels a new sense of purpose.

Mark begins believing that he fits in with the staff. He can handle the work and he has reason to believe that he is beginning to do some good in Africa. Importantly, he is maturing on his own terms: he feels confident, satisfied, and more positive about the impact he can have on the world. He is making friends and meeting fascinating people. This is becoming a transformative experience.

*Mark sits in the middle of the action at a staff party at Lambaréné. On the far left is Dr. Margrit van der Kreek. Siegfried Neukirch is in the foreground. Dr. Lindner Reichert (with glasses) sits in front of the map and the Danish carpenter Poul Erik Rasmussen relaxes in the corner.*

One afternoon a 13-year-old boy is carried into the clinic after being hit on the head by a falling branch. His skull has been cracked open and the boy's brain exposed. Catchpool asks for Mark's immediate assistance in the surgery suite. Mark watches in amazement as Catchpool operates on the boy and saves his life. "I have seen the inside of a man's brain! God!" Mark exclaims in a note home, as he gains an appreciation for the fragile line between life and death.

Mark spends more than a few quiet evenings in his room, reflecting on where he is, how he views life, what he thinks about the world around him, and considering his next steps. Gifted with an exceptional ability for expressing himself, Mark records his impressions in the form of prose and poetry. He saves these compositions in hopes of publishing them someday. They are a treasury of his innermost thoughts.

He continues his education on his own terms. He considers the two college applications in front of him, only partially completed, and leaves them that way. Philosophy fascinates him. He has brought with him some heavy reading, and twice goes through Plato's *Republic*. He has picked up some calculus, and is teaching himself German from a French textbook so that he can be better understood by the nurses.

Patricia Getz, his stepmother's niece who was so close to him before his involuntary confinement at Hartford, is on his mind again. He holds dear the days they spent together at parties with Mary's extended family and the long idle days they shared at Brooks Pond. Mark has heard that Pat is now traveling in Europe, and he asks Mary for Pat's address.

Back home, whenever someone in Worcester receives a letter from Mark, it is big news. He writes notes to his mother and Nick Doman and to his little half-brothers Alexander and Daniel who are only six and four years old. He draws pictures of African animals that delight their young eyes. He writes to Mary and his father, who circulate his letters to other adults in the clan. Mark had become especially close to Mary, who writes to him quite often, and he shows her genuine affection. He also pays special attention to his grandparents, and includes personal notes or references to them in many letters.

Mark writes about everything he is working on, primarily the gardening, his assistance with the lepers, and describes animal antics. A portion of a spirited letter that Mark sends to his mother in New York begins with the lines:

*Hi, ho, ho, hum, here I am in the middle of Africa. I sit at my desk, with my mongrel dog at my left foot, and Ooka, my pet chimpanzee, playing with my shoelaces. A goat is walking on the roof.*

Mary writes to him more often than anyone else, sharing family news and asking what Mark might need.

Mark's enthusiasm for his work grows along with his appreciation for his new station in life. He remains aware of his place in the Higgins clan, and as Thanksgiving approaches, he composes a letter to be read during the huge annual family banquet which will take place this year at the Higgins Armory Museum. His grandfather is hosting the entire clan, 86 people, at his museum for a traditional feast. Long tables placed amidst the "100 Men of Steel" stretch the length of the main hall and down the other side.

It will be the social highlight of the year for the whole Higgins family. Although Mark missed the last few Thanksgiving dinners, he wants everyone to know that he is thinking of them. Well aware that his greetings may be read aloud, on October 11 he composes a letter to the whole family:

*Darkest Africa*

*Dear Parents, Grandparents, Brothers and Sisters, Uncles and Aunts, Cousins (first, second, removed & otherwise) and sundry other relations (I would like to greet you all personally, but you are too weighty a list for air mail),*

*It is now three years, due variously to illness and distance, since I have attended one of these gatherings, though I have tried never to be separate from the spirit of these Higgins Family Thanksgivings. This year, as I sit down to my feast of crocodile, elephant, or (if I'm lucky) goat, I would like to be more tangibly present, by means of a few words and thoughts. For, though Thanksgiving should be a personal ceremony, it can and must not be a private one; an inseparable part of Thanksgiving, as illustrated by the presence of this group, is the communication of the feelings and beliefs which it represents.*

*In recent months I have been witness to many circumstances which have pointed out to me my own personal debt of gratitude, and I have newly become aware of another blessing: the chance to help.*

*Which of us has thought to be thankful not only for our good chance, but for our lack of calamities? Who thinks to thank God for his freedom from the multiple curses of leprosy, trachoma, tuberculosis, elephantiasis, or the crippling effects of simple malnutrition? What child, among those here present, sleeps with a light by his bed, not out of simple mis-*

*trust of the darkness, but to distract malaria-carrying mosquitoes and to ward off passing snakes and predators? Our seemingly untarnished but unblest represent, in fact, the extravagance of God's generosity, our occasional pitfalls rare good-fortune.*

*Through the lack of these problems, we have yet another, still more important blessing: the opportunity to help others. The varied public services provided by this plant, plus our own, individual, public and private helping-hands yield yet another reason, not for mutual back-patting, but for mutual thanks for having had both opportunity and means to have helped. The potential present in this family gathering for service are one more of God's blessings, and for this I give particular thanks today.*

*Sam, my parrot, is watching over my shoulder with great interest as I write; Ooka, my chimpanzee, having tired of swinging on my curtains, is showing equal interest in avoiding my eye, while he eats my cigarettes in the corner. The three of us join in sending best wishes back from this far-flung branch to the sturdy main trunk of the Higgins family. Special regards to Grandparents John and Clara, whose interest in the family tree is as basic to them as they are to the tree itself; to my parents, to whom, notwithstanding my recent lack of letters, I am still firmly and inextricably rooted; and to many nearby leaves & branches - brothers, sisters and friends.*

*Mark Higgins*

Back in Africa, news from the outside world comes in sporadically. No television or radio connects with the outside world. Mark keeps up with the world thanks to the gift subscription to *Time* magazine provided by Grandmother Higgins. It lets him keep an eye on Bobby Fischer's chess championship matches, on business in the United States, and to some extent on politics in Africa, though American news organizations are not yet stationing correspondents in African outposts. Much of the news concerns tensions in Europe and the cold war confrontations with the Soviet Union. The magazine also comes in handy as Mark comments on events in the steel industry. A three-and-a-half-month steel strike in the U.S. has shut down every steel-making plant in the country from July 15 to October 26. The Higgins steel business is affected, and inventories are running critically low. Mark watches these developments and writes to his father about them.

Mary writes Mark that she and his father are sailing for Europe again on behalf of Worcester Pressed Steel. They will visit Switzerland, and one of their side trips will be to Auschwitz where the Nazis had imprisoned her. On November 12, Mark responds with a long, newsy letter:

*Not having written in so long, your frequent letters only made me feel all the more guilty. But your mid-ocean letter so full of enthusiasm must deserve a reply. All is well here. My house is long since finished, a gem, and is now occupied by 24 TB patients. I have now been promoted to a job of greatly increased responsibility requiring much more work and longer hours, but yielding far greater rewards. I am now spoken to as Docteur Mark (and occasionally Docteur Long-long), and officially titled Chief des Piques, and am in charge of giving all the injections to the entire hospital. That's something, isn't it, for someone once so afraid of injections, but it's what I wanted.*

*I work 6 a.m. to about 6:30 p.m., two out of three Sundays, and give up to 300 injections a day. My lack of medical knowledge makes me doubly aware of the dangers involved, and doubly afraid of something going wrong. I am consequently worn to a frazzle by the end of the day and ready for bed by 9 p.m. But for the past week I've had to get up at midnight and 3 a.m. for injections to a fractured skull man. (I saw his operation. I saw the surface of a living brain. God!)*

*The low spots are many - I've had 14 men, women and children die in the last two months - but so are the high spots. The elation, the gratitude to a force I thought I couldn't believe in, the joy, and if I may be so conceited, the satisfaction of watching a pair of dying eyes come back to life is something I thought I could never know.*

*I plan to stay here till late January, then to strike out. I'd like to take the steamer from Leopoldville to Elisabethville via Lake Victoria, thence by rail to Portuguese West Africa (Angola), 1,000 miles, 18 days by express. Thence around the Cape to Johannesburg or Durban, where I have a friend. I expect that, by this point, my funds will have run out, and I'll have to take a job, possibly at the Norton in Transvaal. Thence after a few months until I can build up some savings, by freighter up the African East Coast, possibly toward Israel, which I yearn to see. Lack of funds will preclude most side trips, but still.*

*My money is holding up surprisingly well. I am living on the absolute minimum and, though I regret having nothing to spare for various objets d'art and some of the disappearing handcrafts, am surviving as comfortably as one can here.*

*On the question of college, I am still unsure. I have several applications here filled out, but as of yet unsent. I am aware of the need for a college education, I know of its benefits, and I now recognize a thirst to learn on my own part. But I question whether my mental health will stand up to the rut, whether my spiritual stamina will hold out; in short whether I am yet ready to face up to that side of myself yet. Perhaps I'll be wiser to work longer here, longer in South Africa, work on a kibbutz in Israel, maybe even work my way around the world, and put college still another year away. It might be best if you refused to send me to college, made me fight my own way some more. I must be sure!*

*I am learning in any case. My French I can honestly and proudly say is fluent. It is the French spoken here, that is with an argot vocabulary and very flexible grammar, and I still can't write it. But I can carry on relaxed conversations, without piecing out my sentences in advance, and what's more, I can argue. This latter, as you know, due to the speed, emotion, volume and confidence necessary is the supreme test.*

*I've learned a surprising amount of medicine. But all these accomplishments I consider quite secondary to the practical knowledge and to what I've learned about myself.*

*Everything I can remember having asked for has arrived except for photos of the US in general to show to people here. I need a steak 1 ½-inch tenderloin rare, as the only fresh meat I've had since arriving has been crocodile, elephant (once) and goat. On alternate weeks we have slat pork or corned beef, there is rice six times weekly, macaroni or noodles three times (plus) and either bananas or dried apples for dessert every day. But steak!*

*I would appreciate some cheap and lurid novels for a relaxation of diet plus Romain Gary's "The Roots of Heaven." Please do send a canteen of the army type, belt not shoulder hanging. I am receiving Grammy's thoughtful Time magazine very regularly.*

*How is Dad's steel inventory holding up? Will you be early enough*

*in line to receive any under the injunction and, if not, will you be forced
to shut down? Aren't plastics wonderful? Dad's stay in Europe must be
made as long as possible. He needs it desperately.*

*Xmas? A few light gas cartridges (Ronson Varaflame) a letter or book
and steak. If I am going to spend a greater length of time here a rifle
might be dandy. (.308 H&H 7x67 Scholz & Larsen .375 Weathersby are
all interesting).*

*Oh yes, send me my binoculars left behind in my closet. They're very
low quality, so there's nothing to lose.*

*Be sure to send this letter on to Dad - heaven knows when I'll find
time or spirit to write to him. Thence to Mum and Nick - they've been
exceedingly patient in waiting since the one I sent them in September.*

*Enjoy yourself in Europe, Mary. Look at the bright spots, at what's
new. Don't avoid, but don't burden yourself with the nostalgic spots.*

*I love you, Mark*

*Dad, Was my Thanksgiving note too syrupy or seemingly hypocritical
(that always happens when I try for sincerity)? Save it; I want to read it
when I'm down. I love you, too.*

*Mum, Nick et al.: your turn for the next letter. It's been pretty silent
from your side, too. Your being last in this list indicates no preference,
for I love every one of you.*

Mark remains filled with wanderlust. He is actively exploring options
for where to go after Lambaréné, destinations that most pointedly do not
include home. Amazing opportunities are unfolding right in front of him.
He is working in Africa! Nobody else in his Milton Academy class can claim
that. Rather than hurrying back home to join the rat race and becoming
another man in a gray flannel suit, Mark is dreaming about traversing the
Belgian Congo, of working his way around the Cape, visiting a friend in
Rhodesia, sailing up the east coast of Africa, studying in Israel, working in a
kibbutz, or visiting other parts of Europe. He hopes Patricia Getz will agree
to see him in Europe. He writes home and asks for the address of John
Mason Bigelow, his mother's brother, a novelist who has taken a job as a
correspondent for the *International Herald Tribune* and is based in Turkey.

As Mark envisions these next steps, something else is happening around him. Mark's friends Frank Catchpool and Adriana Calles Eller have fallen in love. Olga Deterding does not know this until Catchpool works up the courage to tell her that he has asked Adriana to marry him. That produces an explosive, emotional scene with Olga, a woman already given to outbursts. The ugliness soon involves Adriana, and considerable tension prevails among the staff. Ali Silver quickly reports all this to Schweitzer in Europe. Olga is furious. Within a few days she leaves Lambaréné abruptly without telling anyone where she is going. Ali Silver advises Adriana that it would be better if she also leaves right away.

The situation plunges Mark into sadness and feelings that he finds hard to express. After Adriana packs her bags, he escorts her to the Lambaréné airfield to await her flight. As she is about to board the plane, Mark puts a bundle of papers in her hand and says to Adriana, "This is how much I think of you. These poems are me! Please don't show them to anyone. When I return I will write more and some day publish them."

Adriana understands the depth of Mark's sadness. He is losing a special friend. She knows that this is not the way Mark hoped or expected that things would turn out. She reminds him that he has discovered many new things about himself and that he is well on his way to becoming his own man.

The upheaval means that it is also time for Catchpool to move on. Linus Pauling has offered him a research job at Caltech. Catchpool leaves Lambaréné on November 16, and the clinic logbook records simply, "our best wishes go with him."

After leaving, Frank Catchpool reflects on his experience with his protégé: "Mark had such a fearless spirit and such a headstrong sense of what was right and just, that I could imagine him intervening on some scene of injustice or brutality, whether of white to black or black to black. I recognized Mark as an exceptionally intelligent man who had been an emotionally disturbed boy. During my three years at Lambaréné he was the only man with whom I could converse freely. I felt that I could help him and that he could help me. We spent many evenings talking together and talking with the natives. I felt his interest in medicine was one of the best ways out. I was amazed at his perception and comprehension. I could discuss problems that I dared not discuss with my colleagues as Mark was always ready to approach a problem with logic and expediency."

Catchpool tells Mark that he has overcome his problems of growing up. He says that if Mark were to return home now, he would be a totally different person – so much so that his family would hardly recognize him.

But Mark has no intention of returning to the United States anytime soon.

As Christmas comes to Lambaréné, it is natural for some of the staff to feel homesick. They support one another, partying and making small decorations with the materials at hand. They adhere to a beautiful custom on Christmas Eve: after dinner they visit the hospital rooms to sing hymns and then walk over to the *Village des Lumières* where each person holds a candle and everyone joins in singing "*Stille Nacht.*"

On Christmas Day Mark opens a special gift from his aunt Beverly, the mother of his favorite niece. It's a chessboard with carved wooden pieces depicting wild animals. But for Mark this is more than just a chessboard: it is a reminder of his past success as well as recognition of the complexities of African travel, and of the need to think 15 moves ahead.

# Eight

# The Path to Independence

Africa in 1960 is at the top of the world's agenda. It will be the year of African freedom and the face of the continent will change forever. Between January and December, 17 sub-Saharan African territories are scheduled to gain independence from European colonial powers.

Fifteen years after the end of the Second World War, many European monarchies still cling to the last vestiges of colonial rule. Great Britain, Spain and Portugal each have several colonies. France had recently decided to liberate its 14 colonies, including French Equatorial Africa, that great swath in the middle of the continent which is about to spawn five distinct nations: French Congo, whose capital is Brazzaville; Cameroon; Chad; Oubangui-Chari (soon to be known as the Central African Republic), and Gabon. But the biggest African landmass is owned by tiny Belgium, which for three-fourths of a century has appropriated great mineral wealth from the Belgian Congo, a central African territory 76 times more vast than Belgium itself.

Some of these territories seem prepared to steer their own destinies, some do not. From a geopolitical perspective, the African evolution to freedom is already producing a dramatic change in the global balance of power. New states will join the United Nations as equals with their former overseers. Will the Soviets influence them? Will they side with the West? Who will have access to their mineral wealth, their markets and their strategic ports?

The emerging nations of Africa are about to become the most politically important pawns in the Cold War. The eyes of the world are on Africa.

It's the place to be, and Mark Higgins is in the thick of it.

On December 31 Dr. Schweitzer sails into Port Gentil, Gabon, on the passenger ship *General Leclerc*, then by steamboat and pirogue to Lambaréné, completing the five-month journey that will be his final sojourn away from his beloved hospital.

On the first day of the New Year, the pace picks up in Lambaréné as Schweitzer leads an inspection of his entire clinic and takes detailed reports from every one of the 23 people on the staff, including Mark.

Within a few days, his friends begin showing up in anticipation of Schweitzer's 85th birthday. Harold C. Case, the president of Boston University who had been a theologian and Methodist minister, brings his family. Case created an African Studies program at BU a few years earlier. Accompanying them is Joseph "Kivie" Kaplan, a Massachusetts philanthropist and shoe manufacturer who owns the Colonial Tanning Company, and works as a prolific fundraiser and board member of the NAACP. Kaplan is as concerned about Jewish causes as he is about the emerging civil rights struggle in the United States. Case and Kaplan are soon joined by the president of the American Heritage Society, Gabonese officials, reporters and cameramen from everywhere.

Schweitzer usually receives messages from long-term friends, world leaders and admirers for his *geburtstag*, but one traditional salutation is missing in 1960. President Dwight Eisenhower's diplomatic advisors in Washington have decided that it would be politically unwise to send birthday congratulations to a man whose outspoken opposition to testing nuclear weapons has been scrutinized carefully by the intelligence community. The Soviet Union has also opposed nuclear weapons testing. Schweitzer, Western analysts suspect, might be siding with the Communists. The President of the United States cannot be seen encouraging the old man. And so it becomes White House policy that there will be no official birthday letter from the President to Albert Schweitzer. But if he knows, Schweitzer doesn't care about the debate in Washington over whether he might get a card from Ike.

Greetings rain in from many places, including heads of state such as Jawaharal Nehru, prime minister of India, fellow Nobel laureates and other accomplished world citizens. Schweitzer tries to respond personally to every letter he receives. Each night he stays up late scratching out responses in his tiny longhand script with his fountain pen in French, German or English.

One of those who have struck up a pen-pal relationship with Schweitzer is a Greek-African businessman who lives in a far eastern province of the Belgian Congo. Lambros Passialis works in the commercially important town of Kasongo in Maniema Province. By chance, several years earlier he read an article about Schweitzer in *Reader's Digest*. Discovering the philosophy of Schweitzer has changed his life. In honor of this landmark birthday, Passialis commissioned a handsome portrait of the old doctor and shipped it to Lambaréné. Schweitzer graciously writes back his appreciation. Mark inquires about the man, and makes a note of where he lives.

In the first few months of 1960, Schweitzer welcomes a steady flow of high-profile visitors. Some come from the medical community, some represent religious missions. Others have been long-time admirers of his peace efforts, his philosophical writings, or his scholarly work on Bach, Goethe, the Apostle Paul, and Jesus. Mark meets all of them.

Hardly could there be a better place to spend quiet time in discussions with world-famous and globally accomplished intellectuals. For Mark and the rest of the staff, this is like participating in a graduate seminar on world affairs.

On January 22, Hal Bruce Dallke, a 37-year-old Methodist minister from California, visits Lambaréné. Dallke strikes up a conversation with Mark. He is impressed. "Young men such as he who have the courage of their ideals and the wonderful foolhardiness not to be deterred by a cynical world give hope for the future," Dallke observes. He asks Mark to pose for a few photographs, which he then mails to Mark's grandparents and to his mother. Dallke's pictures show Mark at work in the jungle hacking away at the overgrown brush. Mark wields in his right hand a machete – the indispensable tool of the African man.

What stands out in the Dallke photos, however, and which the minister would not know, is something that is frowned upon, if not outright forbidden, at Lambaréné: on his right hip Mark wears a holster holding a pearl grip Colt Python, a .357 Magnum caliber revolver with an eight-inch barrel. That particular piece of hardware is a top-of-the-line model, built specifically for hunting. Sportsmen call it "the Rolls-Royce of Colt revolvers."

To an American comfortable with guns, it's the most natural thing in the world, but throughout Africa, a sidearm is seen as more of a threat than a defense. Schweitzer has preached reverence for life. Having a weapon simply is not the custom at Lambaréné. Mark usually keeps his gun hidden away in a rucksack, and only a few people know that he has it.

*Mark wears a Colt .357 Magnum as he poses for a photo at Lambaréné, where weapons are frowned upon. He carries a machete in one hand and dangles a cigarette in the other.*

On February 13, a Boston attorney named Paul F. Hellmuth arrives. A major fundraiser and advocate for Catholic causes, Hellmuth is known for his leadership roles in civic groups such as the Boys & Girls Clubs of Boston. He has come representing Medical International Cooperation (MEDICO), the company formed by Dr. Thomas A. Dooley.

Unknown at this time are Hellmuth's controversial ties to senior people in the U.S. government and his association with Central Intelligence Agency front companies. Hellmuth is the sole trustee of a fund called the J. Frederick Brown Foundation, which receives regular contributions from four CIA-linked funds. Most of that money is funneled to him through Cord Meyer, the World Federalist founder who is an old friend of Mark's father. Meyer has risen through the ranks to become a senior official in the covert operations directorate at the CIA. Hellmuth is co-trustee of another CIA-linked fund, the Independence Foundation, along with David B. Stone, the Boston philanthropist who founded the New England Aquarium. Both foundations operate out of Hellmuth's law office in Boston. The J. Frederick Brown Foundation has been a key funding source for MEDICO, which supplies dental equipment for the Schweitzer clinic, and absorbs the travel expenses for the various dental surgeons.

The Hellmuth-Dooley-CIA interest in Schweitzer merits a closer look. In the late 1950s most Americans recognized Tom Dooley as a selfless and patriotic young doctor who had founded a jungle clinic in Laos. He is sometimes compared to Schweitzer, but there are notable differences: Dooley is a blatant self-promoter and a former U.S. Navy officer who has quietly been discharged for his reckless homosexuality. At the same time, the ultra-Catholic Dooley is a virulent anti-Communist, an author of best-selling books, popular speaker and ardent promoter of the American way of life. He regularly briefs the CIA about Communist troop movements, and his clinic near the border with China operates in part as a military intelligence-gathering outpost.

In fall of 1959 Hellmuth affiliated with Dooley and became his attorney, patron and most trusted confidante. Hellmuth then conducted an intense behind-the-scenes lobbying effort to persuade his alma mater the University of Notre Dame to confer upon Dooley an honorary doctorate of science degree. Dooley becomes one of three honorees, the other two being President Eisenhower and Giovanni Cardinal Montini, shortly to become Pope Paul VI.

Shortly after Hellmuth signed on, MEDICO's celebrity doctor became seriously ill with malignant melanoma. By December 1959 Hellmuth was casting around for ways to build on Dooley's American medicine-and-propaganda program by creating or funding clinics in Africa and other parts of the Third World which could possibly serve as *sub rosa* listening posts and sources of intelligence on other fronts of the Cold War. Thus, one purpose of Hellmuth's trip to Lambaréné is to learn where Schweitzer really stands on the plane of East-West relations, and whether the old doctor will lend his famous name to MEDICO and help raise funds for creating clinics around the world based on the Dooley model.

Given Hellmuth's distinguished Boston roots, Mark Higgins seeks him out. In the evenings, there is plenty of time for a private talk. Finding Mark is an unexpected bonus for Hellmuth: the eager young American frames up Catchpool's familiar litany about the out-dated clinic: the under-utilization of donated modern medical equipment, the lack of up-to-date facilities such as electricity and fresh water, the resistance to new ideas and the patriarchal nature of Schweitzer himself. The place had been run with tight controls for nearly 50 years and Schweitzer always resists measures for improving the sanitation, or for adapting his outpost to the standards of a modern Western hospital. No matter how long he or anyone stays there, Mark realizes that things will always be done the same way.

Hellmuth comes away with the distinct impression that Mark yearns to leave, an analysis he shares with the nearest CIA station in Africa, then in Leopoldville in the Belgian Congo. These impressions make their way into the notebooks of selected media in the Congo and in the United States. Whatever Hellmuth and Schweitzer discussed does not appear in the Schweitzer archives. Immediately upon concluding his fact-finding and analysis mission in Africa, Hellmuth flies straight to Thailand for a three-week stint with Dooley, who will die within a year.

Rene Dubos, the French-born American microbiologist, experimental pathologist, environmentalist, humanist, and future recipient of a Pulitzer Prize for Nonfiction, arrives the following week. Dubos, an editor of the *Journal of Experimental Medicine* on the staff of Rockefeller University, has devoted his professional life to the study of microbial diseases and to the analysis of the environmental and social factors that affect the welfare of humans. His pioneering research in isolating antibacterial substances from certain soil microorganisms led to the discovery of major antibiotics. He researched and wrote extensively on subjects such as tuberculosis, pneumonia, and the mechanisms of acquired immunity, natural susceptibility, and resistance to infection.

At the suggestion of Emory Ross, the treasurer of the Schweitzer Fellowship program in the U.S., a nationally syndicated columnist for the Scripps Howard newspaper chain named Robert Ruark visits Lambaréné.

Ruark turns out to be a swashbuckling old African hand who has spent much of his career writing about the continent. Importantly for Mark, Ruark is also a big game hunter who had written several best-selling novels

about Africa. His popular safari book *Horn of the Hunter* recounted his
nine-week hunt in British East Africa. Another of his books, *Something of
Value*, was made into a 1957 motion picture starring Rock Hudson and
Sidney Poitier. It depicted a Mau Mau uprising in Kenya against British colonial rule. Ruark is a man who is actually experiencing part of the life that
Mark wants to live. He has contacts all over Africa, and just before arriving
at the Schweitzer clinic he had met with Emperor Haile Selassie in Ethiopia,
and then with tribal chiefs in the Belgian Congo. His outlook for the African independence movement is that the Congo in particular faces a violent
future. Although most of Ruark's reporting focuses on politics, he is a great
admirer of Schweitzer and the "miracles" that the old man performs in Gabon. Talking with the notoriously hard-drinking adventurer intrigues the
young man from Massachusetts.

One of Ruark's three Schweitzer columns, printed in the *Worcester
Daily Telegram* on March 14, refers to Mark. "A blonde American college
boy is in charge of 'injections'," Ruark writes, adding in a jocular way,
"That covers a lot of skins." Excerpts from Ruark's column provide more
insight:

> *It is hot . . . steaming hot. And there is beer in the communal mess
> only on Thursdays and Sundays, unless somebody occasionally has a
> birthday.*
>
> *They are Austrian and Dutch and Japanese and Czech and Swiss and
> German and French and American and African.*
>
> *They plead to work with Schweitzer. He has not sufficient beds to
> house the people who want to give their lives to help him in his work. He
> does not want star-eyes - he wants people who can fix Diesel engines or
> repair roofs or carve off the hideous bulges of elephantiasis, who will not
> cringe at leprosy, who can sew clothes and make bandages, and who will
> answer to the master's iron hand.*
>
> *A Japanese doctor runs the culture in the leprosy lab, assisted by a
> native who has had three occurrences of the disease after coming "clean"
> three times. One of Schweitzer's most delicate woodworkers is a leper
> who has no fingers, but clasps his knife and chisel between palms. A
> pretty girl is his chief surgeon, and she does routine night work with a
> flash lamp rather than overtax the temperamental generator. A blonde*

*American college boy is in charge of 'injections'. That covers a lot of skins.*

*The families (of the lepers) cook outside each hospital shack, in individual pots over private fires, while the chickens wander in and out of the wards and the goats perch on promontories or slide down the steps to the main dining room.*

When Carter and Mary see this story in the *Worcester Telegram*, they circulate copies of the column to the grandparents, and to Mark's mother and Nick in New York.

To be sure, not all journalists are willing to bestow the status of deity upon Schweitzer. Two English reporters pay an anonymous informant to give them a different slant on the old man. They sell their un-sourced story with multiple photos to *The American Weekly*, a Sunday newspaper supplement published nationally in the U.S. by the Hearst Corporation. The story is headlined "The Women around Dr. Schweitzer: The Greatest Man Alive is not only a magnet for the ladies but may be succeeded by one." The story is filled with unflattering descriptions of Schweitzer's domestic life, his role as a father and the primitive sanitary conditions at the clinic. The authors strongly infer a very close relationship with his long-time trusted assistants Mathilde Kottman and Ali Silver.

Schweitzer ignores news stories, good or bad, and keeps at his work. He has no time for quibbling with what some reporter might write. Instead, he always takes the long view and falls back on his refrain, "My life is my argument."

Day after day they come, each outsider seeking some time with *le grand docteur*. Schweitzer treats them all kindly, so long as they respect his time. Among February's visitors are a photographer from the *National Geographic*; medical researchers from Sweden and France; adventurers crossing Africa, and Beatrice Gould, the editor of *The Ladies Home Journal*. There are teachers, missionaries and artists; professors of tropical diseases; medical and dental students, and always more journalists. An employee of the Pfizer drug company named William Elliott Rose passes through on his motorcycle.

On February 25 a 23-year-old Danish carpenter walks in to Lambaréné. Poul Erik Rasmussen has arrived in Gabon on a freighter accompanying crates of equipment donated by an association of Danish dentists. On the long transit from Europe, he has endured an Atlantic hurricane, an engine break-down, being adrift at sea for several days, and other delays. Rasmussen informs Dr. Schweitzer that his orders are to construct a new building and install the dental equipment. Schweitzer informs the carpenter that he may stay but that he has no intention of building a separate structure just for dentistry. Schweitzer has allocated only a portion of the main examining room for the purpose. Schweitzer tells the Dane that there are, however, many other uses for a skilled union tradesman. He hires the Danish Army veteran as the staff carpenter, supervising construction crews of native laborers.

One afternoon an American man and woman drag themselves into the Schweitzer clinic, exhausted from their two years of anthropological research and living among indigenous people in Cameroon and Gabon. James Fernandez and his wife Renate are bush-beaten and have come down with some jungle illness and they are in need of some respite. Schweitzer welcomes the young professionals to his dinner table that night as if they were guests he had been expecting. He even seats Renate at the place of honor. Schweitzer ignores the frightening electrical storm brewing in the African skies as he concentrates on his guests and listens to their reports on bush life in the outlying regions.

Up and down the table, the staff listens to the discussion that focuses on life in the tribal villages, and the mystical religious and medical practices of West Africans. It's fascinating for most of the staff because they rarely have time to venture beyond the confines of the hospital grounds. It's also an opportunity for individual doctors to ask about patients they have treated from those villages. Margrit van der Kreek, the surgeon, asks about the witchcraft practices among certain tribes, which in some ways compete with the Western medical treatment at the clinic.

From his end of the table, Mark listens carefully to this discussion. The next night, after the Bible reading, sermon and hymns, he approaches the young scholars. Mark tells them that he likes the fact that as anthropologists they were working outdoors, and that he is impressed with their positive appraisal of local culture.

Mark wants to hear more about anthropology and about their study of the folkloric art of oral narration. African tribesmen are known to be great story-tellers who keep alive their heritage without putting it on paper. This fascinates the anthropologists as well as Mark, who has earned a minor reputation as a story-teller in the Lambaréné tribal village huts.

After most people go to bed, Mark and James and Renate sit in one corner of the dining room and talk well into the night. Fernandez tells Mark that he has been out in the bush studying Bwiti, one of the few West African religious movements that draws its potency from the use of psycho-reactive drugs.

They talk about anthropology, culture, food and religion. Mark tells them why he loves working at the clinic, and shares his ideas about improvements that could be made at the hospital, including architectural ideas that he has developed, knowing that Schweitzer will never implement them. Mark confides that he feels a bit constrained working in the presence of the patriarchal Schweitzer.

Because the Fernandez couple has traveled and lived in the bush, their story appeals to him and Mark lets them know that he is anxious to get into the rest of Africa and away from the "colonial" situation that he says Schweitzer manages. Mark tells them he is envious that they have had the opportunity to learn to know African life as it really is.

James and Renate encourage him to pursue his dream of going out and living among the tribes for a while.

———————

Mark now actively studies the big African wall map in his room. He outlines a plan for the next leg of his own journey into the world, and charts a route that has him passing through some places of dubious stability. He decides on an ultimate goal of Israel and working on a kibbutz, at least for a while. Besides the fact that both of his stepparents are Jewish, the communal farming and mutual support concepts appeal to him. The attractions of life on a kibbutz had begun to attract him in his youth while he and his stepmother listened to an album of Jewish folk songs recorded by the actor Theodore Bikel. The songs were about milking, plowing, watering trees and sowing seeds. On the cover was a shapely suntanned girl carrying a hoe, walking through a farmer's field. Mark had stared at that picture for hours as a boy. Are there more like her? Now, to reach Israel, he will have to travel across the continent by land and water through the fabled Belgian Congo. Beyond there he will traverse the beauty and the rich animal plains of East Africa.

He seeks advice from people who have seen more of Africa. He asks his relatives and friends for their contacts in Africa. All this will bring him closer to realizing the fantastic dream he had described in his Milton yearbook: actually hunting big game.

The only way of navigating through central Africa is to retrace the adventurous passage of historical figures such as Henry Morton Stanley and Joseph Conrad. That means traversing the Belgian Congo by water, rail and overland.

As he sketches out this portion of his trip to East Africa, Mark recalls the experience of the father of his old Milton classmate Randal Whitman, who had taken a Harvard trip in 1927 across the Belgian Congo that nearly foreshadows the route Mark will have to take:

The Harvard expedition left Leopoldville on Dec. 10, 1926, and traveled steadily upriver with brief wood stops and two longer stops adding up to nine days, their paddle boats traveling under five miles an hour up more than 1,300 miles of river. Short train segments that bypassed non-navigable parts of the river added another several hundred miles (at a bit over 12 miles an hour). The last segment was a train that passed Kasongo a few hours before stopping at Kabalo, where they caught another train east to Lake Tanganyika, exiting from the Belgian Congo January 20, 40 days after they started from Leo.

Mark tests his draft itinerary with visitors who have been to the Middle Congo, one of the territories of French Equatorial Africa. Few of them, however, have crossed the Congo River or had gone very deeply into the interior of the Belgian Congo. Fewer still believe this is a good idea. In fact, before they left Lambaréné, Adriana and Frank Catchpool had tried to dissuade Mark from traveling through the central and eastern portions of the Belgian Congo. The regions are unpredictable and unstable because of tribal warfare, they warned him, and on the eve of Congo independence they could be seething with anti-European sentiment.

Schweitzer, too, argues with Mark about making a journey across the

Congo. But one other element alarms the old man: Mark's gun, which Schweitzer of course has found out about. Any black man in Africa who sees a white man carrying a weapon considers him a threat, Schweitzer says. He pleads with Mark not to travel with a weapon and offers to hold it in safe-keeping until Mark comes back.

———

One morning early in April, Mark finds a telegram next to his plate at the breakfast table. It's from a former Milton classmate, John Bart Gerald, who had been only a casual acquaintance. Bart, as he calls himself, is now a sophomore at Harvard with weak grades and girlfriend problems. He sees himself an aspiring writer. Bart says his social conscience has been awakened by an incident in South Africa, where on March 21 police in Sharpeville opened fire on a political demonstration, killing 69 black South Africans. Some people claimed the crowds at Sharpeville were peaceful, while others said the crowd had been hurling stones at the police and that the shooting started when the crowd started advancing toward a fence around the police station.

Bart simply announces that he will arrive in Gabon on April 15 and that he, too, wants to work for Albert Schweitzer. Mark is not enthusiastic about this intrusion but he gets permission to put an extra cot in his room. Sure enough, Bart Gerald shows up in Lambaréné. Now Mark has a roommate he barely knows sharing his small space, and carrying a bunch of sad stories from back home as well as heavy new socio-political concerns. Of course, Bart also insists that Mark introduce him to Schweitzer. Mark arranges for Bart to help Isao Takahasi in the leper village. Bart works there for a few weeks, then prevails upon Schweitzer to introduce him to people at the Protestant mission down the river, which Schweitzer is glad to do. He pays for Bart's transportation away from Lambaréné.

Bart urges Mark to join him in mission work but Mark adamantly resists because he wants to plan his journey across the continent and toward Israel.

It is obvious that what Mark really loves about Lambaréné is his work with the Africans. Everyone who meets him there remarks upon his unique ability to relate to the patients and their families. With his broad smile, gentle sense of humor and sparkling blue eyes, he tells them stories, sings them songs, and wins them over. He has come from his life of privilege where anything he wanted was within reach. These people don't have such advantages.

Learning about the suffering people of Africa, whether they are patients at the Schweitzer clinic, hungry villagers struggling for food and cherishing their secret rituals and dances, or parents trying to educate their children, provides an endless source of fascination to him, and a stark contrast to his own upbringing. Being able to help provides Mark reassurance that he has made the right choices. He is finding peace within himself. He wants to learn more about how the people of the world live. Yale or MIT or Worcester Pressed Steel can wait.

Albert Schweitzer recognizes Mark's cultural curiosity, and the young American's unique ability to relate to the native population. He understands Mark's enthusiasm and considers how to put it to the best use. In fact, Schweitzer already has in mind an assignment that he believes is perfectly suited for Mark Higgins, one that will take him deep into the Gabonese jungle.

# Nine
# From the Hearts of Gabon

The prevalence of heart disease among African patients had long troubled *le grand docteur*. For years, many of them showed up complaining of chest pain. So Schweitzer was delighted to have heard from the Harvard doctor Paul Dudley White, known as the founder of preventive cardiology. White, who had treated President Dwight D. Eisenhower following his heart attack, had met with Schweitzer at his home in Gunsbach the previous fall. The National Heart Institute, a division of the National Institutes of Health in Bethesda, Maryland, had set aside grant money for studying cardiovascular disease outside the United States. Schweitzer and White agree on a plan under which a team of American doctors will spend half their time directly treating patients at Lambaréné, in return for Schweitzer's help in gaining access to tribes in Gabon. It will be a very ambitious undertaking with a substantial amount of field work. White chooses David C. Miller and Steven S. Spencer of the Mayo Clinic to carry out the field research.

They arrive in March to begin working among Schweitzer's patients. Mark meets Spencer, who describes the proposed cardiovascular research. The study calls for a large-scale sampling of patients at Lambaréné as well as in seven native villages representing different tribes and ethnicities across southern Gabon. As Schweitzer knew he would, Mark expresses keen interest in helping with the study. Schweitzer quickly approves. If anything can persuade Mark to postpone a dangerous cross-continent trek, this is it. Mark agrees to delay his departure and the start of his personal journey until this important and fulfilling project is complete.

To refine their technique and establish baseline data, the doctors and their tall young assistant arrange examinations of 371 in-patients who live at the Schweitzer clinic.

The doctors hope to compile a complete medical history of each person as well as measure blood pressure, and record an electrocardiogram on film. Nothing will be easy about this. They work under the constraints of heat, high humidity, fungus growth, and the continuous challenge of obtaining fresh batteries and film. All the film has to be processed in makeshift dark-rooms in the bush.

Mark helps scope out the most efficient routes. They arrange to lodge with French and American missionaries in each region. Mark provides value because at Lambaréné he has already met patients from most of the tribes to be visited. His French is good, and he has picked up conversational phrases in several West African languages. He helps Spencer and Miller pack their Land Rover 4x4 with x-ray machines, portable generators, chemicals and film, medicine, tools, food and goods to trade. Having collected census data and secured the permission of the local government administrator, the team drive down the rut-scarred N1 dirt trail, Gabon's only national road, deep into south-central Gabon.

Their first destination is the most remote. The village of Mbigou lies at the base of the densely forested Massif du Challu region. Just coaxing the Land Rover up the narrow trail is a huge challenge. This is the home of the Nzabi tribe. As soon as Mark and the two doctors arrive on site, they confer with the tribal chief and the medicine man, equally respected figures. Here in the deep jungle, Mark already knows that before trying to get anything done, it is essential to start with blessings from the top guys.

With the formalities done, the two doctors accept the offer of local mis-sionaries to sleep in the parsonage. Mark chooses to sleep in a *tudi*, a mud hut in the center of the village. The hut is a simple structure, constructed in less than a day from bent saplings overlaid with wide leaves. This night, he joins in native night life and bonds with his temporary hosts. He knows that his success in doing this will prepare him well for the unknown parts of his cross-Africa trip. Among the simple pleasures he enjoys that night are palm wine drunk from a crooked-neck squash gourd, and plenty of boiled manioc and plantains. He drifts off listening to the noises in the steamy jungle: the insects, the birds, the monkeys.

Although tucked away deep in an obscure part of Gabon, the work of Nzabi artisans is well known in the Western art world. Native sculptors here use hard, talc-rich soapstone to carve statuettes that frighten away ancient spirits. They also craft the Punu-Lumbo masks eagerly sought by collectors of primitive art. Authentic masks used in ceremonies are full-headed, helmet-like carvings. The oval masks feature narrow eyes, arched eyebrows and small ears. Male ceremonial dancers wear *mokuyi* white-faced masks which usually contain nine scale-like patterns on the forehead representing either a central eye or a flowering tree.

The doctors set up their mobile clinic and proceed to examine 57 members of the Nzabi tribe. They present each person with a card written in French that describes the findings and offers recommendations for whatever future therapy might be needed.

A few kilometers north, a tribe of the Bantu people known as the Itawa lives in the small village called Massongo. The medical team repeats the procedure here and collect data from another 36 natives.

Making their way down the mountain range and then west on the red dirt trail along the bank of the Upper Ngounié River, they pass the night in the town of Mouila. The next day, Mark and the two doctors drive along a similar trail to a village occupied by members of a tribe that is

*A carved wood Punu-Lumbo tribal mask made by the Nzabi tribe.*

the second-largest ethnic group in Gabon. The Bapounnou, Punu for short, live on the shores of a place of remarkable beauty called Lac Bleu, a remote fresh water lake made famous by an ancient legend.

The legend holds that a group of nine dwarves once lived there. One day a dwarf dropped his axe into the water. The water was so clear that the dwarf thought he could reach in and retrieve the ax. Instead, he tumbled into the lake and disappeared. Each of the other dwarves in turn went into the water to look for their friend. To this day all nine dwarves and their axes remain submerged. The shoreline of Lac Bleu is lined with offerings to the dwarves' spirits. Mark and the doctors observe cups inexplicably filled with Coca-Cola, orange slices and wildflowers along the shoreline. Interpreters of the myth tell them that the lost axe is a sign from the spirits that says: "Be careful what you do. There are limits to the destruction you may bring to the forest."

The Punu live in small villages, sometimes only three or four huts comprising a family. They share the lake with gorillas, chimpanzees, hippopotami and forest elephants. Mark and the two doctors evaluate 67 members of this tribe.

The Punu, Mark learns, have a taboo against eating the flesh of dogs, cats and snails. A Punu woman will not eat any animal that she is familiar with such as a hen, goat, civet, screech owl, fox, or valuable animals like roosters, drakes and sheep. They won't eat snakes, either, because they believe that a woman who does so becomes wicked and starts behaving like a man, therefore failing in her duty as a mother and neglecting the education of her children.

Mark notices that these women have very elaborate hairdos. Before they plait one other's hair, they first coat it with palm oil, then tie it into long parallel ridges. Styling their hair in this manner takes several days, but the perm lasts for months. The Punu men are largely traders. Until the later part of the 17th century, the Punu monopolized the trade in salt and imported European products. But according to oral history, they also traded slaves, usually criminals. This active role in the slave trade supervised by Punu chiefs enabled them to become rich by selling to European slave traders, as well as to expand their population by buying captives for themselves. Some slaves, particularly women, were directly integrated into the master's clan along with their children.

Fear of evil spirits governs the lives of most tribal groups in Gabon. Illness and death are not considered natural: these are events deliberately caused by someone. That belief paves the way for the work of fetishers, who not only protect the people but also tell them how to honor the ancestors who will protect them from evil spirits. The disruptive spirits who bother the Punu by taking away their sleep and making life unbearable can be appeased by the performance of certain rites. Punu priests were re-nowned for their experience with the supernatural. These fetishists or witch doctors incorporate ancestor skulls, certain plants, animal blood and flesh into their rites. A fetisher claims to cure illnesses by driving away evil spirits and offering protection to a tribal member who calls on him. In return, the fetisher receives money or gifts.

Mark now understands why at night the Punu villagers keep a fire burning under a shelter in front of protective fetishes or ancestor figures. Ancestors are the source of life. Improperly treated or neglected, they become vindictive ghosts.

Mark watches the Punu demonstrate how they use their distinctive white pigmented masks and statues during a funeral ceremony. White symbolizes the afterlife and the spirits of the dead. Dancers wear these carved full-helmet masks displaying protruding eyes, curved, high domed foreheads, T-shaped noses, and high ridged hair arrangements. Some performers stand on stilts concealed under colorful costumes, and perform strange acrobatic feats.

As he closes his eyes late that night and tries to sleep, Mark smiles and remembers that he is a long way from Worcester, Massachusetts.

◆──✦──◆

After the first three field examinations, the team returns to Lambaréné for rest and re-supply. The next set of examinations will take place in riverine villages. In a few days, they stock a motorized pirogue and set off along the Ogoué River heading south to the lakes region. Mark and the cardiology research team progress to the village of Bonga, the central home of the Eschira people, where they collect data from 46 of the 68 villagers. Eschira ancestors had migrated into the Bonga area in the 1700s after wars with the Akeles and other northern tribes. As early as the 1800s they were known for their tobacco as well as for raffia cloth.

The next stop is with the Bakele tribe in the flat riverside village of Azo. It is, as expected, a friendly reception. Albert Schweitzer himself had once visited this place, and they remember him well. For the two doctors and Mark, the Bakele consent to 54 full examinations. Besides historically having been skilled hunters, their tribal heritage includes active participation in the not-too-distant slave trade. But by 1960, the tribal population and influence is diminishing. The Fang, a larger tribe, have displaced many of the Bakele. Venereal disease has resulted in a substantially lower birth rate. The remaining members of the tribe now live peacefully along the river, where their diet consists of fish, fish broth, fruit such as mangos and grapefruit, plantain, manioc and the occasional piece of bush meat. They can still per-

*Life in the lakes region consists of fishing, and soaking manioc in the river to get rid of the cyanide.*

form exotic dances such as the maringa, ilombon, mamboumba, ondokoue, ongono and lechembe.

Ezolwe, the sixth village that the team examines, is also located on the lower reaches of the Ogoué River. But this village is well concealed high on a bluff overlooking the river and accessible only by a long series of terraces. African black parrots populate the trees, and monkeys swing from the branches. Mark notices one of the most remarkable floral phenomena right here: a small green plant whose leaves, when touched or blown upon, shrivel up. It is known as the *mimosa pudica*. But that's not its only magic: when the leaves and bark of the little plant are extracted, dried and smoked, they produce hallucinations more intense than cannabis.

Here, the Galoas have long served as intermediaries between the tribes up the river and along the coast. The Galoas allow the team to examine every one of the 62 persons who live in the village and surrounding areas. Their very hospitable welcome includes sharing several group meals with the medical team. The tribe's diet is richer in bush meat – usually monkey, pork and pangolin – than that of other peoples examined. However, at less than 10 grams per day, one serving is "far poorer than our usual American diet," which the researchers conclude "in all probability is an important factor in their low coronary disease rate."

In all, the field work is largely a success. After two months of collecting and analyzing data at Lambaréné and in the native villages, the doctors begin drawing some preliminary conclusions. Yet they find themselves at an impasse. They cannot imagine why diseases of the coronary arteries are so rare and diseases of the cardiac valves so prevalent.

"As compared with the classical emotionally tense, physically soft, overfed, hyperlipemic white American male candidate for coronary thrombosis, these Africans are different in almost every respect. Most of them are remarkably easy-going, they tend to be hard and thin, and their diet is sparse and lean," they observe.

The medical team decides that they need a detailed study of native diet to help isolate contributing factors.

In the Fang tribal village of Nzorbang just a few miles northwest of Lambaréné, they find a tribe willing to permit lengthy observation. Here is the perfect assignment for Mark. He will be paid to live among the natives and learn about their history, culture and eating habits for five days. So during the second week of June, Mark goes to live in Nzorbang, with a mission of eating, working and sleeping in their midst, and recording everything that a typical Fang working adult consumes for five consecutive days.

"Very few persons could have observed their food pattern so unobtrusively, yet so carefully and thoroughly as did Higgins," Dr. Spencer writes. "During his residence in Lambaréné he had come to know the people and had become greatly liked by them. As other villagers had done, these villagers shared their bed and board with him, with very little if any change in their usual eating habits."

Mark's analysis leads to an important conclusion. His data shows that the daily native diet consisted of 2,250 calories. Manioc, a staple of the African diet made from the cassava plant, is the principal component. It has a much higher caloric content than potatoes. Manioc has to be soaked in water to remove the cyanide before it can be prepared for eating. The root is very rich in starch and contains significant amounts of calcium, phosphorus and vitamin C but is poor in protein and other nutrients. Manioc leaves, while a good source of protein, are deficient in certain amino acids, but are often mixed with spices and nuts to create a tasty mushy soup.

Big green sweet-tasting plantains make up the next greatest source of calories, followed by fruit, palm oil, peanuts, taro, and meat or fish. Small amounts of okra and gourd seeds round out the diet. The villagers tell Mark that they eat fish or meat only once every five or ten days.

But Mark learns something else important while he lives with the Fang: he learns about their rudimentary iron-making practices. The Fang tribe, he finds, gained a great deal of regional influence because they could produce iron for axes, spears, arrows and knives. The tribe occupies a region rich in small deposits of high grade ore. Mark believes the methodology of this early steel-making process will interest his father, so he writes a narrative analysis and sends it home. "The Fang would set up a furnace on the side of an ore deposit, work the deposit, and then leave," Mark writes. "The furnaces were small and made of fire-baked clay with a stone grating. The ore was poured in at the top of the furnace, and heated by the fire under the grating. Air was blown in by wood and skin bellows through passages under the ground, lined with hollowed stones, and the pigs were cast in the ground. The pigs were not only used for weapons, but also as money, principally to purchase brides." Carter is so impressed with his son's report that he sends it to the editors of *Metal Progress* magazine.

Altogether, the cardiology team makes 416 field examinations, along with another 371 back at Lambaréné. The cardiology research team reviews Mark's field data and concludes that the usual daily intake of animal fat is well under 10 grams per person and that this is "an important factor in their low coronary disease rate." The three doctors publish their results in *The American Journal of Cardiology* under the title, "Survey of Cardiovascular Disease among Africans in the Vicinity of the Albert Schweitzer Hospital in 1960." Rheumatic heart disease is the most common cardiologic affliction. Hypertension and congenital cardiovascular diseases are also common, but coronary heart disease is practically non-existent.

One of their principal discoveries has an immediately positive and long-term impact on the lives of Fang tribesmen. Unlike members of the Galoa tribe, who show no evidence of rheumatic heart disease, the far more populous Fang are found to have an astonishingly high prevalence of a surgically correctible heart condition called mitral stenosis, a narrowing of a key heart valve. Richard Friedman, the gruff Czechoslovakian physician and Auschwitz survivor at the Schweitzer hospital, embraces this finding at once, and begins performing valvuloplasties on Fang patients who complain of chest pain.

This single discovery is expected to save and extend the lives of hundreds of Fang tribesmen in the years ahead. This contribution to African life is one of which Mark is justifiably proud, and the doctors agree.

The cardiology study has given Mark everything he hoped for: a purpose in life, helping others, living among other cultures. It helped him find meaning in life. He has come a long way in one year. But now the study is over.

Spencer, Miller and White recommend follow-up studies. Most importantly, they also recommend surgical correction of rheumatic and congenital heart disorders. The study concludes:

> *The high prevalence of mitral stenosis is astonishing. With our present knowledge of the cause and surgical relief of rheumatic heart disease, we believe strongly that it is a duty to help bring to these sufferers the benefits of better penicillin prophylaxis and of cardiac surgery when indicated. The same responsibility exists for those with correctable congenital cardiovascular defects. . . . We hope, however, that this report may increase the reader's awareness of our opportunity and obligation to share more generously the life-saving measures of modern medical science with those elsewhere who need so much and have so little.*

Mark's old friend Gene Schoenfeld, with whom he had snuck away to observe native dances in the middle of the night the previous summer, returns to help doctors Spencer, Miller and White finish writing and analyzing the cardiology data. During Mark's last days at Lambaréné, they enjoy a boisterous reunion. Capitalizing on Mark's new friendships in the African villages and his rudimentary comprehension of local languages, they venture out for a few more evenings of tribal rituals.

While Mark was living and eating with the Fang tribe down the river, new arrivals were temporarily lodged in his room at Lambaréné. The guests are the famous sculptor Kalervo Kallio, whose father had been president of Finland, and his wife Sylvia, a French countess. Kalervo has begun research for a bust he wants to create of Albert Schweitzer. Sylvia had lived in the French Congo. Fluent in seven languages, she served as an interpreter for the Allied Forces in France during the Second World War, raised money for the French Red Cross and procured false identification cards for Jews living in occupied France.

When Mark returns, all of his things were still stored in the room occupied by the Kallio couple, and as he decides what to send home and what to discard and what to take with him, he and Sylvia Kallio have many long talks. Mark makes the new guests feel at ease. Sylvia enjoys Mark's stories about life out in the bush, and she discovers that he has a repertoire of American songs. She begs him to sing "Ol' Man River" for her again and again in his deep bass voice.

Mark ships home his accumulated artifacts including two gorgeous African masks and carved soapstone statuettes, books and extra clothing. Where he plans to go requires that he travel lightly and nimbly, with most of his stuff in a rucksack.

The world beyond Lambaréné is frequently on edge. In May, the Soviet Union shoots down an American U-2 spy plane piloted by Francis Gary Powers; the fallout from that incident results in the cancellation of a summit meeting between Eisenhower and Soviet Premier Nikita Khrushchev. The Cold War is heating up. Tensions between East Germany and West Germany run high. The new Cuban premier Fidel Castro nationalizes all American-owned businesses, including oil refineries, factories and casinos, which prompt the United States to end diplomatic relations and impose a trade embargo. The presidential campaign is getting underway, and the vigorous young Senator from Massachusetts, John Kennedy, is an early favorite to win the Democratic Party's nomination based on his pledge to get America moving again.

Mark has heard from any number of sources, notably the journalist Robert Ruark, that unrest has been brewing in the interior of the Belgian Congo. More recently, stories of tribal warfare have been surfacing. In April, an enterprising 23-year-old Scripps Howard journalist named D'Lynn Waldron filed a series of reports about the atrocities in Luluabourg in which she described the fighting between the Lulua and the Baluba tribesmen there. This fighting occurred right in the path of Mark's intended travel. In fact, one could not cross the Congo without going through Luluabourg. Some of this violence, instigated by the soon-to-be-departing Belgians, includes horrors such as cannibalism, rape, village burning and torture. *The New York Times* had reported on May 7:

> *New fighting between the Lulua and Baluba tribes threatens to cause chaos in the final weeks before Congolese Independence June 30. In Luluabourg, where the Constituent Assembly is scheduled to meet next month, Belgian authorities are unable to keep peace between the hostile clans. Yesterday the mutilated bodies of seven Lulua men were found in tall grass on the outskirts of the city. They had been ambushed by the Baluba three weeks ago. An ambush on Easter weekend near the headquarters of the American Presbyterian Congo mission ended a truce of several weeks.*

By May 11, reporter Waldron is in Leopoldville, the capital of the Belgian Congo. As one of only about 2,000 Americans in the country, her sources include senior operatives at the American consulate. They have studied her highly edited dispatches, which had appeared in her hometown newspaper, the *Cleveland Press*. They also tell her what they know about Mark Higgins, who is expected at the embassy the following month.

Waldron developed contacts with the incoming prime minister, Patrice Lumumba, and for a while tried to pass messages from the Lumumba camp to the outside world. In late May, the Belgian Congo held elections for legislators who would set up a government after the territory received independence. There were numerous irregularities, as Reuters reported on May 26:

> *A state of emergency was declared in an eastern region of the Belgian Congo today following reports of increasing violence and intimidation during elections there. Congo-wide elections are being held for legislators to set up a Government after the territory receives independence. Election results were held up in part of Kasai Province, adjoining Kivu, today after a ferryboat carrying boxes of uncounted votes had sunk in a river near Lusambo. Ten persons were drowned, including some polling officials.*

Back home in the United States, life in the Higgins family has been moving ahead. Mark's father has gained more visibility in the steel industry, authoring articles for trade magazines such as *Iron Age, Steel, Metalworking, Management Review*, and *Purchasing Week*. He is advancing up the ranks of the World Federalist organization and is now next in line to become vice chairman of the national executive council. Lisa has been accepted into the University of Colorado at Boulder, where she will enroll in the fall.

In mid-June Mark receives a rare and rambling two-page letter from his brother Dick. Now 22 and living in Greenwich Village, Dick will soon graduate from Columbia University with a degree in English. Dick tells Mark that one of his electronic operas has just been staged in New York, and "was a whopper of a success" as acclaimed by *The New York Times*. But his main reason for writing is to announce that he will be getting married to Alison Knowles, an "insanely attractive" artist five years his senior. Dick says he intends to flaunt family tradition at the reception by jamming it with their bohemian friends: "nice people, but from a non-Higginsish world. Imagine Grammy being confronted by a cheery-sad abstract painter, probably high, and very very dark." For their honeymoon, Dick says, he and Alison will fly off to a secret destination and go hunting for mushrooms, his latest passion. He cautions Mark about going to work in a kibbutz in Israel and warns that life can be lonely there for those who are not Jewish or who don't speak Hebrew. He suggests Southeast Asia might be a better place to explore. But what startles Mark is a Latin phrase at the very close of Dick's letter. "*Ave atque vale*," he writes. Mark recognizes the line, which roughly translated means "hail and farewell." Those are the famous last words that the grief-stricken Roman poet Catallus spoke in a eulogy over his dead younger brother's ashes. Mark wonders why Dick would choose that haunting sign-off.

Monday, June 20, is Mark's last official day working for Schweitzer. For his final meal in the staff dining room, Mark sits next to his friend Siegfried Neukirch, the adventurous bicyclist. Neukirch likes Mark, whom he has come to know as "a peaceful man who did every task he was asked to do."

Although they had worked in different parts of the clinic -- Siegfried has been driving the truck and running errands outside the hospital -- they share the bond of Schweitzer's philosophy. Neukirch recounts the words of their mentor: "Dr. Schweitzer taught us that the most important thing in life is to leave traces of love with your friends. The most beautiful monument to yourself is in the heart of your friends."

Later that day, as is his custom for a departing colleague, Albert Schweitzer orders a special bell rung: the *"Ehrfurcht Vor dem Leben"* (Reverence For Life) bell that hangs in a frame structure overlooking *la grande pharmacie*. Its chime summons everyone at the hospital to walk down to the Ogoué Rover pirogue landing for a cere-

mony. Schweitzer hands Mark an envelope containing a cash gift – a token of his appreciation for Mark's work. Then he looks directly at the young American, shakes his hand and says simply, *"Viel Glück."* Mark steps into the pirogue. As he waves back to Albert Schweitzer, the doctors and nurses, patients and friends, four chanting oarsmen push his pirogue away from the shore and steer the boat into the downriver current. In a few minutes it goes around the bend.

Ali Silver writes neatly in the log of the clinic: *"Depart Mark Higgins pour Sindara. Il se rendre a Brazzaville via N'Djole. Il nous a aide pendant 13 mois."* Her notation indicated that Mark is headed for the small town of Sindara, and that he will then make his way 75 miles upriver by steamer to the small town of N'Djole. The only way to proceed to Brazzaville on the French side of the Congo River is to fly there from the airstrip at N'Djole.

As he leaves Lambaréné, Mark reflects on what he has learned and how his life has changed in the past 13 months. He is well aware of the irony that he had left one patriarchal structure for another; that he had left the relatively safe protective confines of one home for another; that he had left a hard-driving autocratic father who was religious, passionate about classical music and desperately concerned about the state of the world for another man who exhibited many of the same characteristics.

In Lambaréné, Mark has grown. He had put himself in unfamiliar surroundings, starting at the bottom, and gained the respect of many men more senior to him. He continued his intellectual growth by teaching himself German, calculus and philosophy. He was promoted to greater responsibilities, learned to be on his own socially, and made friends outside of his prep school and his family. He has matured into a man.

Mark acquired a high degree of confidence while living among the native tribes of Gabon. Now it is time to apply what he has learned, and to explore on his own. He seeks authenticity, adventure, and awareness. Surely he will be able to trade on all this accumulated experience, knowledge, empathy and self-confidence as he makes his way across the rest of the continent and up the east coast of Africa toward Israel.

From now on, however, he must carry out his detailed and bold plans without a safety net.

# Ten

# Knights on a Chessboard

Mark knows that the best time to travel across equatorial Africa is during the dry season, when the roads are most likely to be passable. Like all travelers leaving Lambaréné, Mark must make air connections through Brazzaville, capital of the French-owned Republic of the Congo. It is a four-stop flight from N'Djole on Air France. It's a town he wants to explore and he finds that the best way to do so is on two wheels.

The summer solstice marks the beginning of the dry season in central Africa, where for two months temperatures average between a low of 64 and a high of 84 Fahrenheit. Rainfall averages a third of an inch in June, and a tenth of an inch in July.

Brazzaville, the capital of the Republic of the Congo, lies a few degrees south of the equator on the north side of the Congo River. Brazzaville was built specifically so the French could compete with the Belgian city of Leopoldville on the opposite bank. This is the only place in the world where capital cities face one another on opposite sides of a river.

Yet Brazza, as it is known, more closely resembles a small provincial French village than the capital of a country. Larry Devlin passed through the city in June 1960 enroute to taking up his duties as the CIA Chief of Station in the soon-to-be-independent Belgian Congo: "Brazzaville was a small, sleepy town with a strong French flavor," he said, "low-lying stucco buildings with green tin roofs, sidewalk cafes, bars with zinc countertops, a few high-rise hotels, and walled gardens brimming with bougainvillea, cannas and hibiscus. It could have been the tropical version of a rather run-down French provincial town."

Charles DeGaulle, the president of France, is wildly popular in Brazza. The city was his headquarters during the Second World War. A stone house built for him there in 1943 was the house to which he returned in August 1958 to announce that the colony, then part of French Equatorial Africa, could choose to become an independent country, or remain associated with France. DeGaulle's historic decolonization proclamation set in motion the movement for African independence. It has had a ripple effect across the continent, most definitely on the other side of the Congo River. As Mark has heard, this is the cause of much of the tension brewing in the Belgian Congo.

June 26 is Mark's 20th birthday. He celebrates by renting a bicycle, finding the afternoon ride through the quaint European section a delightful experience. The next day, while riding that bicycle around town, Mark spots his new friends the Finnish sculptor Kalervo Kallio and his wife Sylvia, the couple who had moved into his room at Lambaréné and for whom he sang the *Show Boat* ballad "Ol' Man River." In Brazza for a few moments the three friends look out on the Congo River, the Ol' Man River of Africa. Sylvia remembers, "He seemed so happy to see us and we were certainly glad to see him. We chatted. He told us that he was leaving the next day."

Mark explores Brazza for a few days while he puts the finishing touches on his plan. He has a good sense of where he wants to go and how he wants to get there. Because he will be on the move and without regular access to a telegraph office, he identifies American consulates and mission outposts as primary points of contact. Family members can send packages or leave messages for him that he will pick up at these intermediate destinations. He writes ahead to those places, and advises them of his travel plans. He knows he will be in for an adventure that permits him to continue meeting native people just as he had in Gabon, getting to know them through art, music and story-telling and their varied lifestyles.

Mark has good reasons for wanting to see the Belgian Congo. Travel guides describe what a beautiful place it is. The new book published by Pan American Airlines in 1960 says: "The eastern part of the Congo known as the 'Gem of Africa' is becoming increasingly popular with Americans and Europeans. Its scenery is most diverse. It includes active volcanoes, lakes, impenetrable forests, high plateaus and grassy meadows. The people are friendly."

The Pan Am guide recommends starting one's central African experience at the Relais Hotel in Brazzaville, a "commendable hotel with excellent French cuisine." Rates are about $6 per night. American cigarettes are available throughout the Congo for about 24 cents a pack, a bargain price for a regular smoker like Mark. For those who might require medical attention, the Pan Am guidebook notes that in the Congo that "there are excellent doctors, dentists and good hospitals. The various Protestant missions have hospitals with modern equipment and outstanding doctors 'in the bush'."

The airline's booklet recommends that sightseeing in Leopoldville should include the native market (a 'must' for color photographers); the Zoological Garden, and a tour of the European quarter covering the Museum of Native Life, St. Anne's Cathedral, the King Albert Monument, the Pioneers Monument and the Stanley Monument. Outside of Leopoldville, tours of the Congo are offered by train, auto and boat. But the main attraction for natural beauty awaits in the eastern Congo:

"Most picturesque scenery in the Congo is in the Kivu region, with its volcanoes, lakes, mountains and national parks. Principal places of interest include Lake Kivu, called the 'Jewel of Africa' where at Bukavu to the west you can see the famous seven-foot-tall Watussi natives and to the north the still-active Nyamuragira volcano, among others; the broad mountain-bordered plains of Albert National Park where you see the great variety of wildlife at farther range but in great numbers than at Kruger." Furthermore, the travel book recommends the famous Ruwensori Mountain range, called 'Mountains of the Moon' and the Ituri Forest, where one could see the home of the pygmies, "and go hunting in organized trips."

All of that is close to the last waypoint Mark has set for himself in the Congo, the town of Kasongo in the far eastern province of South Kivu. This is the hometown of Lambros Passialis, the Schweitzer admirer who had commissioned that handsome portrait for the doctor's 85th birthday.

From there, if all goes well, he will fly onward to Uganda, his gateway to some of the most spectacular scenery and hunting in all of Africa. Known as the Pearl of Africa, it is in the heart of the western branch of the Great Rift Valley, the place from which *homo sapiens* walked out of the savannah

60,000 years ago to populate the world. But first, to get there, Mark must travel 1,500 miles on his own along waterways, railways and rough roads cut through the jungle and savannah.

⸻

Two and a half miles across the Congo River from Brazza lies Leopold-ville, the capital of the Belgian Congo, a territory administered and exploited by Belgium for almost 80 years. Belgians named the capital city in tribute to Leopold II, their king who once owned all of the Congo but had never set foot there.

The Congo River and surrounding rainforest shroud the mysterious land of pygmies, mythical beasts, dreadful plagues, and cannibals.

Portuguese explorers in the 15th century were the first white people to enter the place called the Kingdom of Kongo. Nearly half a million people lived in its capital city of Mbanza Kongo and created an extensive trading network.

Merchants traded raw materials such as ivory elephant tusks as well as goods such as copper and ironware, raffia cloth and pottery. Even before the Europeans arrived, a flourishing slave trade existed. Only when the great Victorian missionary David Livingstone found that quinine prevented malaria, the scourge of explorers, could Europeans explore the interior of Africa. But Livingstone disappeared into the jungle. *The New York Herald* sent Henry Morton Stanley to locate him and of course when that happened in 1871, Stanley uttered the famous words, "Dr. Livingstone, I presume?"

After Stanley's famous voyage was reported in the European papers, Leopold summoned Stanley and commissioned him to return to the Congo and negotiate with the local chiefs. In five years, Stanley signed hundreds of treaties with the Congolese chiefs. The Africans had no idea they were sell-ing their land. They thought they were signing friendship treaties and re-ceiving trinkets and cloth in return. At an 1884 conference in Berlin called to divide up Africa (no Africans attended), Leopold persuaded Otto von Bismarck that, in order to exclude Britain and France from the region, a better solution would be to declare the Congo a free trade area and let him own it and run it according to the humanitarian principles he had articu-lated. Leopold II was handed control of a territory that he named the

Congo Free State. But it wasn't a Belgian colony; it was his personal property.

The northern political boundary of the Congo Free State was marked by the magnificent Congo River, Africa's most powerful river and the fifth longest river in the world. It flows from the east, starting near Lake Tanganyika. After a series of rapids, it gives way to the Middle Congo, a thousand-mile stretch of navigable river, nine miles wide in some parts. Along one quiet stretch of that river was the city that the explorer named Stanleyville. Near the end of the Middle Congo, the river slows to a virtual standstill for twenty miles, a section known as Stanley Pool. Here the river is two and a half miles wide and flanked by Leopoldville and Brazzaville. Downstream to the west, travelers stop at Livingstone Falls, a 220-mile-long series of rapids and cataracts having as much power as all the rivers and falls in the United States combined. The last hundred miles to the Atlantic Ocean is fully navigable.

Leopold's Free State consisted of nearly a million square miles of unmapped jungle. The territory was 76 times the size of Belgium itself. Although greed for ivory inspired the land grab, it was the invention of the pneumatic tire for vehicles that began a worldwide boom in rubber. In the Congo, rubber grew almost everywhere on wild jungle vines. One had only to persuade the natives to scrape it off into big baskets. Leopold did this by setting a quota of both rubber and ivory for each village. They received a fixed price for the labor, a miserably low rate set by Leopold's enforcers on the scene. Each community was told to provide ten percent of their number as full-time forced laborers, and another twenty-five percent part-time. It was slavery. The advent of the automobile in Europe and the Americas increased the demand for rubber dramatically. In 1902, rubber constituted eighty percent of the exports of Leopold's Congo Free State. The tool for enforcing production was a whip made of raw hippopotamus hide. This was cut into long sharp-edged strips which when applied repeatedly -- dozens of lashes at a time was a common punishment -- was sufficient to tear the skin off a man's back.

The king established a militia known as the Force Publique to enforce his rubber quotas. Its soldiers were black, many of them from the fiercest tribes of the upper Congo. The white Belgian officers who led them also supervised the burning of non-compliant villages and the torture and rape of workers slow in meeting quotas.

The penalty for actually failing to meet a rubber quota was to cut off a worker's hand. Bonuses were paid for enforcement, so the Force Publique collected hands by the basketful: they severed hands from living people as well as from corpses. Joseph Conrad, the captain of one of the riverboats that transported the ivory and rubber, wrote a book about this period, a narrative that forever influenced the way colonial Africa would be remembered. *Heart of Darkness*, one writer has said, describes "fetid fever-ridden ports in an Equatorial river basin surrounded by dense tropical rainforest. Its climate of high temperatures and humidity enveloped a world of madness, greed and violence." The memorable last words of the fictional ivory trader reverberate in the minds of all who read Conrad's book: "the horror, the horror."

A 1904 report commissioned by the British House of Commons suggested that at least three million people had died as a result of King Leopold's exploitation.

A series of investigations provoked international outrage. Mark Twain wrote a savage piece of sarcasm called *King Leopold's Soliloquy*. In Britain, Arthur Conan Doyle penned *The Crime of the Congo*. After deliberating for two years and negotiating with Leopold, the Belgian Parliament annexed the Congo Free State and renamed it the Belgian Congo. Leopold received £ 2 million as compensation for his troubles. The government of Belgium oversaw a somewhat less brutal administration. As reporter Paul Vallely of the British newspaper *The Independent* summarized:

> *In the decades that followed the transfer of responsibility to the gov-ernment of Belgium, large amounts of the wealth produced in the Congo were spent there by the alliance of church, commerce and state. Mission-aries built hospitals and clinics to which large numbers of Congolese had access. Doctors and medics achieved great victories against disease, man-aging to eradicate sleeping sickness. Many villages had medical posts, and bigger cities had well-equipped hospitals. Churches ran schools to which 10 percent of the people were admitted. Colonial authorities built rail-ways, ports and roads. The mining companies built houses for their staff,*

*provided welfare and technical training.*

*By the Second World War, production and profits had risen to the point where the Congo was Africa's richest colony. In the 1950s, life expectancy was 55 years. By 1959, the year before independence, the Belgian Congo was producing 10 percent of the world's copper, 50 percent of its cobalt and 70 percent of all industrial diamonds. What was missing, however, was an educated class of Congolese to run their homeland. The Congolese had no rights to own land, to vote or to travel freely. There were curfews in towns and forced labor in the countryside. The only higher education was for those who wanted to become priests. The Congolese could become clerks, medical assistants and mechanics, but not doctors, lawyers or engineers.*

As a result, on the eve of independence, out of a population of 60 million, there are only 16 university graduates in the entire country. The Congo is perhaps the least prepared of any African colony for independence.

Nearly 90,000 Belgians live and work in the Congo as managers, owners, officials and operators of the machinery of business and government. They rotate through a tour of duty but do not provide training to the locals. The Congo exists only to make Belgians richer.

The party of the charismatic orator Patrice Lumumba, the *Movement National Congolaise* (MNC), has won a plurality of the parliamentary seats. Founded in 1958 as a nationalist, pro-independence group, Lumumba's MNC had substantial support throughout the Congo, while most other parties were based primarily on tribal allegiances and garnered support in their respective provinces. Lumumba campaigned on a national basis. In a last-minute compromise with a rival candidate, Joseph Kasavubu, he received the approval of the Congolese House of Representatives to form the new government that would take office in six days. Yet, incredibly, the still-subservient Congolese were required to radio their cabinet nominations to Brussels where the list was signed by the Belgian King, the Belgian premier and the Belgian minister to the Congo.

Media take liberties in their characterizations of Third World residents, as does *Time* magazine in its summary of the situation on the eve of independence in the issue that appears on newsstands June 20:

*BELGIAN CONGO: A Blight at Birth*

*Streaming into Leopoldville last week, the delegates to the Congo's first Parliament were a strange-looking lot. Some had the sharply pointed heads of a tribe that practices infant skull bandaging. Newly elected Senators in elaborate robes sat soberly at sidewalk cafes sipping beer, looking somewhat dazed. Others were tieless and in shirtsleeves, but sported bright, beaded caps with dangling horns and tassels as they gawked at the sights. Most were obscure villagers who had never before been to the city, but some of the faces were already nationally and even world famous.*

*Wiry, goateed Patrice Lumumba, 34, the Batetela tribesman from Stanleyville, whizzed about grandly in a black limousine as he dickered desperately to get control of the first government. Chubby, 43-year-old Joseph Kasavubu, loyal to his Bakongo people, was also deep in negotiation with key faction leaders such as Paul Bolya of the Mongo tribe and Jean Boli-kango, the Ngombe spokesman. The corridors of Leopoldville's new Palais de la Nation echoed to the jabber of a score of languages and dialects, for the Congo's first legislators represent a nation of more than 150 separate tribes, each with its own interests and jealous point of view, its own savage and mystic creed, its own desire for power.*

*Political Potpourri. Out of this tribal nightmare must come a national cabinet, a prime minister and a chief of state in time for independence day on June 30; but bloody tribal fighting has raged for months through the Congo. Bitterest of all was in the land of the Lulua. Since the 19th century, when Arab slave raiders drove the frightened Baluba westward into Lulua territory, the Baluba had happily tilled Lulua soil in semi-serfdom in exchange for the right to remain in the area. Then last year, when whispers of Congolese independence filtered out from Leopoldville, the Baluba began declaring themselves free men, tried to take over some of the Lulua land for themselves.*

*The warlike Lulua reacted with spears, knives and sharpened sticks, killing hundreds of Baluba, burning their huts and carrying off their women. Only Belgian armed intervention, coupled with the mass re-moval of tens of thousands of Baluba to another region, stopped the blood bath.*

*Thus, tribalism may yet tear the vitals out of the new Congo before it even gets its start as a nation, just as it has been the political plague everywhere in Africa. For to conservative tribal rulers, democracy is a mysterious and not entirely welcome concept. Tribal elders do not like the idea of upstart youngsters challenging their authority in the tribe's affairs. Warrior clans, like the Lulua, whose hegemony was built with spears and brawn, are outraged to find themselves outvoted by the humble Baluba, who have adopted such unmanly professions as clerk or typist. Many tribes had less interest in establishing a new nation than in protecting their own traditional home areas from outside interference.*

*Said a neutral diplomat in Leopoldville gloomily: "I have an uneasy feeling this place is tottering on the brink of disaster."*

As Mark prepares to embark on his cross-Africa trek, his family can only hope that he will do so safely and wisely and that he will continue writing his colorful, descriptive letters. They will certainly read the magazines and newspapers more carefully, because Africa's emergence from colonial rule has suddenly become a very important news story.

People who plan great adventures, vacation travels, construction projects or careers put considerable thought into what they wish to achieve, and how they wish to achieve it. Preparedness, training and knowledge are important keys to success. But kismet also plays an important role. Making the right transportation connections, having the right person greet you at your destination, expecting that civil order will prevail, and knowing where to find food and shelter are all components of a travel plan that can be written, but execution of the plan is also dependent upon a measure of good fortune. There's a lot of wisdom in the old saying, "No amount of good planning ever replaces dumb luck."

Nowhere is that more true than in Africa. The whole continent seems to have its own timetable, driven by factors beyond the control of any one man. No one trying to make transportation connections across its breadth should be in a hurry. Mark Higgins or anyone setting out to cross the African continent requires a certain amount of luck. Mark has proven to himself that he is resourceful. He knows he can live amongst natives, befriend them, make them laugh, share their stories, eat the same food, and stay in their villages. He is likeable and friendly. He has listened to a lot of opinions, assessed the risk, and decided that he has the stamina, the health, the courage and the wherewithal to complete a solo trek across the Congo. He is an American, not a European. So here he stands: adventurous, confident, determined, independent, intelligent, and with time to spare. He has been very lucky so far.

On June 28, as he had so carefully planned, Mark packs his essential clothing, his malaria pills and other necessities into his rucksack. He takes a taxi to the pier in Brazzaville, boards the ferry to cross the Congo River and half an hour later lands at "the Beach," the chaotic port of entry that is the entrance to Leopoldville, capital of the Belgian Congo. The city of Leopoldville is a maelstrom of activity. It is the second-largest city in sub-Saharan Africa and the third largest in the whole continent after Lagos and Cairo. After struggling through the customs line, he hires a taxi to take him to the office of Ted Koton, an American businessman with whom Mark has arranged to stay.

Months earlier, Mark had appealed to the whole Higgins family for any contacts they had across Africa. His uncle Charles Wilding-White, a business professor at Rensselaer Polytechnic Institute in Troy, New York, had responded that Cluett Peabody & Company, Inc., owner of the Arrow line of shirts, was running a very popular operation in the Congo. Koton, a native of Montclair, New Jersey, had been assigned to the Congo in 1959, and was enjoying great success selling Arrow shirts. In fact, the incoming Prime Minister Patrice Lumumba and most of his ministers wore Arrow shirts which are considered "high-style." Koton was proud that it had become the local custom for a groom to present his new father-in-law with cash plus three Arrow shirts. Business was booming: Arrow had sold 196,000 shirts in the Congo during 1959 alone.

At a sidewalk café, Koton introduces Mark to another one of the great national institutions of the Congo, Primus beer. While they drink, Koton discusses with Mark the local excitement over independence and offers some tips on how to stay safe. Most Congolese recognize Lumumba's national political party, the Movement National Congolais (MNC). Just to be on the safe side, Mark acquires and carries an MNC card. Outsiders of course have to be cautious about allegiances and alliances, yet one might never know when it would be prudent for a white person to show empathy with the national cause.

In preparation for the Independence ceremony, Leopoldville has taken on a festive air. Lining the streets are thousands of the new Congolese flags bearing a large golden star on a field of dark blue, with six small stars for the provinces running from the top to the bottom down the left side. The next day, June 29, the Belgian King Baudouin arrives in Leopoldville. Belgian and Congolese officials sign a treaty of friendship and collaboration that includes aid to the new Congo Republic, and allows for Belgium to maintain military units in certain bases on a temporary basis for an unspecified period of time. Since the Belgians haven't trained any native Congolese to become officers of the Force Publique, the white Belgian officers and senior non-commissioned officers will continue to lead the military, which serves as an army as well as a police force.

———◆———

In front of Mark is a chessboard far more complex than he had ever seen in his matches at Milton Academy. White kings stand on one side, black kings on the other, with their pawns lined up in front. If he believes that he can deftly navigate his way across this board, this is really the time to think 15 moves ahead. He will have to move as deftly as a knight, sometimes making two moves in one direction and then sidestepping a space.

His newly polished French language skills should come in handy here. Outside of Paris, Leopoldville is the largest French-speaking city in the world. After four solid years of French at Milton Academy and a year of immersion in Gabon, he can now read, speak and, as he had boasted to his stepmother, argue in French. This is the language of government, schools, newspapers, public services and high-end commerce. On the streets, however, and importantly, within the Force Publique, people speak Lingala. This language of many dialects evolved from Bantu and consists of words borrowed from ancient tribal languages, mixed with elements of French, Portuguese and Dutch. Across the Congo, 22 languages are spoken.

Mark's welfare while traversing the Congo will be directly affected by national and international political and military events, long-simmering tribal rivalries, and the raging currents converging in the early days of Congolese independence. It's obvious that many Congolese do not understand the word "freedom." Some believe it means trading places with their Belgian oppressors. Some see it as assuring instant wealth. Some see it as the end of white European control. No one, certainly not the Belgians, has prepared the populace for the hard work ahead or equipped them with the fundamental skills or training to take over what the Belgians had been doing -- or forming a government and running a country.

The Rev. Jack Mendelsohn, the newly appointed senior minister of Arlington Street Church, a prominent Unitarian-Universalist congregation in Boston, happens to be visiting Leopoldville and captures the upbeat mood in the capital city on June 30, the morning of Independence Day:

> The gray-uniformed Congolese Police Band played 'Way Down Upon the Swanee River' and 'Marching Through Georgia'; some 7,000 smartly-outfitted school children paraded down Avenue Gouverneur General Ryckmans; a few small army howitzers blasted away on the lawn of the Palais de la Nation; a single helicopter circled noisily overhead; and the Congo was magically transformed from a Belgian colony into an independent, sovereign republic.

> When the great moment of independence came, to this nation, which is larger than the U.S. east of the Mississippi River, the surface atmosphere was so calm it seemed as if most of Leopoldville was unaware of the history being made. The crowds for the various festivities in the inner city were comparatively small and orderly. Cordons of helmeted Congolese troops, still under the command of Belgian officers, were completely in control of all ceremonial areas. Everything, except the hotels and cafes, was shut down.

The formal event transferring power takes place in the colorfully draped circular hall of the Palais de la Nation, a newly built place that was to have been the residence of the Belgian Governor General. Both houses of the Congolese legislature attend, as well as senior diplomats from around the world.

*Prime Minister Patrice Lumumba, in bow tie, flanked by Joseph Kasavubu and King Baudouin of Belgium.*

Baudouin, the 29-year-old King of the Belgians, speaks of the historic relationship between his country and the Congo. He mentions with pride the achievements of his uncle King Leopold II, who, he says, helped the Congo in so many ways.

President Joseph Kasavubu responds with diplomatic grace. As the new nation's Chief of State, he expresses goodwill toward Belgium and receives hearty applause from the members of Parliament. Kasavubu deletes the last sentence of his prepared address, which was to have ended with the declaration: "I proclaim in the name of the nation the birth of the Republic of the Congo!"

But from that instant forward, the ceremony veers off course. Prime Minister Patrice Lumumba, a dramatic orator, had not been scheduled to speak. At the conclusion of Kasavubu's remarks, however, he strides to the podium and delivers his own fiery speech boldly reminding the king and the people of the Congo of the oppression that Belgium had imposed on central Africa over the years. Lumumba is charismatic, with extraordinary powers to move an audience. He launches an attack on the heart of colonialism. He references the "terrible suffering and exploitation" that had been experienced by "we niggers" and he promises: "We shall make of the Congo a shining example for the whole of Africa." He says that June 30, 1960 will be known for the "glorious history of our struggle for liberty." He asserts that no Congolese will ever forget the struggle in which "we have not spared our strength, our privations, our sufferings or our blood."

It was a struggle that was indispensable, he says, for putting an end to the "humiliating slavery which had been imposed on us by force." Colonialism has left wounds too keen and too painful to be wiped from memory. Lumumba reminds members of the new Parliament of "the ironies, the insults, and the blows that we had to submit to morning, noon and night because we were Negroes." He declares that Congo must be made the "rallying point of all Africa" and that the nation must put an end to the oppression of free thought and give to all citizens the fundamental liberties guaranteed in the United Nations Declaration of the Rights of Man.

By some accounts, Lumumba now ad libs at the conclusion of his remarks, *"Nous ne sommes plus vos macaques!"* ("We are no longer your monkeys.") Irrespective of whether he uttered those exact words, that is the precise sentiment he conveys. It has a stunning impact. No Congolese had ever spoken like that to Belgian royalty. By playing a populist political hand, Lumumba wins the support of the people as quickly as he wins the antipathy of the Belgians.

Two hours later at a state dinner, the meteoric Lumumba has calmed down a bit. He toasts King Baudouin and praises Belgium for the magnificent work done in building the Congo. He notes that Belgium was ready to provide help and friendship and that the treaty they have just signed will be profitable to both countries. He says the Congolese people are grateful that Belgium has given them freedom without delay and that the two countries will remain friendly.

But it's Lumumba's Independence Day speech that is the talk of the town. It produces reactions of surprise and disappointment among Belgian and other Western representatives. Soviet diplomats seem to enjoy the occasion, but the Eisenhower Administration does not know what to make of the man who now stands front and center of the most important new country in Africa at the new nexus of Soviet-American cold war contention. The United States immediately recognizes the new Republic of the Congo. The Americans upgrade their diplomatic presence from a consulate to an embassy and assign the first ambassador, a man named Clare Timberlake.

Back in the United States, sitting at his desk at Worcester Pressed Steel, Mark's father reads the *The New York Times* on the morning of July 1, as its correspondent summarizes the challenges facing the new country:

*Congo Rises from Stone Age to Statehood in Few Decades*

> *Fifty-five years ago, in the heartland of darkest Africa, which formally became the independent Republic of Congo today, the wheel was not used, language was not written, cannibalism and witchcraft were common, and the site of the capital, Leopoldville, was still a dense jungle.*

> *That area became known to the outside world only eighty-five years ago. At that time the British-born American newspaper man Sir Henry Morton Stanley, who had earlier tracked down the missing Dr. David Livingstone, undertook a long exploration of the Congo River.*

> *Sir Henry later tried to interest the British in the new land but failed. However, he succeeded with King Leopold II of Belgium, who decided to use his own great wealth to develop the Congo as a kind of personal estate after the Belgian Government had refused to show interest. King Leopold set up the Independent State of the Congo, which lasted until 1908, when the Belgian Parliament took it over as a colony.*

> *The Belgian Government set out to substitute the carpenter's hammer for the tribal drum, introducing the twentieth century overnight to a primitive people divided into many warring tribes.*

> *The 13,600,000 Congolese, scattered over an immense area of equatorial forest and savanna about a third as large as the United States, are still divided into about 200 tribes, some of them still warring.*

> *More than 400 dialects are still spoken in the Republic of Congo. The range of social evolution almost covers the range of human growth, starting with the Stone Age aborigines in the Pygmy tribes, who use arrows*

*and spears dipped in poison. The new state is home not only to the world's smallest human beings--the four-foot Pygmies--but also to some of the world's tallest--the seven-foot-tall Watussi.*

*There is also a "lost greatness" for the Congolese to remember in their new struggles. The Kingdom of the Congo flourished from the fourteenth century and even exchanged envoys with Portugal, the Vatican, Brazil and the Netherlands. But the kingdom fell victim to the slave traffic and began a rapid decline in the eighteenth century.*

*Today barely half of the Congolese can read and write, and only sixteen Congolese are university or college graduates. There are no Congolese doctors, lawyers or engineers, and no African officers in the 25,000-man Congolese Army.*

*The independence movement began among Congolese working for the colonial administration or for commercial companies in a land that is rich in copper and cobalt and industrial diamonds. At first, after World War II, the Congolese talked only of "equal pay for equal work," but following quickly upon this came talk of political rights.*

*In December, 1957, the Belgian colonial administration gave the Congolese their first measure of self-rule by holding elections in Leopoldville, Elisabethville and Jadotville. A year later the cry for "immediate independence and departure of all the Belgians" had become common.*

*The Belgian Government tried to carry out a plan for independence by stages, but rioting in Leopoldville in January, 1959, aroused pressure for early independence. That independence was agreed upon at a round-table conference in Brussels earlier this year.*

Mendelsohn, the Unitarian minister, notes in his journal the first signs of trouble: "While the inner city retained its placid atmosphere, trouble brewed in some of the outlying communes on the night of July 2. The Balubas and Luluas began skirmishing. The new Congolese government cracked down hard. The new Republic of the Congo flag now flies over the heroic Stanley monument, overlooking the mighty Congo River and the great, modern city of Leopoldville. It is the ultimate symbol of what happened in June when 'uhuru' (freedom) came to the Congo."

Until Independence, the U.S. State Department has had few intelligence sources within the Congo. Diplomats have grown accustomed to relying entirely on Belgian officials for situation reports. The consulate prior to independence had a very small staff. As events now unfold, the American diplomats turn to the best and most knowledgeable experts they can find: international journalists. Andrew Steigman, the Consular/Economic Officer in Leopoldville, explains: "We were working very closely with the American press. There were some top reporters that had come out there, and they were, in effect, almost extra political officers for the embassy because we were very open with them. They would bring us the stories that they picked up, and we would tell them whether or not we had information that could confirm or if we had totally contradictory information so that their reporting would be as accurate as possible."

The journalists, with their mobility, speed, accuracy and more resources, provide immediate information with up-to-the-minute sources. The embassy now relies on these dispatches.

The family scrutinizes The New York Times and Time Magazine with increasing anxiety as Mark stands at the beginning of his cross-Congo journey. The United Press International wire service reports on July 2:

> Fighting flared between rival tribesmen in Leopoldville and the provincial capital of Luluabourg today in the wake of a two-day celebration of the Congo's independence from Belgium.
>
> ... the violence broke out while 1,500 guests were being entertained by the Government at a reception in the Palace of the Nation. The brawling and fighting went on throughout the night in L'ville's African community of Dnjii. It grew worse this morning when groups of Bakongo tribesmen looted a half dozen dwellings belonging to Bakayas.
>
> ... In Luluabourg, the capital of Kasai Province, the long-standing feud between the Lulua and the Baluba tribes erupted into renewed fighting last night. ... Authorities canceled a fireworks display that had been scheduled to conclude the independence celebrations.

Saturday, July 2, is the 78th birthday of Clara Carter Higgins. Mark's grandmother is enjoying another lovely summer at Breaknolle, the family coastal retreat in New Hampshire. As was his practice, Mark tries to call her. But the telephone operators in Leopoldville are on strike for the "Independence Holiday" and there is no telephone service on Sundays in the Congo.

On Monday, July 4, Mark attends a reception at the American Embassy, a four-building complex in the European sector. In other U.S. embassies around the world, diplomats and expatriates are celebrating the Fourth of July by hoisting the new 50-star flag, which commemorates the recent addition of Alaska and Hawaii to the Union. But in Leopoldville, more pressing concerns dominate the agenda. Guests all want to meet the new American ambassador Clare Timberlake, his wife and their five children. Larry Devlin, the new CIA station chief, attends the reception, as does another American official who has already been there for a few months.

Frank Carlucci, a 30-year old State Department employee, serves as vice-consul and second secretary. This mid-level rank is an important stepping stone in the diplomatic career path. Carlucci had graduated from Princeton University in 1952, where his roommate Donald Rumsfeld had also been a teammate on the wrestling team. Carlucci served two years in the Navy, got married and earned a Harvard MBA before joining the State Department in 1956. In March 1960, he was assigned to the Congo. He holds a diplomatic posting but is very close to the CIA station chief and has already been briefed about Mark's experiences with Schweitzer at Lambaréné. Apparently he has shared some of this information with the young American reporter D'Lynn Waldron, who has since left the Congo but kept detailed notes on interactions with her contacts.

At the embassy, Mark finally meets Rev. Jack Mendelsohn, the man whose name he had often heard. Mark tells the Boston cleric that his grandfather Higgins is a Unitarian, and admires his preaching. Mendelsohn, physically imposing and eloquent, is an activist in civil rights and human rights causes. He has come to Africa researching his book, *God, Allah and Ju-Ju*, an assessment of the roles of religion in Africa, coupled with his observations on the impact of Communism. While in the Congo, he has even talked about religion with the new Roman Catholic prime minister Patrice Lumumba, who "seemed even younger than his thirty-four years as he described his disenchantment with the Roman Catholic faith in which he had been raised," the cleric tells Mark. Lumumba is "content to be a secularist" and holds that the Church is incapable of understanding the "humanistic society" African nationalists will build.

Mendelsohn tells Mark that he was inside the Palais de la Nation when Lumumba made those inflammatory and extemporaneous remarks. The Boston minister's discussion with Mark, who has just come from a year with Albert Schweitzer, is an eye-opener and it is also a great coincidence: Mendelsohn's church had hosted Schweitzer in 1949. Mark makes a good impression on Mendelsohn, who relates this encounter to the Higgins family. It is a small world.

Mark by now can hold his own in these settings. By the time he arrives in Leopoldville, he realizes how far his family pedigree can carry him. It has opened doors and revealed opportunities. When necessary, in just a few minutes of conversation, Mark knows he can establish himself as an up-and-coming member of the establishment club. Even here in Africa, at the American embassy, his unique credentials work for him. Every boy growing up in New England has spent a scouting trip or a school overnight at the Higgins Armory Museum. Well, yes, Mark acknowledges, he is from that Higgins family of steel men and authors and civic leaders. Far from home, his surname serves as an instant identification, a conversation-starter, and a ticket of admission into an elite world. He doesn't have to embellish his standing; those who have gone before have prepared the way for him. This works as long as he remains in the company of Europeans or Americans who know something of his family background.

<hr>

While the festive reception is underway at the embassy, Congolese troops form other ideas about the meaning of independence. The Congolese armed forces, the Force Publique, have had both police and military functions. All officers and senior non-commissioned officers are Belgians and even though the Congo has been granted its independence, the old uniformed leadership has remained in place. The 24,000 members consist almost entirely of illiterate and poorly paid indigenous troops, with an officer corps made up entirely of white Europeans. Since June 30, resentment has begun to arise among the army privates and non-commissioned officers who see little opportunity for advancement. Further discontent is caused by

Lumumba's decision to raise the pay of all government employees except the military.

Signs of unrest within the military start almost at once. The political officer at the embassy, Frank Carlucci, recalls:

> I had heard rumors that rioting was occurring at the Parliament building so I grabbed a Lingala-speaking driver and went to the Parliament building where the troops were indeed rioting. I went up to them and through the driver asked what they were rioting about. The answer was interesting. They were upset not so much at the Belgians as at their own leadership, Patrice Lumumba and others, who had suddenly sprouted big cars, big houses, and flashy suits. They asked, 'What's in it for us? Everybody else gets something and we get nothing.'

On July 5 the Belgian commander of the Force Publique, Lieutenant General Émile Janssens, not known for his diplomacy, calls a meeting of the Leopoldville garrison. Reminding the soldiers of their oaths of loyalty and obedience, he reiterates his philosophy by personally writing on a blackboard, "After independence = before independence." In other words, the white Belgian officers are still in charge, and there will be no pay raise for the troops. This is not the message the rank and file want to hear.

Soldiers of the Force Publique garrison at Thysville, near Leopoldville, drunk and high on hashish, suddenly mutiny against their white officers. Then they begin attacking European targets. Armed bands of mutineers roam the capital looting and terrorizing the white population. Thousands of Europeans begin seeking refuge across the river in Brazzaville and up the river in Stanleyville.

That is all the Belgians need to hear. They quickly mobilize a military re-intervention into the Congo to ensure the safety of their citizens. Obviously, the arrival of these forces violates the national sovereignty of the new nation. In an effort to placate its soldiers, Lumumba's fledgling government decides to "Africanize" the army. All personnel are promoted by one rank but the flight of white officers has left the armed force totally leaderless. The government has no effective instrument of law enforcement. *Time Magazine* summarizes the developments:

*All 1,000 Belgian officers were removed from their positions, and re-placed with Congolese. With or without an Africanized officer corps, the soldiers are running amok throughout the Congo, and panic-stricken whites are fleeing in all directions. Numerous European targets have been attacked.*

The outbreak causes fear among the Belgian and other civilians and officials still resident in the Congo. Word spreads fast by missionary radio. The white community in Luluabourg is besieged in improvised fortifications and holed up awaiting a rescue by Belgian Army paratroopers. At least 10 Europeans are killed in armed clashes in Elisabethville in the south and in Leopoldville. Lumumba meets with the Force Publique and tries to calm them down. But the troops remain undisciplined, leaderless, armed, and angry at the Belgians.

Mark is eager to get away from Leopoldville as quickly as possible, and into the smaller towns of the interior.

# Eleven

# Upstream

_⤙⤛_

The terrain and climate of the Congo Basin present serious barriers to cross-country road and rail construction. The distance between places is enormous. In addition to the topographic challenges, chronic economic mismanagement and internal conflict has led to serious under-investment over many years. Development of infrastructure has been ignored. As a result, surface transport in the Congo is very difficult. On the other hand, the Congo has thousands of miles of navigable waterways. Traditionally, water transport has been the primary means of moving around approximately two-thirds of the country. The Belgians created a single company called the Congolese Transport Office known as OTRACO that manages all the vital commercial traffic on the rivers, the railways and the roads.

Mark books passage on the once-a-week river service that will depart Leopoldville on July 6. OTRACO operates a twin-engine Integrated Tow Boat stern-wheeler named _Inspecteur Mahieu_ that carries passengers aboard the main vessel and a mixed-cargo service with pusher tug barges. The 175-foot steamer operates on a semi-weekly schedule.

Before departing the embattled capital city he wants to let his grandparents know he is thinking of them, so he writes them a letter:

_Leopoldville, Rep. du Congo_

_Dear Grammy & Granddad,_

_Happy Birthday! As you undoubtedly know, I planned to call on your birthday. I was so looking forward to hearing your voices again, to having personal contact after a year. But Saturday the operators were on_ *strike ("the Independence" holiday!) On Sunday there's no service. On Monday there was service but no circuits available for me, and Tuesday, due to a storm somewhere, they lost radio contact with the states. Today, Wednesday, I must leave. What a disappointment!*

*I hope that you had a good birthday anyway and that, as usual, Little Boars Head (Breaknolle) was full of family.*

*I leave today, by boat, for Port-Franqui, thence by truck to Usumbura. In about a month, I should arrive at Kampala, Uganda, and you can write me there c/o the American Consul.*

*Happy birthday again, from your loving grandson,*
*Mark*

As Mark boards the *Inspecteur Mahieu* he meets the master, a Belgian officer named Pierre Camerman who in normal times lives with his wife Henny and their two children in a cabin on the top deck. Mark pays the fare in francs, not the nearly worthless Congolese currency. Added to the fare is a mandatory surcharge of $12.80 per day for three meals per day. To his surprise, Camerman offers Mark his choice of staterooms. The third deck offers the best vantage point for viewing the passing scenery.

*OTRACO steamboats on the Congo River and the Kasai River such as the Inspecteur Mahieu would often push or pull smaller boats, a custom and courtesy of African riverboat captains.*

As the *Inspecteur Mahieu* slips her lines and heads up the Congo River, Mark has his first surprise: there is a lot of cargo piled up on deck, but he is the only passenger. On the left side of the river is the French Congo, and on the right side, the now independent Republic of the Congo. It will be a slow ride; the steamboat makes only about eight mph against the current. The sailing plan calls for a voyage 128 miles up the Congo River before turning into the Kasai River, its major tributary, towards Port-Franqui. The boat will anchor in the stream every night. In all, it will be a seven-day voyage against the current.

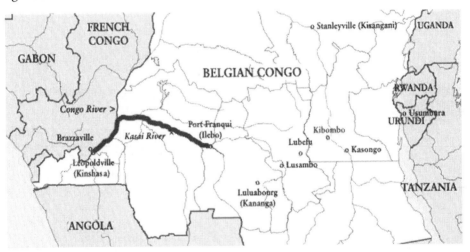

*Mark's plan calls for him to depart Leopoldville on the Belgian-operated stern-wheeler Inspecteur Mahieu on its bi-weekly departure up the Congo River and into the Kasai River toward Port-Franqui.*

Mark's plan is to continue from Port-Franqui by train to Luluabourg, and then continue by truck, with an indefinite number of stops along the way until he reaches Usumbura, at the northern end of Lake Tanganyika. As he outlined in his letter home, he hopes to proceed from Usumbura across Rwanda. After about a month he will arrive in Kampala, the capital of Uganda, where he will check in with the American Consul and retrieve mail and messages. Until then, there will be no way for the family to contact him.

As Mark looks out on the scene ahead, he recalls passages from Joseph Conrad's classic work. Conrad had piloted a steamboat on the Congo River on a boat very much like this one and had used the experience as an inspiration for his famous anti-colonial novel *Heart of Darkness*. What Conrad saw in 1890 shocked him profoundly and shaped his moral view of all exploration and trade in newly discovered countries, and indeed of civilization in general.

As a youth Mark had memorized parts of Vachel Lindsay's thumping, rhythmic poem "The Congo." He had often recited its dramatic verses with his mother and his siblings because they all had a personal connection to the poem: Lindsay had been a personal friend of his maternal grandmother Elisabeth MacDonald. Now as he looks out the window of his cabin at the great river, in his head he recites the refrain:

> *Then I saw the Congo, creeping through the black*
> *Cutting through the forest with a golden track.*

He smiles and then shudders involuntarily as he remembers the rest of the words.

After 16 hours, the vessel turns east into the Kasai River, and proceeds another six hours to a wood fuel stop at the small town of Mushie.

Mark sits on deck and writes a letter to his family. He has been talking with Captain Camerman, and from the wheelhouse has observed the passing parade on the river. Now he watches as shirtless native workers load aboard cord after cord of wood. When the refueling finishes, he hands the letter to one of the natives onshore and asks him to mail it. The nearest postal facility is at Mpukumbu, a small village on the north side of the river.

*At wood stops like Mushie on the Kasai River, natives work fast to bring fuel aboard the steamboat.*

The voyage resumes promptly after the refueling. Four hours later the boat arrives at Banningville, the first scheduled port of call. Here the company faces an unusual decision. Camerman monitors radio reports about rioting in the interior. A number of high-level consultations take place within

OTRACO about whether Camerman should continue the voyage, given the level of unrest and violence reported ahead. He believes it is his duty to offer safe passage to Belgians and others who want to escape the troubles. Many of those he wants to rescue are people he knows who have been working at the wood and palm plantations along the Kasai River.

Any six-foot-five English-speaking white man going the opposite direction of everyone else stands out in the Congo. "Mr. Higgins was a passenger on board of the *ITB Inspecteur Mahieu*," writes Neuville Kleber, an OTRACO shipmaster stationed at Banningville. "Moreover, he was the only white passenger on the arrival of this boat at Banningville. I was also there. It was on July 8. Because of the events in the Congo, it had been decided that the boat would stay at Banningville, for an undetermined period. Mr. Higgins liked to continue his travel to Port-Franqui. It was proposed to him to take a place on board a small boat going to Port-Franqui towing a boat with Congolese passengers (2nd and 3rd class)."

Mark has a reason for wanting to hasten his arrival at what he anticipates will be the security of Port-Franqui, so he accepts Neuville Kleber's suggestion that he embark on a small boat towing a separate craft, a common practice in the Congo. Native Congolese routinely lash to the sides of the barges other boats which cannot travel under their own power, but which accommodate many more passengers.

The moon is full on the night of July 8, and it bathes the Kasai River with sparkling light. At dawn, Mark leaves Banningville riding slowly upstream with a group of Africans.

When Camerman receives clearance to get underway again, he soon overtakes the slower boat pulling the Congolese barge on which Mark is riding. "On July 10, about midday, the *ITB Inspecteur Mahieu* was continuing to Port-Franqui," Kleber recalls. "It joined the boat Mr. Higgins was on board. He took again his place on board of our boat enroute to Kasai."

The special correspondent for the *Cleveland Press* D'Lynn Waldron had reported from this area only two months earlier. "Most of the river boats were tiny Victorian relics, half rusted away and painted the color of rust so it wouldn't show," she said. "Many of the larger riverboats had been towed across the Atlantic after outliving their usefulness on the Mississippi. These were big, old-fashioned, flat-bottomed, stern wheelers that drew only a few feet of water."

*The Integrated Tow Boat Inspecteur Mahieu, here taking on cargo, makes a transit every other week up the Congo and Kasai rivers from Leopoldville to Port-Franqui, the end of the navigable waterway.*

Mark spends hours on the navigation bridge with Camerman, who has skippered this vessel for twelve years. In normal times, the impeccably dressed captain and his wife visit with passengers, share the lore of river life and try their best to make passengers happy. Mark's story about working with Schweitzer interests him.

But what really concerns Camerman as he talks with Mark is what might lie ahead in the newly independent Congo. A whole way of life is at risk. Up until now, he explains, life has been good for Belgians working in the Congo. Every three-year tour is followed by a six-month vacation. At the end of every one of his vacations, Camerman can hardly wait to get back to piloting his ship. He takes his wife and children to Belgian parties on Saturday night. He runs as tight a ship ashore as afloat: any boy wishing to dance with his daughter Alfonsine first must approach the captain and ask permission. But now, as a precaution against the difficulties brewing in the Congo, Camerman has sent his wife and his young daughter to safety over in Brazzaville. He has a son about Mark's age who is studying back in Belgium.

The chatter monitored from radio operators upstream indicates a great deal of restlessness. The situation is considerably more uncertain than company officials had anticipated in the months prior to independence. Captain Camerman has good sources along the waterfront and is a keen observer of the nuances of the Congo, but it doesn't take an expert in African politics to see that things are changing rapidly.

The captain has earned the trust of his black crew, who find him to be a decent and fair boss. He helps them solve whatever problems arise. Whenever there was an engine failure, Camerman would work alongside the

*Pierre Camerman has spent 12 years as a riverboat captain in the Congo and enjoys a good relationship with his crew.*

native crew to fix it, crawling into the dirty engine room with his tools. He would help his men fix a puncture in the hull on the Inspecteur Mahieu or on one of the barges they inevitably would be pushing.

Like any captain at sea, he also has to resolve everyday disputes. When crew members get into a fight over money, or over a woman, they look to the captain to settle things and dispense justice. At the same time, he is the ship's paramedic, and sometimes has to nurse back to health an injured crewman. He insists that his men do things right, and if they make a stupid mistake, he shouts down from the command bridge in Flemish, *"Twintig frank uwen boek van,"* which means "20 francs from your pay!" Yet on payday, he smiles and relents, and gives them what they earned.

One of the pleasures of the voyage Mark experiences is the steady flow of native merchants who row out from their villages in produce-laden pirogues to the passing boat. They offer fresh fruit in abundance: an unbelievable choice of bananas, large and small, red or yellow, mangoes right from the tree in all shapes and sizes, oranges, grapefruit and lemons. One little lemon costs only 10 francs.

As Mark's boat continues east, the radio reports indicate that thousands of whites, mostly women and children, are fleeing Leopoldville while mutinous African troops run wild through the city. The next day, the only escape route for whites -- the ferry across the Congo River to Brazzaville -- is temporarily shut down. Hundreds of Belgians and others hoping to leave the city resign themselves to another night of uncertainty. Mark feels relieved that he has left all that trouble behind.

But across the Congo, the developing situation is considered so uncertain that United States and British Consuls in the southern provincial capital of Elisabethville order their countrymen to evacuate Katanga Province as swiftly as possible.

In the far northeast Kivu Province, mutinous troops set up road blocks around the border town of Goma. The Associated Press wire service reports eruptions of violence in two eastern Congo areas, "where rebellious troops killed two Europeans. This first slaying of Europeans by Africans in the current disorders serves to hasten the mass flight of whites from the seething Congo." Fears of more bloodshed send Europeans fleeing eastward across the border into Uganda.

If all this was hard for outsiders to understand, Henry Tanner, a Swiss-born journalist who reported from the Congo for The New York Times, laments in print that even the ordinary English phrases he uses in his stories cannot possibly convey the accuracy of meaning required for an understanding of daily life in the Congo. He writes, for instance, regarding the Congolese police force:

> *Whenever the dispatch contained a reference to "rampaging soldiers," the box might well include a passage like this: "These Congolese soldiers belong to the Force Publique which lost all but a dozen of its officers, all Belgians, at the start of its mutiny immediately after independence. Be-*

*fore that the Belgians kept the Force Publique like a good police dog on a short leash but lean, mean and hungry. Whenever there was trouble in the villages, they let it loose to deal with offenders in its own unceremonious way." The box might add that what happened after independence was that the dog broke his leash and jumped his master in the way he had been trained to attack others.*

On July 10, as the Belgian government decides to defend its citizens and its business interests, the Belgian army begins airlifting 10,000 para-commandos into the Congo. At the same time, the Belgian national airline Sabena begins airlifting Belgian citizens out of the Congo. Over the next three weeks, the airline would fly home more than 25,000 Belgians, many of whom would never return. Now, besides Leopoldville, trouble spots include Luluabourg, the provincial capital of Kasai, and Elisabethville, the capital of Katanga whose governor Moise Tshombe detests Lumumba.

With the quiet encouragement of the Belgians, Tshombe has proclaimed Katanga an independent country, and seceded from the Congo. The Katanga province has been the profit center for the Congo; without its mineral resources, the national treasury will be considerably poorer and the Congo as a nation might disintegrate.

Tshombe petitions Belgium for military aid. Lumumba counters by asking the United Nations to intervene and help keep the country intact. The intervention of the Belgian troops, Lumumba says, has been based on "fallacious excuses." White residents across the Congo continue to flee in the wake of attacks and pillaging by Congolese soldiers.

In Elisabethville, 800 Belgian para-commandos attack mutinous Congolese soldiers after six Europeans attempting to reach the center of the city are dragged from their cars and killed.

———————

Despite the radio reports, Mark cannot gauge how serious the situation ahead of him has become. Missionaries at the American Presbyterian Mission in Luluabourg are forced to watch in dismay and horror as their congregation crumbles into fratricide. Mary Crawford, a white American missionary who has been translating the Bible into Tshiluba, the local language, writes to benefactors back home:

*At Luluabourg there are two great problems - that of the mutineering soldiers, and that of the tribal warfare which is yet to be resolved. The Bena Lulua are still determined to drive the Baluba out of the city and the Baluba do not want to go. House-burning and attacks with bows and arrows and home-made guns had begun again on the 4th of July.*

*Sometime after dark on the 9th we began to hear shots coming from the European quarter of the city and after some time had a telephone call from one of our friends who told us of the mutiny of the Luluabourg soldiers following the pattern in Lower Congo.*

*During Sunday (July 10) the soldiers were racing up and down our newly paved street, making everybody wonder what was happening. Our Congo friends would not let us out of our houses because they feared our white skins would bring trouble upon us. About the middle of the afternoon some dozen soldiers were put out of a truck near the home where we were all staying and eating together, and we wondered what they were doing. Later we learned they had set up a machine gun on the corner trained on our house and asked the watchman at the school across the street who we were. When he told them we were not Belgians, but Americans doing missionary work in Luluabourg, they told him he was lying.*

*While all these things were happening, the paratroopers arrived, and it was quite exciting to see them bail out and float down. They took control of the European sector of the city with no gunfire. The big boxcars flew right over our houses and we watched them make their turns.*

Crawford and the other Presbyterian missionaries, men and women alike, evacuate Luluabourg on July 12 and fly to Southern Rhodesia. They have no idea how long they will be away from their work and the flocks to which they have been ministering.

The paratroopers that Mary Crawford had seen drop in on Luluabourg rescue several hundred Europeans who have been besieged in the formerly luxurious Paix Hotel.

"The Congo is falling apart," declares a British diplomat in Leopoldville. "This has become a country which is a body without a head. Everything is crippled. All is chaos. Law and order are rapidly disintegrating."

Besides transportation, other public services such as mail and communications are being seriously disrupted. Food supplies are uncertain.

The sternwheeler churns slowly up the Kasai River. From Banningville it will take 30 hours of daylight to transit the 240 miles to Port-Franqui. On the top deck, Mark smokes cigarettes and exchanges stories with Captain Camerman and First Mate Van de Velde as he nervously eyes the passing scenery and makes notes for his letters home.

Although the river is two and a half miles wide in some places, the navigation channel runs very near to the shoreline. There is an art to navigating the shallow Kasai River and skirting around the many underwater rock formations. Sailing requires a captain to hew close to the channel, not straying more than a few meters from the track. The fear of running aground and the constant vigilance exacts a toll: Camerman once told a colleague who asked whether he ever had a chance to sit down, "Not while I'm working."

The upper deck offers a view of the dense green jungle and the many tributaries that feed the mighty Kasai. Mark observes that most of the little villages are on the south side of the river. In the riverside villages nets are hung out to dry. Families sit near the river and soak manioc stalks. Some young girls sit on rocks cleaning fish. Pirogues are everywhere. Many of the people in the villages they pass have prepared piles of wood, indicating their attractiveness as a fuel stop. From the river, it looks like people are going about their routines. Much of this looks familiar to Mark, not dissimilar from what he has seen along the rivers in Gabon.

And yet, despite the natural beauty of this place, Mark is hearing that the Congo is disintegrating into pieces even as his steamboat progresses deeper into the country. Gauging by what he has seen of the river traffic and his conversations with the ship master, he knows something is dreadfully awry. He describes the scene in a letter to the family back home:

"It is purely and simply panic," he writes. "I have passed seven boats headed downstream, all dangerously loaded with fleeing [Belgian] families. I am the only passenger headed into the interior -- all alone on a 32-passenger steamer."

Referring to his sojourn aboard the boat pulling the African barges, he adds: "I have had only friendly reactions from the Africans and anticipate no problems ... They ask why there aren't Americans out here where they're needed and wanted."

Being seen as an American is a good thing. Being perceived as a *Flamande*, the nasty word one used referring to a Belgian, would invite trouble. He knows it is safe on the water. Any trouble, if it comes, will be ashore.

# Twelve
## Into the Heart of Darkness

When Captain Camerman ties up the *Inspecteur Mahieu* at the Port-Franqui pier on the morning of July 13, it is a relief as well as a challenge. Port-Franqui normally hums as a commercial, industrial, and agricultural center. But now, on the other side of the fence line, Mark peers into the eyes of terrified and restless people hoping to board the big boat and get away from the interior.

Here is a decision point: should he turn around and go back to Leopoldville with the boat, or continue his journey despite the risks? Feeling the odd combination of caution and confidence, Mark decides that he has something to prove and somewhere to go. His goal is to get through the Congo in the dry season, spend some time in East Africa, and to reach Israel. From where he stands, there is no other way to get there than the way he has mapped out.

Mark shakes hands with Pierre Camerman and thanks him for the hospitality. As the courageous young American turns and walks down the gangway, the captain calls out to him, *"Bonne chance, mon ami."*

Port-Franqui is the end of the navigable waterway in central Congo, and here the railway begins. Years earlier, at the expense of enslaved natives, the Belgians had constructed the railway that linked Port-Franqui to Luluabourg and points south down to the provincial capital of Elisabethville. Everything being shipped, passengers as well as cargo, must be off-loaded from the boats arriving at Port-Franqui onto the southbound trains. Of course, OTRACO ran the railway as well as the big riverboats. Not a single road connects Port-Franqui to Luluabourg, so the train is the only way to travel that 155-mile route.

But now in the midst of the civil upheaval and tribal warfare in the central Congo, the trains on this vital route are running on a chaotic schedule.

Mark walks to the nearby railway terminal to await the arrival of a passenger train. He knows the service is spotty; he considers whether it might be worth the risk to hop on a freight train if one comes through. It is essential for him to get as quickly as possible to Luluabourg because he believes that the people he made contact with at the Presbyterian mission will give him shelter, respite and advice for the next phase of his journey. He is dependent on their goodwill.

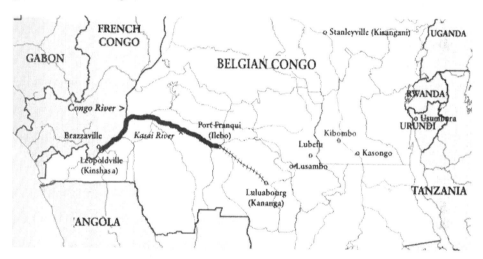

*The water route ends at Port-Franqui. From there, passengers heading to the interior cities of Luebo and Luluabourg travel by train. Fierce fighting had broken out in Luluabourg several times in early 1960, and again while Mark is there.*

His luck holds: the OTRACO train actually has been waiting for the boat to come through that day, primarily to carry badly needed supplies down the line. Soon after he boards, the train's steam locomotive, wood-fueled like almost everything in the Congo, begins pulling the elegant old European-style sleeping cars, followed by freight cars. Ahead of it the train pushes the much more crowded "African cars," which are far less comfortable and less expensive. The whole assemblage chugs along at about 20 mph, pausing at villages to let people on or off the African cars. It creeps across the tropical savanna through steamy jungles, sometimes slowing down so an OTRACO man can walk in front. He is looking for bombs on the track. Natives looking for food and treasure sometimes ambush the train.

Mark's train passes through the town of Luebo, about halfway between Port-Franqui and Luluabourg. Here, too, without the discipline of the Belgian-run army, tribal warfare has broken out. A Presbyterian missionary named J. Hershey Longnecker recalls the scene on the ground:

> *After independence the tribal war between the great Baluba and Lulua tribes reached Luebo. During the years since 1891 a town of 10,000 people had grown up around the Mission station. Most of the people belonged to various branches of those two tribes. The town was split wide open. There was fearful fighting. Whole sections of the town were burned. Horrible things happened. Neither of those tribes owned the land, which had belonged to the Bakete. The Baluba outnumbered and outfought the Luluas, and drove them across the Lulua River.*
>
> *Luebo remained a depleted town, those remaining being Baluba or their friends. Many Baluba who had been scattered in the Lulua country fled to Luebo. The town was filled with refugees.*

At the end of this long day, the train finally approaches Luluabourg. Scattered over the flat hilltop grassland, cut by sharply descending valleys of thick, tropical marsh-type vegetation and streams, Luluabourg is a city shaped into nine zones by these valleys. Until about 1940, it had been simply a train stop between Port-Franqui and Elisabethville. But Luluabourg has now become the center of exchange for European products coming in from the north, and African products coming in from the south. That cargo usually consists of copper and other essential minerals coming out of Katanga. The Belgians have constructed warehouses and made Luluabourg an administrative center. It is home to a museum and an airport. During the negotiations for the independence of the Congo a year earlier, consideration had been given to making Luluabourg the new country's capital due to its central location.

Mark's plan is to check in with the American Presbyterian Mission. The Presbyterians have been preaching in the Congo for nearly a century. Now, with 160 missionaries, it is one of the largest and most successful ministries in the Congo. About a third of the people in the region who declare a religion identify themselves as Presbyterian. The Presbyterians have set up their mission station out in the bush behind a walled-in compound resembling a college campus.

Luluabourg by now has become the scene for considerable pillaging, with disputing tribes trying to dislodge one another. It is no longer a safe haven for white people. Only weeks earlier, the center of European life in Luluabourg had been the Paix Hotel whose café on the sidewalk faced the town square. Intertribal war in the period before independence, coupled with efforts by the Force Publique to establish control and settle scores, and then by the Belgian military trying to restore order, have wreaked havoc here and left the once-peaceful town square vacant and dangerous.

Arriving at Luluabourg, Mark goes looking for his contact at the American Presbyterian Mission, James Halverstadt, the secretary-treasurer. Mark finds only a few natives remain. Halverstadt has fled to Southern Rhodesia. At this point he realizes how serious the civil situation in the interior has become. The city's native population of 1,400, including 800 women and children, having taken refuge in apartments, has been under siege by Congolese forces for several days. The entire European and American population has been evacuated.

Back in America, the *Time Magazine* that lands on the newsstand on July 18 alarms Carter Higgins. His frustration is compounded by the fact that he has no way of communicating with Mark. The magazine reports:

> *By week's end an estimated 60,000 of the 80,000 Belgians had fled before the rampaging soldiers. In Luluabourg only 54 of 3,600 Belgians were left, and mutineers still roamed the streets looting European shops and homes. From outlying districts there came more reports of rape and mayhem. In the Equator province a Roman Catholic priest was tied to a stake, forced to watch as ten nuns were repeatedly raped.*
>
> *The Congo treasury is empty, and there is virtually no chance of collecting taxes since most Congolese firmly believe that independence means freedom from taxation. Foreign investors have been thoroughly scared off, and each morning Congolese workers line up hopefully before the closed doors of factories whose white owners and managers have fled. The government bureaucracy ground to a halt as 10,000 Belgian civil*

*servants left the country. The Leopoldville radio was off the air for 48 hours last week because there were no white men left to run it and inexperienced Congolese blew fuses every time they turned on the power.*

Mark has to find shelter in Luluabourg quickly. Native Congolese friends of the Presbyterian Mission provide a safe refuge for him. He hunkers down with them for five harrowing days.

Politically, across the Congo, events now move even more rapidly. On July 11, attempting to pacify the out-of-control Force Publique militia who have turned against their white officers, President Joseph Kasavubu and Prime Minister Lumumba began flying around the country to meet with troops in key cities and try to restore order. As they are doing so, a new development takes place in the southern mineral-rich province of Katanga.

The American consul in Elisabethville is William Canup, a career foreign service officer who has had a remarkable career after coming face-to-face with death in the Second World War. He had participated in D-Day, gotten shot down and had been held as a POW. The Congo assignment is new. With him in Elisabethville are his wife and their two young sons.

John Andregg, program officer for the State Department's East Asian and Pacific Programs, reports the situation:

*The American consulate in Elisabethville issued a recommendation that all American citizens should leave immediately. Consul Bill Canup and vice consul John Andregg prepared their families to drive south in a convoy to the copper belt in Northern Rhodesia. The previous night, they had received advice from the Belgian army contacts that there would shortly be a conflict between two factions of the Force Publique (the local Congo army). One faction was supporting the current elected governor of Katanga Province, and the other was supporting the defeated candidate, who was connected to Patrice Lumumba. The convoy departed in good time.*

*Several hours later, as darkness came to the town, we could hear gunfire coming from the direction of the barracks. This lasted until the following morning, when a strange calm came over the city. We had warned everyone not to move about during this time. However, we learned that the Italian vice consul, looking for Italian citizens, had been stopped at a roadblock and shot. Then we learned that the pro-Lumumba group of soldiers had surrendered and were being shipped off to Kasai province, from whence they came. At the request of the provincial government, Belgian troops flew in, and that seemed to calm things down, at least temporarily. We brought our families back from Northern Rhodesia, safe and sound. July 9 is my birthday, and Bill Canup and I cracked open a bottle of champagne to celebrate my reaching the advanced age of 32.*

But there is no celebrating back in Worcester, Massachusetts, as Carter Higgins continues reading the *Time Magazine* on his desk. He reads the story headlined "Monstrous Hangover":

*With a primeval howl, a nation of 14 million people reverted to near savagery, plunged backward into the long night of chaos. Tribe turned upon tribe. Blacks turned upon Europeans. The deserted streets of great cities resounded with delirious gunfire and war cries in a dozen tongues. The 25,000-man Force Publique mutinied against their white officers then turned their anger on their new government, against all whites, against all authority. There seemed no logical explanation for the madness that swept the Congo. The Congolese involved gave no coherent answers except to ask bitterly where were the pay raises and easy jobs and plentiful food that had been promised by the politicians.*

*Startled Europeans found the streets suddenly filled with disheveled troops, their sports shirts sticking out of their unbuttoned tunics. Carrying clubs and iron bars and swinging their belts like whips, the mutineers shouted alternately "Kill Lumumba" and "Kill all whites." They overturned a car driven by a white nurse, smashed the cameras of a LIFE photographer, roughed up reporters and Belgian officers.*

*Under the dust-red light of a nearly full moon, thousands of Europeans flocked to the "Beach," the starting point of ferries making the two-mile run across the mighty river to Brazzaville in French Congo. Terrified whites crowded onto paddle-wheel steamers, motorboats, skiffs—anything that would float—in their panicky flight.*

*Prime Minister Lumumba, encouraged and accompanied by Foreign Minister Bomboko, who emerged last week as the coolest and most cou-*

*rageous member of the Congolese government, went to the Leopold II Barracks to negotiate with the army mutineers. A compromise was effected: President Joseph Kasavubu would become commander in chief of the Force Publique in place of General Janssens; the garrison would get native officers; and the army would be run by a general staff, part Belgian and part Congolese.*

*Returning to Leopoldville, Prime Minister Lumumba gratuitously added new fuel to the flames. He blamed the mutiny on General Janssens, who, he said, had refused to accept proposals for the Africanization of the army; he blamed the scare about Soviet "invaders" on Belgian agents, and summoned the Belgian ambassador to make the fantastic charge that he had uncovered a Belgian plot to murder him. "The assassins were discovered and arrested in my residence," cried Lumumba. "They were armed to the teeth." Everything that was happening, Lumumba insisted, was a Belgian plot to discredit the Congolese government.*

*At week's end the Belgian government decided upon armed intervention to rescue and evacuate its citizens in the Congo, who are estimated to number 80,000.*

On July 13, just as the Belgians are sending in more paratroopers, Prime Minister Lumumba severs diplomatic relations with Belgium and appeals to the United Nations to put an end to the secession of Katanga. One faction in Katanga is opposed to the secession and soon gangs of young Baluba tribesmen are rebelling against Elisabethville, while another group proclaims the creation of a province of Lualaba in North Katanga.

That day, hundreds of refugees on mercy rescue flights from Katanga begin arriving in Salisbury, Southern Rhodesia. Many of the American missionaries fleeing from the Congo are blaming "subversive Communist activity" for the disorders.

Across the country, mutinous Congolese soldiers are forcing the ouster of their Belgian officers and are harassing Belgian civilians in various parts of the Congo.

The Force Publique interference with fleeing refugees results in a clash with Belgian troops at the Leopoldville airport. The Belgians control the airport and two main highways leading to the city and have patrols at main intersections in the downtown area. Belgian paratroopers occupy key positions in the European part of Leopoldville, despite bitter objections by the Congo Government.

That evening, Secretary General Dag Hammarskjöld calls an urgent meeting of the Security Council to determine whether to dispatch United Nations peacekeeping troops. The Security Council votes unanimously to send U.N. forces to restore order in the Congo and in Katanga, and to request that Belgium withdraw its troops.

The resolution authorizes Hammarskjöld to facilitate the removal of Belgian troops, maintain law and order, and help to establish and legitimize the post-colonial government. This mandate extends to maintaining the territorial integrity of the Congo, and to removing the foreign mercenaries supporting the secession of Katanga. The first U.N. forces troops, drawn from Ghana, Guinea, the Mali Federation, Morocco and Tunisia arrive the next day, on July 14.

On that same day, Lumumba appeals for help from Soviet Premier Nikita Khrushchev, who responds not with troops as Lumumba had hoped, but with a harsh denunciation of the Western powers who are threatening the independence of the Congo. Khrushchev wasn't ready to commit the Soviet army to a land war in Africa.

From Luluabourg United Press International correspondent Ray Moloney files this ominous dispatch:

*Murder, rape, pillage and arson made Luluabourg what it is today - a dead city.*

*The 54 whites who remain, including 10 women and four children, insist they will never leave. Belgian paratroopers guard them. But food is running short. Utilities are haphazard. And the memory of a nightmare is with them as they see the mutinous Congolese troops who rule most of the city. About 900 whites have fled.*

*... There was the absolute quiet that comes with fear. The heat was sticky. Downpours drenched and smashed the heart of Luluabourg and added gloom. Few whites walked the streets.*

*...Professor Paquay, primary school principal, set out Saturday night refusing to believe the rumors of a Congolese army mutiny. He went to their barracks to investigate. They shot him.*

Day after day, huddled with his protectors, Mark listens to the battles in the streets, and he remains in hiding. On the fourth night, listening to the crackling sounds of a short-wave radio, Mark hears a few bits of world news. In addition to what was unfolding in Africa, the BBC reports that the Democratic Party convention in the United States has nominated Senator John F. Kennedy of Massachusetts for president. They broadcast an excerpt from the soaring rhetoric of Kennedy's acceptance speech during which the nominee articulates his theme:

*We stand today on the edge of a New Frontier -- the frontier of the 1960's, the frontier of unknown opportunities and perils, the frontier of unfilled hopes and unfilled threats.*

*... the New Frontier of which I speak is not a set of promises. It is a set of challenges. It sums up not what I intend to offer to the American people, but what I intend to ask of them. It appeals to their pride -- not to their pocketbook. It holds out the promise of more sacrifice instead of more security. The New Frontier is here whether we seek it or not.*

It is a powerful speech delivered by his home state senator and it is great to hear a familiar voice from back home. But just then Mark Higgins of Massachusetts has his own new frontier to explore and his own set of challenges to meet. And he knows he has to get moving.

On the following morning, July 16, Mark sees his opportunity. There is finally a big truck coming through and headed east toward Lusambo, the direction he wants to go. He bargains for a ride. This vehicle, a truck known as a *commercant*, is a two-and-a-half ton, 10-wheel, three-axle, all-wheel-drive workhorse of the type known to soldiers everywhere simply as a "deuce-and-a-half." But no matter what the truck size, overland travel in Africa is a rough business. The roads consist of narrow red dirt trails with random potholes and divots. Breaking down or encountering a vehicle coming the opposite way can add untold days to a trip. Mark fears that he is about to find out how rough a passage that can be, even in places where the track is dry. He has to get out of Luluabourg. But arranging a ride on a *commercant* doesn't guarantee a seat. In fact, passengers are an after-thought. Merchandise and goods have the first priority. Only after a truck is fully loaded are paying passengers given space atop the cargo. And they must supply their own food.

Mark knows he has narrowly escaped Luluabourg. The next day, a unit of 1,000 Tunisian soldiers wearing United Nations uniforms physically takes control of the city and forces a Congolese army garrison of 3,000 men to lay down their arms.

If Mark is seeking authenticity, this is as real as life gets. There is no such thing as road maintenance here. Trucks often break down, or became stranded behind other trucks that need repairs. The jostling and jolting ride atop a *commercant* is uncomfortable as well as physically exhausting. If the vehicle breaks down, the load had must lightened so the truck can be pushed through the mud. Passengers may have to walk for a few miles. A vehicle might reach its destination on schedule or might be delayed for twice the expected length of the journey. Hence, adhering to a schedule while crossing the Congo is simply not a concept anyone can embrace. A truck gets there when it gets there.

The terrain eastward of Luluabourg slopes down rapidly, with the road intersecting many small streams through the tropical forest. Old railroad ties and pieces of lumber constitute bridges. The noisy diesel truck rumbles down into the town of Lusambo, a small town near the confluence of the Lubi River and Sankuru River, the longest tributary of the Kasai.

This is a good place to stop for the night. In the central Congo, the rare visitor is usually welcomed in the small villages. It is the African custom for inhabitants to show their hospitality by vacating their own mud hut, finding a mattress somewhere and making the visitor comfortable. For dinner, they will catch a chicken, kill it and cook it in palm oil. They cook a version of polenta with manioc, break off a piece with their hands and dip it into the chicken gravy. This is incredibly tasty to a hungry and haggard young man.

Night cools the air quickly, and sleeping is comfortable. In the morning, the diesel engine of the truck roars to life, and Mark resumes his journey.

The Belgians have now taken control of 20 towns in the Congo. They

methodically go town-to-town rescuing their citizens. It's a long and meticulously detailed evacuation process.

On July 17 Kasavubu and Lumumba, unhappy with the United Nations'
progress in pressuring Belgium to withdraw its troops, take the unprece-
dented step of giving the United Nations a deadline: if Belgian troops are
not withdrawn within 48 hours, the Congolese leaders will invite the Soviet
Union to send troops.

On July 20 in Leopoldville, the Congo Cabinet formally decides "to appeal to the Soviet Union or any other country of the African-Asian bloc to
send troops to the Congo" unless the United Nations Security Council takes
effective action that night to expel the Belgian troops. "We know that the
Soviet Union is ready to help us," Lumumba says. "We solicit unilateral intervention to a peaceful end." Lumumba prefers that any Soviet military
action be taken "unilaterally" and not through the United Nations channels.

— ◆ —

People notice Mark wherever he goes, and he is aware that he stands
out in a crowd. A six-foot-five Caucasian male with a distinctively trimmed
beard traveling alone and wearing khaki shorts and a broad-brimmed hat
makes a lasting impression. The longer he stays in one place, the more of a
memory he creates. The truck he is riding atop pauses for several hours at a
place called Lubefu, which is bisected by a river of the same name. People
speaking Lingala call out to this *mondele*, this white man in their midst.
Mark talks with Henrique Fernandes Figueredo, who sends a dispatch to
Radio Brazzaville: "This man passed through this locality (Lubefu) the 18-
20 July from Port-Franqui to Luluabourg, and this city (Lutebo) by way of
Lusambo. The man appeared to be 20 years old, had blonde hair, was
dressed in a khaki shirt and shorts, with a wide-brimmed hat. He stopped
here several hours."

During this land-based stage of his journey, like many explorers before
him, Mark lives off the local economy, sharing meals with Africans. Wherever the truck stops, he eats the standard daily diet consisting of manioc,
fruit, nuts, rice and plantains. Africans take the starchy paste made from
corn flour or manioc and make it into dough called fufu. They roll this into
golf ball-sized balls and dip into a spicy stew. Mark follows the local custom
and makes an indentation in the fufu with his thumb to bring up a thimble-

ful of sauce. Bushmeat and fish thoroughly cooked and mixed with vegetables and manioc paste round out the meal. He washes that all down with a bottle of Primus beer and then with a gourd of *nsamba*, the plentiful and popular local palm wine.

The natives tell him that only a few decades earlier, Belgian colonial authorities were forcing the local peasants to grow cotton against their will. They collected and shipped this haul to the big cotton processing plant over at Kasongo. Brutal penalties were imposed on those who refused to grow the crop. The residual evidence of those penalties includes a few one-armed men Mark sees around the village.

Eventually, the resourceful and resistant population took to boiling the seeds before planting them, which prevented them from germinating. Residents then claimed that the hot soil itself was burning the seeds. That put an end to the forced cotton-growing.

Mark takes time to compose a colorful eight-page letter describing wildlife he has been seeing in the Congo, and sends it to his young half-brothers Daniel and Alexander Doman in New York. The letter contains vivid descriptions and hand-drawn sketches of jungle wildlife. In this letter, Mark writes about a fable similar to the one told by Rudyard Kipling in the Just-So stories, that he has told to African friends. It is *How the Leopard Got Its Spots*. The moral of Mark's fable is "never judge a leopard by his spots." The tale reflects Mark's  non-judgmental attitude on the question of black-white relationships.

Mark's friends back home certainly have not forgotten him. Now Neil Goodwin, one of Mark's Milton classmates, tries to contact him. In his second year at Yale University and working for the literary magazine, Goodwin wants Mark to write an article about his African experiences for *The Yale Literary Magazine*. He calls Mark's mother and finds her deeply worried since she has not heard from him for a very long time. She tells Neil that she knows how dangerous it is where her son is traveling.

Political and military events throughout the Congo now move swiftly. With the army in rebellion, Katanga seceding, Belgian paratroopers seizing cities from rebellious and avaricious militia, diplomatic ties between Belgium and the Congo severed, the friendship treaty signed three weeks earlier in tatters, and Lumumba and Kasavubu flying around the country trying to pacify various factions, the prime minister issues an ultimatum to the U.N.: get the Belgian troops out now.

Belgians and other white Europeans continue fleeing from the terror. It is clear that the new government is incapable of administration, diplomacy or restoring order.

Lumumba, as ever, is unpredictable. In Leopoldville on July 22, in the midst of the chaos, he surprises everyone by calling a press conference where he announces the signing of a 50-year contract with Edgar Detwiler, an American businessman. Representing a previously unknown United States company, Detwiler says his plan would develop the Congo's mineral and hydroelectric resources. Lumumba says the deal will "permit the immediate start of the exploitation of the country's mineral resources and energy" and it will lead to "full employment, the improvement of living standards of the people and stabilization of currency." Detwiler has quickly negotiated the deal with Lumumba, who says the project would cost $2 billion and that 500 technicians and workers are ready to come to the Congo immediately; both claim that the project will eventually employ 11,000 persons.

When Lumumba finishes the news conference, he calls the American embassy and says he wants to visit the United States. Political officer Frank Carlucci tells a friend what happens next:

> *The Deputy Chief of Mission McIlvaine said the prime minister had just called him and he said that he wanted to go to Washington. McIlvaine had said, "Fine, we will be glad to welcome you in Washington. Could you tell me when the visit will take place?"*
>
> *The answer was: "This afternoon." McIlvaine instructed me, "Frank, you've got to organize this."*
>
> *I went to the consul, who was a rather strong-willed woman named Tally Palmer-Allison. I said, "Tally, I want you to prepare about 20 visas on blank sheets of paper." She looked at me like I was crazy. I said,*

*"Now, just do it." Sure enough, all of a sudden a delegation appeared on her doorstep and said, "We want 20 visas." She was able to issue these visas on blank sheets of paper.*

*I then went to the airport. I couldn't find an airplane. I couldn't fig-ure out how they were going to get to the U.S. So I went to the control-ler's office and said, "Do you have an aircraft coming in that is going to take the prime minister of the Congo to the United States?"*

*He said, "No. The only thing we've got in is a Ghanaian Air Force plane that just landed and disembarked some troops."*

*So, I went back to the radio room and at that moment, Lumumba and his entourage pulled up. I stopped them and said, "Mr. Prime Minis-ter, we would like to welcome you to the United States, but do you know how you are going to get there?"*

*He said, "Do you see that plane over there?"*

*And I said, "Yes. It's a Ghanaian Air Force plane."*

*He said, "We're going in that plane."*

*I went over to the plane and said to the pilot, "Did anybody give you any instructions to take a group of Congolese to the United States?"*

*He said, "No." And at that moment Lumumba and company ap-proached the plane. The pilot looked at me and he said, "What should I do?"*

*I said, "You better salute and let him board and take them wherever they want to go," which is precisely what the pilot did. In fact, there was a humorous sequence when he got out on the tarmac ready to take off. A straggler came running out and stood in front of the airplane and would-n't let them take off until they put him on board. They lowered the lad-der and put him on board. They flew to Accra where apparently they got a plane to go to the United States.*

The Lumumba delegation of 20 arrives in New York shortly after dawn on July 24 after an overnight flight from London and heads straight for a two-hour conference with Secretary General Hammarskjöld. Lumumba tells a cluster of reporters that the meeting has been "fruitful" and that they have discussed "the general situation in the Congo."

The Security Council convenes in an extraordinary session to consider Lumumba's appeal. The American ambassador Henry Cabot Lodge argues that the Congo problem should be solved by Africans. Ultimately, the U.S. backed a Tunisian resolution that authorizes the dispatch of a U.N. military force to the Congo and demands that Belgium withdraw its armed forces.

Mark continues his eastward journey atop the heavily laden Congolese truck. As the path narrows, tree branches and tops of tall savannah grasses scrape the sides of the truck, and he reminds himself that he is lucky to be traveling during the dry season.

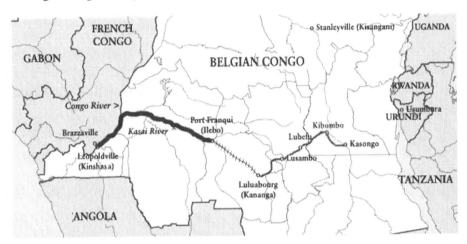

*Travelers headed east from Luluabourg had little choice but to travel overland. An occasional commercial truck, called a commercant, would travel the rough dirt road. Mark hitched rides to Lusambo and Lubefu enroute to Kasongo. The old city of Kasongo on the east side of the river was the European merchant center where a grass airstrip allowed the occasional supply plane to come in. The "new" Kasongo on the west side of the river was where most native Africans lived and there was a guest house.*

Hour after hour the truck jostles along the red clay trail through the town of Lusamba and into Kibombo, important diamond-mining town of 20,000 people. Although it has been another jarring day, by this point Mark is within a few hours of Kasongo, his last waypoint in the Congo.

When they arrive at Kibombo, Mark leaves the truck and sets up his camp for the night. In the morning he finds the Post & Telegraph office, and mails a letter to his family. It was one of the letters he had started writing 12 days earlier while on the Kasai River enroute to Port-Franqui. He knows the letter from Kibombo will take weeks to reach them.

One way of getting from Kibombo to Kasongo has been to ride the Lualaba River ferry into Kasongo. In the stretch between Kibombo and Kasongo, the river is navigable for about 60 miles. But in July of 1960, not all services are functioning, and the ferry is a casualty of the strife. The trail parallels the Lualaba River and the road becomes more of an open savanna, with a relatively smoother ride. In the dry season, this leg of the journey can be covered in one day. Mark finds a truck making the trip to Kasongo, and pays the driver up front.

The northern portion of Kivu province is known as "the country of the volcanoes" and the "African Switzerland," nicknames that reflect the number of mountains and lakes scattered throughout the province. Within the Ruwenzori Range, the biggest of the extinct volcanoes reaches 22,000 feet above sea level. Although it lies on the equator, its peaks are permanently snow-capped. Along with Kilimanjaro and Mount Kenya, they are the only such peaks in Equatorial Africa.

On July 23 Mark arrives in Kasongo, the second-largest city in the province of Kivu. He is exhausted, dirty, hungry and in need a few days' rest. Over the past two weeks, against incredible odds, he has succeeded in traveling alone by steamboat, by train and by truck over rough roads more than 1,100 miles across the Congo during one of the most divisive and dangerous periods in the region's history.

In Kasongo, of course, one of the first items on his agenda is to locate the 30-year-old man named Lambros Passialis, the Greek-African who has been corresponding with Albert Schweitzer. For Schweitzer's 85th birthday party in January, Passialis had commissioned and sent an oil painting portrait of Schweitzer. Mark had noted the man's name. Now, after an incredible trip across the Congo, he is close to meeting someone who has been corresponding with the great jungle doctor. He expects a friendly welcome.

Mark walks around the historic old *cité*. Kasongo had been built in a river valley and the hills sloped upward on both sides of the Lualaba. Kasongo has played an important role in the development of Belgium's interests. In the previous century it had been the center for slave trading, which in 1892 led to a war between Belgium and Arab slavers. "The Arabs had developed it into the capital of their slave state," author Tim Butcher writes. "It was near here that Livingstone witnessed the raids that made him such an ardent opponent of slavery. In Kasongo the Arabs had built slave markets where tribesmen, caught by raiding parties, were traded; prisons where slaves had their necks wedged into timber yokes, so heavy and cumbersome they made escape impossible; storehouses where elephant tusks and other booty pillaged from the local villages were collected before being hauled back to Zanzibar by chain-gangs of slaves."

Kasongo earned its place in literature when the town supplied 400 men for Henry Morton Stanley's third expedition in 1888. The workers, probably slaves, were procured by Major Edmund Musgrave Barttelot, the horribly abusive and ultimately mentally deranged English officer whom many historians regarded as a model for the character of Kurtz in Joseph Conrad's novel *Heart of Darkness*.

This was also one of the places where the representatives of Leopold II once had enforced production of rubber and ivory at whatever cost they deemed necessary in terms of life and limb.

Despite its violent past, the Kasongo of 1960 shows some signs of sophistication, civilization, prosperity and religious devotion. A large Muslim population is served by the Grand Mosque which stands 30 feet tall and displays artfully crafted brickwork around the windows and door frames. The Catholic Cathedral of Saint Charles rises at the end of an avenue lined with ancient 120-foot tall mango trees. The apostolic society *Pères Blancs,* known as the White Fathers, has run the mission since the early 1900s, and Kasongo has recently been made a diocese led by Archbishop Richard Cleire. There is a big and well regarded tropical hospital. Clustered around the typical Belgian monument in the heart of town, many shops sell locally made artifacts as well as fruit, smoked river fish and manioc flour.

For large-scale employment of the Congolese, and for their own interests, the Belgians have created a company called COTONCO that purchases all of the cotton produced by African farmers. The company does not have its own plantation, but rather buys raw cotton at a mandated minimum price. Starting about 1920, entire tracts of the Congo in places like Lusambo, Lubefu and Lualaba, places that Mark had just visited, were transformed into one big cotton plantation. It wasn't just by chance: the Belgians actually required that everyone with arable land cultivate at least one acre of cotton per year. Bales were collected in the COTONCO centers and prepared for shipment to Belgium where it was made into clothing, and then sent back to the Congo for sale.

The combination of the tropical medicine hospital and the cotton production made Kasongo relatively prosperous. White Europeans had come to Kasongo to participate in these activities. After two or three generations, they called themselves Africans. Tourists came to see the sites, too, not only the natural beauty in the northern portion of the province, but also the old Arab slave trading market.

The old town had gotten crowded over the years, and because its proximity to the river made it prone to flooding, eight years earlier the Belgians built an entirely new Kasongo nine miles away. It was across the river and at a much higher elevation. Renaming the old town Kasongo-Rive, they moved all of the important regional activities over to the new town: the civil and military administration; the schools; the hospital, and the Ministry of Post, Telephones and Telecommunications.

More than half of the population has moved over to the new Kasongo, but some of the long-term residents, especially the Europeans whose homes had been there for years, prefer not to leave. The only thing of any importance remaining in the old town of Kasongo-Rive is the airport. And the airport is vital to Mark. His research has shown that from Kasongo there are only three ways out of the Congo: by rail south to Kongolo and Kabalo, then east to Kalemi on the shore of Lake Tanganyika; overland by the northeast road to Bukavu, the border city facing Rwanda, or by airplane to Bukavu. There is a grass airstrip in Kasongo-Rive where mission planes sometimes land. An aircraft would be the fastest and safest way out after his visit with Lambros Passialis. But no one can tell him which services might be functioning, which routes might be passable, or when. Still, flying out of the Kasongo area to Bukavu looks like his best choice.

Mark asks around and gets directions to the Passialis house. The Passialis family is well known in town. They have been in Africa for a generation. The father, a trader, left Thessaly in Greece many years earlier, married a black Congolese woman, and took up permanent residence in the Belgian Congo. The four adult children who survive include two daughters, a son who is permanently disabled by sleeping sickness, and Lambros. After the new city was built, this Greek-African family prefers to stay in old

Kasongo. Here at last is the family Mark wants to meet. Mark knows that he and Lambros will be able to share stories about Lambaréné. He is looking forward to this.

At the Passialis home, he finds Lambros' two sisters, who speak neither French nor English. Using gestures, Mark indicates for whom he is looking, and the women communicate that Lambros is not at home. Mark admires the fruit trees growing in their yard and the two women give him several oranges to put in his rucksack.

Mark walks back into the town center and learns what he can about the intermediate air service still operating from the town, and when the next plane might touch down at its simple airstrip. Then he inquires about finding a guest house where he can spend a few nights. The place most recommended is owned by a native Congolese couple in the "new" town across the river.

At the riverfront he sees the warehouses for storing cotton and other materials as well as the piers for the paddleboats and steamboats that work this section of the Lualaba River. The area beyond the landings on both sides consists of thickly forested banks. Ferries and pirogues cross the river shuttling passengers between Kasongo's old town and its new town. Mark signals for a ride, and a pirogue quickly shows up. Three paddlers, two at the bow and one at the stern, make the half-mile crossing in 20 minutes.

Arriving late that afternoon on the west side of the river, Mark walks along until he finds the guest house owned by a man named Ndarabo Kongaboto. "An American citizen came to my home and showed me a MNC card," Kongaboto tells a neighbor. "He was a young tall spare fellow, he had a short beard and wore a shirt and khaki pants. He spoke American. When I indicated to him that he should go to the European town, he told me that he would not be entertained by unknown whites and asked whether he could stay the night at my home. I am the president of MNC, so I accepted him and offered him hospitality. He had a good night."

His wife confirms the description: "The American man was tall and slim, with blonde hair. He looked 20 years old. He had a short beard."

Kongaboto, the Muslim who owns the guest house, had been very active in Lumumba's political party and had helped in recruiting youthful zealots who helped carry the party's message to outlying villages. The youth group considers Kivu Province their stronghold, and had worked hard to run up a big vote for Lumumba in the parliamentary elections in May. More than 79 percent of the 35,500 eligible voted in Kasongo alone. A regional group called the *Centre de Regroupement Africain* (CEREA) won in Kivu Province, and the MNC came in second.

One local tension point that the local Muslim community shares with the Lumumba's MNC is bitter disdain for the Catholic clergy. The new archbishop of Kasongo, Richard Cleire, at first had encouraged the MNC, but then under pressure from Belgian territorial administrators, retracted his endorsement and changed course, advising the priests of his diocese to support an opposition party, the *Parti National du Progrès* (PNP), which the Belgians favored. The bishop even made a Congolese abbot available to the PNP as an advisor. Archbishop Cleire later reversed course again, but too late to change the hostility directed toward the church.

Despite the political tension, life in the Kasongo area has remained relatively peaceful compared to the rest of the Congo. No serious incidents have taken place, and the rebellion by the Force Publique has not spread to this area. Europeans feel no reason to be afraid or to complain.

Having now crossed most of the country, Mark feels relieved to settle into a guest house and a real bed. He plans to stay for several days, and then when a flight becomes available, he will continue his journey.

On July 24, Lambros Passialis crosses the river from his home in the old town and goes into new Kasongo to handle some business. He pays a call on his mother's family in the native village and while there, Passialis hears that a young white man is staying nearby in a black-owned guest house. That is unusual. So out of curiosity Passialis walks over to the guest house to meet this stranger. He has no idea who Mark Higgins is. The dark-olive-skinned Lambros enters the parlor of the guest house.

Passialis finds Mark seated at a table and around him are scattered many sheets of paper on which Mark was making notes. Mark looks up, greets the man and offers him a chair. But Passialis, seeing that the young tourist is busy, asks to be excused.

They do not introduce themselves to one another, so when Mark sees the man standing before him he has no way of knowing that this is Lambros

Passialis, the man whose house he had visited earlier, the man he has actually come to Kasongo hoping to meet.

Passialis takes him for another of the occasional tourists who visit Kasongo. For some reason Passialis does not follow his usual custom of giving a foreigner his name. He stands in the vestibule of the guest house only long enough to extract a promise from the young man to visit him the next day in Kasongo-Rive. Mark asks the friendly man how to find the house, but Mr. Kongaboto interrupts and says he knows where it is and will tell Mark. Passialis leaves and goes back across the river.

On the morning of July 25, Patrice Lumumba and his senior cabinet ministers are in New York at the United Nations. Lumumba tells media there that peace and order in the Congo can be restored "within five minutes" after the complete withdrawal of Belgian troops. Lumumba insists that Belgian forces withdraw from all of the Congo, including the bases reserved by Belgium under the Congolese-Belgian treaty of friendship and cooperation. Lumumba says he will fly to Washington, D.C. the next day where he will meet with Secretary of State Christian Herter and hopes "to pay my respects" to President Eisenhower. Lumumba would then go back to the United Nations in New York for another round of meetings. He doesn't know that Eisenhower is vacationing in Newport, Rhode Island.

The Belgian army, meanwhile, has just a little more work to do. Some Belgian citizens are known to be in Kasongo and in towns throughout Kivu province. Over the past three weeks, highly disciplined para-commandos have rescued and flown out of the country nearly 10,000 Belgian citizens. On July 17 elements of the Third Parachute Battalion dropped in on Kindu, 100 miles north of Kasongo, seized the airport, evacuated the Belgian nationals and disarmed the Congolese militia. Their mission in Kindu, as elsewhere across the Congo, has been simply to extract Belgian citizens and lead them to safety. The next day the para-commandos answered a call to help rescue a fishing boat on the Lualaba River near the town of Lokandu 40 miles north of Kindu. Making this rescue more dangerous is the fact that about 1,200 members of the Force Publique have seized the arsenal there. A dozen exhausted Belgian soldiers volunteer for this assignment, but as they go upriver their boat runs out of fuel. Congolese militiamen soon surround and capture the Belgians, who feared they would be butchered and killed. Following two days of a tense stand-off and negotiations, the para-commandos are released and returned to their regiment in Kindu. But there is one more assignment waiting for them: to extract Belgians from the town of Kasongo.

On July 21 the Second Company of Parachute Detachment 3 starts traveling down the road toward Kasongo in motorized armor. But for some reason the operation is cancelled.

The para-commandos receive new orders to try again early on the morning of July 25. This time they are better prepared, and move aggressively to avoid any chance of being ambushed or captured. It is to be the last rescue operation before the Belgian Army pulls out of the Congo altogether and turns over peace-keeping to the United Nations forces.

—◆—

On Monday morning July 25, Mark wakes up in the guest room of Ndarabo Kongaboto. He washes himself, and then plays some music on the wind-up record player.

He wants to get as much done as possible while the temperature remains cool: at 2,000 feet above sea level, morning temperatures in summer start in the low 70s but easily reached 100 degrees by mid-day.

He has a brief conversation with his hosts, and explains that he has been traveling across the Congo.

Mark is looking forward to another day or so in this far eastern province. He plans to look around, see the sights, and then sometime later cross the river again, hopefully to meet Passialis. After that, he will fly from Kasongo to Bukavu if he can hop on a flight.

He sits in the living room of the guest house organizing his day.

About 9:30 that morning, an advance party of the mechanized Belgian paratroopers arrives at the edge of the city. They encounter and quickly disarm a squad of Force Publique mutineers. The paratroopers then proceed into the city. Here, the rebels open fire on the Belgians. With vastly superior numbers and weapons, the para-commandos return fire, surround and capture some of the Congolese soldiers. The rest of the rebels escape into the bush.

Advancing toward the Force Publique garrison, the para-commandos encounter a platoon of about 50 more rebels and advance quickly while the Belgian leader Captain Desprechins calls out to demand their surrender. In response, the Force Publique leader orders his men to open fire on the Belgians. The para-commandos respond with a fusillade that shakes the whole area. Four of the Congolese troops are killed outright, some surrender, and the rest flee into the bush.

It is a chaotic situation. Crowds of natives follow the rebels, looting and looking for the spoils that follow in the path of war.

In the meantime, the Belgian army begins canvassing the city and encouraging Europeans to head for the shelter from which they will be evacuated. With a high level of tension across the Congo and with the widely held perception that Belgium is forcibly trying to retake the country, the Kasongo populace is at once outraged and terrorized. The sudden appearance of the Belgian troops has startled the European white community in Kasongo, who have not called for a "rescue."

Rioting breaks out all across the city. The Congolese soldiers from the local garrison, fortified by liquor and hemp, begin pillaging and committing cruelties. Out-of-control and underpaid, they are basically operating on their own, seeking both vengeance and booty. The unexpected arrival of the para-commandos has inflamed the situation. During the morning rampage, the rebels shoot and wound two Europeans and destroy most of the boutique shops and the marketplace in town.

For Mark, just listening to this street action unfold is fearsome. Two weeks earlier, he had left Leopoldville just as violence was terrorizing the capital. A week earlier, he had escaped all of the trouble in Luluabourg by the skin of his teeth. Now he has wandered into a new set of eruptions.

As the morning's rioting progresses the white Europeans are hustled into a large public building that the Belgian troops have made into their command center.

Mark does not have time to join them. By 10 a.m. he finds himself alone in the village ... the only white person in Kasongo ... while the firefight rages between the para-commandos and the mutineers.

A rebel militiaman notices him in the guest house. The soldier leaves for a minute and returns with a few comrades. Some of them surround the house, others rush in, shout accusations that the white man inside is a Belgian spy disguised as a civilian.

None of the residents can explain why this *mondele* has suddenly shown up in the middle of the native village just before the raid started. Nobody yet knows who he is.

Suddenly Mark is facing a dozen angry rebels. They smell of liquor and have a crazed look in their eyes.

This squad is led by a non-commissioned officer, an adjutant named Celestin Kumbusa.

He keeps a gun aimed at Mark.

The militiamen see Mark's maps and rucksack in the room. They look at Mark's boots ... the same boots as those worn by Belgian soldiers. And they see his expensive Colt Python .357.

The adjutant shouts at Kongaboto and his wife to wait outside the house.

White with fear, Mark begs the soldiers' forgiveness and protests his innocence. The militiamen shout at him in their native Lingala. Mark argues back in polished French.

Hands shaking, he fumbles for his American passport and holds it aloft to show that he is not a Belgian. He even asks that they tie his hands and feet rather than shoot him.

Mark is sitting down. The adjutant raises his gun and points it at Mark. To protect himself Mark instinctively raises his arm.

# Thirteen
## Recovery

⌒⌒

The mutineer fires point-blank.

Outside the guest house, the terrified Kongaboto says, "We heard a detonation."

The bullet tears through his hand and into his chest. Mark Higgins slumps to the floor.

The soldiers strip away Mark's clothes and drag his body outside. They use their machetes to deliver repeated blows to his face and limbs, badly mutilating the remains.

Seeing this, Kongaboto and his wife and family do what most Congolese do whenever there is violence: they flee into the bush.

Mark's body lies on the ground for three days.

⌒

Passialis learns about this when he returns a few days later. He finds that villagers have dug a hole in a sandbar along the Lualaba River, 150 feet southwest of the home of a man named Jean Kabula.

One of the natives is suspicious of his interest and threatens Passialis "with the same sort of fate as that of the white man." Passialis hurries away and goes home to talk about it with his sisters. They decide to write the United States Consul at Leopoldville. But since Lumumba had set up censorship on all correspondence with white people, they decide it is wiser not to commit anything to paper.

Passialis, a Roman Catholic, goes to the Cathedral of St. Charles in Kasongo and arranges for a Mass to be said in memory of the young man who had been killed.

His family leaves Kasongo-Rive to seek refuge in Usumbura, which remains under Belgian protection. He stays for a few days alone in the family home, but the situation becomes dangerous when he learns that militiamen are looking for him. He joins a convoy of European refugees heading south to Kongolo with hope that he can meet his family again in Rwanda.

His path is blocked at Kongolo, so he decides to go to Elisabethville. Passialis is destitute and desperate. He has lost track of his family, and by now he learns that his home has been looted and destroyed. Everything is gone, even the precious "Bibliothèque Schweitzer" he had so painstakingly assembled.

On August 18 Carter receives a letter from Mark dated July 25. It is the letter Mark had mailed at Kibombo.

In the weeks ahead, the family expects to hear from Mark that he has finally emerged from the chaos of the Republic of the Congo. They send telegrams to the American Consulate at Kampala, Uganda and then to the other places where Mark had been expected in the Congo.

Anxiety mounts back home, but daily life marches on. In August, Lisa makes her society debut in Worcester and is honored at a formal dance given by her grandparents. In early September, she begins her freshman year at the University of Colorado.

Letters that his mother had written to Mark in care of the American Presbyterian Mission in Luluabourg are returned to her in New York in an unmarked envelope mailed from Southern Rhodesia. It's probable that the letters were carried there by the Presbyterian missionaries who were evacuated from Luluabourg.

Carter cables Albert Schweitzer and asks if anyone at Lambaréné has heard from Mark since he left. Schweitzer responds with the names of three doctors with whom Mark might have been in contact. But no one has heard anything.

On September 24, not having heard from Mark for more than a month and with Kitsie's letters to Mark now being returned, Carter decides to ask the U.S. State Department to help find his son. He tells officials that he will pay a financial reward to anyone who provides accurate information. Grandmother Higgins types up one-page summary of a physical description of Mark and lists all of his known travel plans for the period from June through August. She mails that summary to her cousin's husband, U.S. Senator Prescott S. Bush of Connecticut, trusting that he would "do everything possible to locate my grandson" and to get the State Department to act. She adds a personal note: "Mary Walker tells me that Dotty said she felt sure you would do what you could." Senator Bush writes back, saying he will immediately seek the State Department's help.

The fact that Mark is reported missing and that the State Department is involved in the search becomes a big news story. Tipped off that a prominent family's heir is missing in Africa, reporters begin calling Carter and Kitsie for updates every day. The search becomes a public anguish. The Higgins family finds comfort in describing Mark's African odyssey as a noble way of helping people. Sympathetic media reflect this characterization and cast Mark as a role model.

As the family waits for answers, Mark's body lays decaying in a shallow grave of red dirt 6,870 miles from home.

U.S. diplomatic responsibility for the eastern and southern provinces of the Congo resides in Elisabethville, the capital of the breakaway province of Katanga, which by the fall of 1960 has seen street combat, political intrigue and diplomatic maneuvering. Its residents have endured harrowing and violent experiences. Nevertheless, in early September 1960, Lambros Passialis succeeds in making his way there. "When I reached Elisabethville, I decided to tell the United States Consul about it and to put myself in his discretion to keep me anonymous." Passialis walks into the consulate to inform the American government what happened to one of its citizens. He tells what he knows of the American but insists on anonymity. Consul William Canup assures the informer that he will respect his confidentiality.

Canup cables the State Department in Washington about the new information. In a few days, headquarters matches the report from Elisabethville with the Higgins family request. Canup then asks the United Nations battalion commander in Kivu Province to verify the details of the report he has received from Mr. Passialis.

Canup then reveals to Passialis that Mark had been working for Albert Schweitzer. It is the first time Passialis learns of this remarkable coincidence of interests. This knowledge helps him understand why the young white man was in Kasongo: to meet with Passialis himself, the faithful Schweitzer correspondent.

On October 14, the Kasongo Police Commissioner and the battalion commander from the United Nations Operation in the Congo (ONUC) visit the Kasongo guest house where Mark had stayed. The military officials talk with Ndarabu Kongaboto and his wife. After taking statements from the couple, they locate Mark's temporary grave. They unbury his body and place his remains in a coffin. The battalion commander, a Malian officer, reports through his UN chain of command back to Consul William Canup, who cables both the State Department and Schweitzer.

———

By now, headlines about the American youth missing in Africa have been appearing in major newspapers all over Massachusetts and all across the country. Senator John F. Kennedy, now in the final weeks of his presidential campaign, keenly follows African affairs because he serves as chairman of the African Subcommittee of the Senate Foreign Relations Committee. His Senate staff briefs him about the missing constituent.

On October 14, 1960, Kennedy stands up and delivers an impromptu late-night campaign speech on the campus of the University of Michigan. In his brief remarks he challenges the assembled young people to consider volunteering for service overseas. It is the genesis of what will become one of Kennedy's most important ideas. Kennedy asks 10,000 students at the 2:00 a.m. rally:

> *How many of you who are going to be doctors are willing to spend your days in Ghana?*
>
> *Technicians or engineers: how many of you are willing to work in the Foreign Service and spend your lives traveling around the world?*
>
> *On your willingness to do that, not merely to serve one year or two years in the service, but on your willingness to contribute part of your life to this country, I think will depend the answer to whether a free society can compete. I think it can. And I think Americans are willing to contribute. But the effort must be far greater than we have ever made in the past.*

Ironically, Kennedy delivers those remarks at the very same moment that United Nations troops half a world away are recovering Mark's body from its shallow grave in Kasongo.

⌁

The State Department cable to Lambaréné on October 19 advises, in French:

> *Doctor Schweitzer - Lambaréné. Mark Higgins has been killed by Congolese soldiers in the native town Kasongo in Kivu the 25 of July. STOP. His mortal remains have been recovered and are located with the contingent Malieu O.N.U. in Kivu. STOP. Please telegraph what disposition of them you would like to make. STOP.*

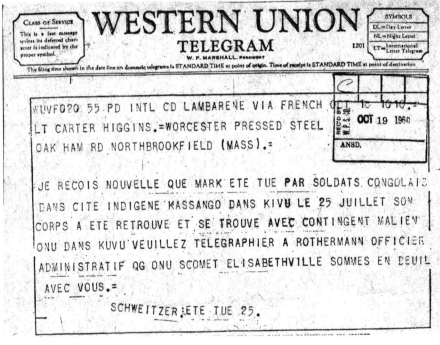

Schweitzer is stunned. It's the worst news he could possibly hear, and yet in some ways he feared this would happen. He carries the telegram with him into the dining room, and reads it aloud before dinner. He then puts his head in his big hands, and with his elbows on the table, offers a prayer for Mark's soul. He tells everyone that he begged Mark not to go to the Congo, and not to carry a gun there. Among those who hear Schweitzer's lamentations are the American restaurateur Herman Reis and his wife who worked briefly with Mark the previous fall during their first tour.

Assistant Secretary of State William B. Macomber writes to Senator Bush that the American Consulate at Elisabethville has cabled confirmation of the identity of the body found near a the bank of the Lualaba River at the Kasongo bar. Senator Bush and Dotty write to Clara that they are "deeply distressed to learn of the tragic death of your grandson" and that they will help return his body from "this troubled area."

That same day, October 19, Albert Schweitzer sends a telegram to Carter Higgins. Schweitzer's telegram reads: "I have received news that Mark was killed by a Congolese soldier in the native city of Kasongo in Kivu the 25th of July. His body is with the Mali contingent of the United Nations force in Kindu. We are in mourning with you."

Carter informs Kitsie and his own parents. He then makes a painful call to his son Dick and his new daughter-in-law Alison. Someone must break this horrible news to Lisa, who has just begun her freshman year at the University of Colorado. Carter commissions Dick to fly to Colorado immediately and tell her in person, and comfort her as much as he can.

Dick is worried that the news will hit the papers before he can talk with her. He stands in the Denver airport and tells her the news very quietly, his eyes brimming with tears. He also tells her not to blame the Africans or Lumumba, that if anyone is to blame for what happened it is the Belgians, who sent in paratroopers and destabilized a fragile, new country.

Lisa is devastated. She takes a long shower in her dorm that night and curls up on the bathroom floor where she expresses her emotions the way she knows best: by composing a ballad about the brother who had been her childhood companion and protector. She keeps the words and music in her head as a private sort of mantra:

*Sleep on, sleep on, my brother*
*The sun shines bright above*
*The hand that cruelly smote you*
*Was the hand that taught you love*

The next day, she and Dick go up into the hills above Boulder and rent horses. They ride silently in their own little funeral cortège.

By chance, Mark's classmate Randal Whitman has been planning to visit

Lisa that weekend in hopes of re-stoking their long relationship. His flight arrives at Denver's Stapleton airport just as Dick's flight is leaving. But there is nothing Randal can do to assuage Lisa's grief. Neither is able to share their thoughts or to set them aside. Lisa knows that although they had become secretly and informally engaged that summer, their relationship is now at an end. Normally clever with words, Randal is unable to reach across Lisa's engulfing emptiness. He knows that all she feels is an impenetrable sense of loss.

A few days later the identity of Mark's body is publicly confirmed. His name becomes national news because he is the first American killed in the Congo uprising, which has been dominating headlines for months. The prominence of the Higgins family in Massachusetts and in New York, coupled with Mark's record of humanitarian service with the famous Albert Schweitzer, makes his death a much bigger story. Accounts of Mark's murder move across the worldwide wires of the Associated Press, United Press International and Reuters.

The front page of the *Boston Globe* features a two-column-wide photo of Mark and refers to a long feature story on the inside pages. Stories appear in *The New York Times, New York Herald, Worcester Telegram, The Washington Post, Boston American,* the *Scripps-Howard* chain of papers and many other media outlets in the U.S. and in Europe.

The family makes available the Polaroid images that Rev. Dallke had snapped, and the nation's two biggest weekly news magazines, *Time* and *LIFE,* each give the story of Mark's death national prominence. On October 31 both magazines run big inspirational photo stories about Mark, praising his initiatives. *Time,* with a circulation of four million subscribers, headlines its story "The Wanted American," a counterpoint to the best-selling novel *The Ugly American.* To underscore the importance of the story, *Time* magazine publisher Bernhard Auer, in his letter to readers at the front of the issue, excerpts three sentences from one of Mark's letters home.

THE WANTED AMERICAN

*In a vague way, Mark Higgins was determined to do good in the world—just how, he was not sure. Tall (6 ft. 5 in.) and high-strung, he could not settle down to the idea of college after boarding school, and the thought of going to work in his wealthy father's steel-fabricating plant in Worcester, Mass, appalled him. He decided that a year working with Missionary Albert Schweitzer at Lambaréné in Gabon on Africa's West Coast might help him sort things out. There the work was back-breaking, but he loved the life; month after month he helped clear jungle thickets and unloaded the heavy supplies that arrived by boat. "Hi ho. ho hum, here I am in the middle of Africa," Mark wrote his mother exul-tantly, typing out a letter on his portable. "I sit at my desk with my mongrel dog at my left foot, and Ooka, my pet chimpanzee, playing with my shoelaces. A goat is walking on the roof."*

*Jeeps and Boxcars. But when he bade farewell to Dr. Schweitzer last June, Mark still could not go home. The 20-year-old youth had become interested in the World Federalists and decided he wanted to see more of the young nations of Africa. He headed south toward the Congo, plan-ning to cross the continent to Kenya and Ethiopia, and then make his way to Israel before returning to the U.S. He made his own way by hitch-ing rides on passing trucks or jeeps, even in boxcars on the occasional trains that passed; often he slept in the mud huts of natives he had be-friended along the route, shared their rude fare at mealtimes.*

*Mark boarded a boat at Leopoldville for the long journey upcountry just as the flames of chaos had begun to spread through the new Congo nation. "It is purely and simply panic," he wrote home in early July. "I have passed seven boats headed downstream, all dangerously loaded with fleeing [Belgian] families. I am the only passenger headed into the inte-rior—all alone on a 32-passenger steamer." He added: "I have had only friendly reactions from the Africans and anticipate no problems . . . They ask why there aren't Americans out here where they're needed and wanted."*

*Terse Telegram. There was one more letter, postmarked July 25. Then only silence followed until three weeks ago when an envelope ar-rived from Southern Rhodesia containing some old letters and photos Mark had been carrying. Alarmed, the family pressed the State Depart-ment to open a search. A check with consulates in Kenya and Uganda, where the boy was overdue, produced no trace. Then a native arrived at the consulate in Elisabethville with grim news: a soldier of the mutinous*

*Congolese army, presumably searching for Belgians, had shot an un-known white man near Kasongo; the body was found on a bar along the bank of the Lualaba River. At first there was hope, but last week Mark's family opened a terse telegram from Washington: DEPARTMENT RE-GRETS INFORM YOU . . . BODY OF PERSON IS THAT OF MARK. HIGGINS.*

But it is LIFE Magazine that most people will remember. With its huge circulation of 13.5 million, its full-page photo and treatment of Mark's service and his death reach the hearts and the homes of decision-makers across the nation. It certainly touches the Kennedy family: both Bobby and Teddy had attended Milton Academy, the same prep school as Mark.

## LAST JOURNEY FOR AN IDEALISTIC AMERICAN

*"This area, which is cleared every dry season for a garden, was grown about 12 feet high, and so thick that it took 12 men with ma-chetes three and a half days of hard labor to level it, leaving for labor all stumps and roots."*

*So, in a letter home, a 20-year-old American named Mark Higgins wrote of an arduous work in which he wholeheartedly joined. Higgins had gone to Africa after graduating from Milton Academy outside Boston to work for a year at Albert Schweitzer's renowned hospital at Lambaréné. There, besides clearing jungle, he had tended patients and trav-eled as technician with a team studying heart disease in Gabon.*

*Last week his parents learned that Mark Higgins had been killed, in a tragic case of mistaken identity. On a trip deep into the Congo, he was visiting with African friends when a Congolese soldier hauled him out of their house. Thinking he was a Belgian spy, perhaps because he spoke French, the soldier shot him. One of the last reports received before his death came from a minister who had known Mark at Lambaréné. "He is so loved and respected," the minister said, "he will surely have no trou-ble."*

America has begun taking note of the need to participate in the world, and to offer the resources of her talented young men and women to im-prove the lives of others.

While those magazines are still on the newsstands, John F. Kennedy gives a formal speech in San Francisco. In his November 2 remarks at the Cow Palace, a huge civic arena, Kennedy formally proposes "a peace corps of talented men and women" who would dedicate themselves to the progress of developing countries. Encouraged by more than 25,000 letters responding to this call, Kennedy decides he would take immediate action as president to make the campaign promise a reality.

No one on Kennedy's presidential campaign staff knows what has led him to mention this idea when he does. One impetus may be that the son of a prominent Massachusetts industrialist was missing in Africa and the story is all over the national news at that time. In Washington, D.C., the idea for a volunteer corps of young Americans to work overseas has been under consideration for a few months. Proposals have been introduced in the House and in the Senate, but these legislative proposals have not advanced. Kennedy found a reason and a venue to test the idea.

As the news is being reported across the country, friends of Carter Higgins and Mary, and friends of Kitsie and Nick Doman, write to share their anguish. And importantly to Carter and Mary, and to Kitsie and Nick, and to Mark's grandparents, the doctors at Lambaréné with whom Mark worked write to share their feeling of loss, and to extol Mark's virtues.

Steven Spencer, the Mayo Clinic doctor with whom Mark worked most closely on the cardiology study, writes to Mark's parents that their son "carried out his responsibilities with remarkable maturity, ingenuity and thoroughness. He exhibited a sincere compassion for his fellow human beings and was more successful than anyone else at the hospital in achieving a real closeness with the natives. He understood them and helped them in every way that he could with a good sense of humor and an ability to make others laugh. The natives loved him very obviously, and hundreds if not thousands of them will always remember him fondly and thank him for the happiness he brought into their lives. I am sure he derived great satisfaction from being able to help other people, and from his obvious success at making friends with the natives and winning their respect. Long, long after the mourning is over he will continue to live in the hearts and memories of those of us who knew him well, and of those hundreds of African natives who were reached by his ministry of service at Dr. Schweitzer's and who will always remember 'Monsieur Mark' with fondness and gratitude as a man who understood them and who made them laugh, and who helped them."

Frank Catchpool writes to assure Carter and the family that "Mark could have returned to the USA a totally different person, so mature that you would hardly recognize him. I am sure that when he left the hospital most of his problems of growing up were over. He was ready to face life."

Adriana, now Frank Catchpool's wife, visits New York and calls upon Kitsie, Lisa, and Mark's little half-brothers Daniel and Alexander.

Closer to Brooks Pond the monks over at St. Joseph Abbey write to say they are offering prayers for Mark and for the Higgins family. The daily chiming of their bells serves as a constant reminder.

Soon after his death is confirmed, Mark's stepmother Mary goes through the children's house at Brooks Pond and in a fit of manic depression begins destroying and discarding Mark's possessions. It is her way of grieving, and hiding from the facts. Soon there is hardly any trace of Mark's papers, or photographs, or a record of his life. She enters into a deep psychosis.

———— ~ ————

Mark's remains, transported by the United Nations forces to Kongolo in Katanga province, and then flown to Leopoldville and back to the United States, arrive in New York on November 6. When his casket arrives in Worcester, Carter is so distraught that he cannot bring himself to identify the body. He writes to Mark's mother that he could not bear "to see what is left of him." The medical examiner determines that Mark died from a bullet wound. The Worcester funeral home managed by Carter's friend George Longstreet handles the arrangements. Mark's body is cremated on November 9 at the Rural Cemetery Crematorium.

With only a few family members present, his ashes are interred in the family plot there on November 26. Carter invites his favorite Episcopalian priest, Rev. Richard Greeley Preston, rector of All Saints Church in Worcester, to conduct a graveside memorial service and eulogize his son. The minister does his best to comfort the family:

*Adjustment to life is not easy for any of us. It is of course much more difficult for those who carry a heavy inner burden, a troubled spirit, which they find so hard to hard to cope with. Such situations we can never fully understand, nor can we help as much as we would like to.*

*It is always a great joy, however, when such a person begins to find himself and to enter into happy relationships with his fellow men. And there is added inspiration when that relationship is established with the less fortunate, the underprivileged, the stranger and the outcast. And this is even more true when that relationship is expressed in terms of service to those in need, those who are just beginning to realize their full status as spiritual beings and take their rightful place, as individuals and as a nation in our modern world.*

*And when such a useful and developing life is taken from us suddenly under such tragic circumstances we feel anew our responsibility to do our full share in promoting racial understanding and world fellowship and good will and a just and lasting peace.*

*As we face the fear and suspicion and hatred which abound in the tragic world of our day, we realize afresh the saving truth of Jesus words, "God so loved the world that he gave his only begotten Son that whosoever believeth in Him should not perish but have everlasting life." When we remember that Our Lord's mission was completed at age 32, it is perhaps a little easier for us to become reconciled to the passing of one whose earthly pilgrimage seemed only it its beginning.*

*So it is with confidence that we commit this young life to His loving care, knowing that God must love him certainly as much as we do, since he was His before he was ours, and conscious that He holds him and us in the hollow of His hand.*

Lisa returns from Colorado before her semester ends, and participates in her brother's graveside service. She never returns to Boulder. Before Mark's death she has been planning to come home for Christmas and is booked on a United Airlines flight into New York on December 16. That particular flight collides with a TWA airliner over New York City, killing 128 people, among them her close friend Susie Gordon.

Consular official Canup in Elisabethville decides that Carter's $2,000 monetary reward belongs to the informant Lambros Passialis, who has put himself at considerable risk to provide the information that led to the recovery of Mark's remains. But Passialis is still frightened for himself and for his still-missing sisters and his brother. In January 1961, he writes Carter Higgins a 16-page letter, in which he thanks Mark's father for the reward money and explaining everything he knows, but insisting on remaining anonymous.

# Fourteen
# Legacies and Lifetimes

On Christmas Eve 1960, the editors of the Scripps-Howard newspaper *Washington Daily News*, in Washington D.C., published a front-page editorial saluting people who during the year 1960 "best fulfilled the spirit of Christmas." At the very top of the page three men are mentioned: Hermann Gmeiner, the Austrian philanthropist who founded the SOS Children's Villages Association; Dr. William B. Walsh, who established Project Hope and converted a retired Navy ship into a floating medical center called the *SS Hope*, and Mark Higgins. The editors wrote:

> We remember, and we wish we could greet, Mark H. Higgins, 20, who went to Africa to work for a year at Albert Schweitzer's hospital, and was mistaken for a Belgian spy and shot by a Congolese soldier during a trip into the Congo.

Under various categories that follow many well-known names appear, including Dag Hammarskjöld, the Secretary General of the United Nations; Jacqueline Kennedy, the new First Lady; Patricia Nixon, the wife of Vice President Richard Nixon, and other world leaders.

The tribute to Mark was undoubtedly inspired by Robert Ruark, the author, explorer and columnist for the Scripps-Howard newspaper chain whom Mark had met in Gabon.

Among the messages of condolence Carter received was one from his old friend Sargent Shriver. They had been personal friends since their days together at Yale, where Shriver was editor of the student newspaper. They were also brothers in the social fraternity Delta Kappa Epsilon, and had shared a pacifist view of the world. Now Shriver's brother-in-law John F. Kennedy had been elected President of the United States.

In his Inaugural Address on January 20, 1961, President Kennedy articulated the sentiment that it was time for Americans to volunteer their educational, agricultural and technical assistance to neighbors around the world. Referring specifically to Africa, he made this cause quite clear:

> *To those new States whom we welcome to the ranks of the free, we pledge our word that one form of colonial control shall not have passed away merely to be replaced by a far more iron tyranny. We shall not always expect to find them supporting our view. But we shall always hope to find them strongly supporting their own freedom -- and to remember that, in the past, those who foolishly sought power by riding the back of the tiger ended up inside.*

> *To those peoples in the huts and villages of half the globe struggling to break the bonds of mass misery, we pledge our best efforts to help them help themselves, for whatever period is required -- not because the Communists may be doing it, not because we seek their votes, but because it is right. If a free society cannot help the many who are poor, it cannot save the few who are rich.*

As his Administration began, President Kennedy asked Sargent Shriver to sketch out the framework for what a "peace corps" should look like. Shriver did so and on March 1, 1961, Kennedy signed an executive order establishing the Peace Corps and named Shriver as its first director. Within the year, volunteers were being sent to five countries, Ghana being the first.

For a specific Higgins family contribution that would create a living memorial to his son, Carter Higgins wanted to fund educational opportunities for native Africans. Educating Africans and teaching them to read and write had been a favorite cause of Mark, one to which he had contributed his own funds. Remembering Mark's letters about the value of education, the family agreed that such a legacy was appropriate, perhaps in the form of a scholarship, a fellowship, or a school. Carter consulted with an organization called the Volunteers for International Development (VID) and agreed to sponsor two educators to go to Africa and continue Mark's dream.

In October 1961 a 27-year old Princeton University scholar named Rene Wadlow went to Gabon under this program. He became an advisor to the Ministry of National Education in Gabon and conducted research about creating an adult school there. Wadlow stayed in Gabon for two years, but from the outset it was apparent that the newly independent Gabonese Republic had little interest in an adult college created by Americans.

Meanwhile, there was the question of where to send the second scholar. Shriver had sent the first wave of Peace Corps volunteers to Ghana, whose national goal was to bring in teachers and build education facilities. Both governments had embraced the idea. Ghana seemed a likely place to establish the living memorial to his son.

The Higgins family contributed money toward construction of and then improvements to a school in Ghana called the Awudome Secondary School. A plaque was placed in the school's chapel honoring the memory of Mark Higgins.

This school was in the same region where the first Peace Corps volunteers were working, and where the new American government was helping finance construction of a large hydroelectric dam.

The anthropologist Margaret Mead served as head of a selection committee for the second scholar. When they announced the program, Mead told the media:

> *Mark Higgins died working toward this ideal after a year of volunteer service with Dr. Schweitzer in Gabon. It is hoped that the elders who thunder against the apathy of young Americans will come forward to underwrite VID's volunteers, who are now ready to go on missions congruent with the opportunities of the 1960s in an endangered, interdependent world.*

Mead's committee selected a man named William H. Wheeler, who held a master's degree from Columbia University and had served with the American Field Service as an ambulance driver during the war. He moved to Ghana and worked as headmaster of the school for seven years, and then remained in Ghana and associated with the school for many years. Wheeler frequently credited the Higgins family for his presence in Ghana. He also appealed to the family for more financial support when things looked bleak.

Under Wheeler, the Awudome Secondary School thrived. It subsequently received substantial government and private support, including significant help from the Higgins family. The school observed its 50th anniversary in 2013.

———

Mark touched hundreds of people during his life. Many of those he touched went on to emulate Schweitzer and continue the kind of selfless work he exemplified.

What follows is a look back at the people who walked into the life of Mark Higgins: his family, his friends, and the people he encountered.

## THE FAMILY:

**John Woodman Higgins.** Mark's grandfather suffered a heart attack a year after Mark's death and on October 19, 1961 died at his home at 80 Williams Street in Worcester. The grand old man with the impish sense of humor and impeccable business timing who had built Worcester Pressed Steel, made a fortune before the Depression, built the nation's finest private collection of arms and armor, and created a lifetime of memories for his grandchildren, was interred in the large family plot in Worcester. He was 87 years old.

**Clara Carter Higgins.** After her husband's death, Mark's grandmother continued living at the family homestead at 80 William Street in Worcester. Much of her life, besides raising her children and making her home welcome for visits from guests and grandchildren, took place at the center of Worcester civic and social life. She took great pride in developing the Worcester Center for Crafts and was deeply involved with the Garden Club of America as well as several historical and conservation societies. Her lifetime commitment to psychiatry oriented many of her family to therapeutic solutions to their emotional turmoil. She died in 1972 at age 90.

**Carter Chapin Higgins.** On July 30, 1964, Mark's father Carter Higgins, a heavy smoker and in his later years a heavy drinker, died suddenly of a heart attack while reading at his home on Brooks Pond in North Brookfield, Massachusetts. He was 49 years old.

**Mary Bechhold Einstein Higgins.** The woman who worked so hard to raise Mark properly, Mark's stepmother became deeply troubled by Mark's death, and sank further into depression. In the days following the news about Mark, she quickly destroyed or gave away many of Mark's possessions, often over the objection of close relatives. After Carter's death, her bipolar disorder exacerbated her drinking. Mary moved to Manhattan, but could not endure the pain of the many losses she had endured. In one of the last letters she wrote, she described the agony that she always felt on July 25, the anniversary of Mark's killing. She committed suicide in her apartment in November 1965 at age 57.

**Kitsie Doman.** Mark's mother Katherine Huntington Bigelow Higgins Doman never stopped grieving over the loss of her son. She and Nick Doman raised their two sons in New York. She deeply regretted having given up the custody of her two oldest sons and believed that some of Mark's problems stemmed from her absence as an engaged parent. In her second marriage, although active in civic and social life, she worked hard at being an involved mother and maintaining both her gracious New York home and a weekend home on Shelter Island, New York. She clung to that tempestuous marriage as a lifelong commitment, having felt extremely guilty about walking out on her first husband. She died in 1991 at age 73.

**Dick Higgins.** An avant-garde poet, Mark's older brother expressed his anguish through poetry. He dedicated a book to Mark, and made a dramatic reading at the Cooper Union theatre in New York City's East Village. Dick took John Cage's legendary Course in Experimental Composition at the New School for Social Research, which formed the early elements of the Fluxus Movement that Dick Higgins would co-create. Fluxus combined imagery, movement and music; he involved John Lennon's widow Yoko Ono in its promotion. Dick also started Something Else Press, a specialty publishing company supporting artists he cared about. Dick and his wife had twin daughters, Hannah and Jessica, before divorcing. Dick chose to live as a gay man for many years, but later returned to his wife, with whom he always had a close working relationship. They remarried and lived together until he died of a heart attack in 1998 while performing at an event in Quebec. He was 60 years old. His art work continues to be shown at major museums such as the Museum of Modern Art in New York.

**Elisabeth Higgins Null.** In the fall of 1960, Mark's sister was beginning her freshman year at the University of Colorado in Boulder. After Mark's death she suffered a nervous breakdown. Two years later, Lisa married a Pennsylvania weekly newspaper editor named Henry Null; they had two sons, John and Jacob, before divorcing. Lisa finished her degree at Sarah Lawrence College, moved to the New York area and co-founded Green Linnet, a record company producing Irish music; she began a career as a performer and producer of traditional folksongs. Later, she earned graduate degrees in History at Yale, in folklore at the University of Pennsylvania, and in Library Science at the Catholic University of America. She taught music at Georgetown University while working as a digital writer at the Library of Congress. She now manages her own writing and editing business while teaching voice and performing in the Washington, D.C., area, where she lives with her long-term partner Charles Baum and performs and records American folk music.

**Nicholas Doman.** Mark's stepfather remarried after Kitsie's death and continued living in New York City until his own death at age 90 in 2004.

**Daniel Bigelow Doman.** Mark's half-brother is a technology and information systems executive in New York where he lives with his wife Jody.

**Alexander Nicholas Doman.** Mark's youngest half-brother Sandy became a sports medicine physician and orthopedic surgeon. He has a keen interest in metaphysical studies and lives in Georgia with his wife Laura and two children.

**Bradley Carter Higgins.** Mark's uncle, as the last male Higgins, continued corresponding with Albert Schweitzer and treasured his letters. In the spring of 1965, Schweitzer wrote a letter to Bradley C. Higgins expressing his thanks for the Higgins family wishes on his 90th birthday. In that letter Bradley told Schweitzer of the death of Mark's father Carter Higgins. Schweitzer responded: "We often think of Mark. Just by chance, Monsieur Lambros Passialis, who found Mark in Kivu, is at this moment visiting with us." Schweitzer died a few months later. The letter to Bradley Higgins was the first time the family learned the name of the anonymous informant whose tip led to the recovery of Mark's body. It became the key to the story of Mark's death. Bradley had his own success in business as an inventor and as president of Electro-Steam, and a civic leader. He died on April 2, 1981 after suffering a heart attack while driving near Worcester. He was 64.

**Mary Louise Higgins Wilding-White.** Mary Louise and her husband Charles Wilding-White had four children before divorcing. After Carter's death, she took control of Worcester Pressed Steel until the company folded, and served as chair of the Higgins Armory Museum until 1980 when it became a non-profit corporation. She kept extensive notes and served as the family archivist, although she edited much of the original source material. She died in Manchester, Massachusetts in 2007, at age 87.

**Patricia Getz.** The niece of Mark's stepmother and one of his favorite childhood companions shared her memories of Mark for this book. After she earned a Ph.D. from Harvard University in classical archaeology, she became an expert scholar on the art of the Cycladic civilization, one of three major Aegean cultures that flourished from 3300 to 2000 B.C. and under her married name Pat Getz-Preziosi and later Pat Getz-Gentle, published two major books on the topic. She lives in Hamden, Connecticut.

**Worcester Pressed Steel.** Carter left a plurality of his shares in Worcester Pressed Steel to his two surviving children Dick and Lisa, and appointed a financial guardian to control the stock. At the time of his death, the company was losing money but still producing high-quality products. A consortium tried to buy the company but wanted to divest it from the Higgins Armory Museum, a plan opposed by Carter's sister Mary Louise, a minority shareholder. She gradually pooled her shares with other minority holders and gained complete control of the company and the Museum. Mary Louise appointed a boyfriend to manage the factory, but the business went bankrupt in 1975, and was closed.

**The Norton Grinding Wheel Company.** The globally successful abrasives company that was the source of the family's wealth and that had been founded by Mark's great-grandfather was sold in 1990 to Saint-Gobain, a French firm specializing in manufacturing engineered materials. It remains a thriving firm.

**The Higgins Armory Museum.** The world's largest collection of arms and armor remained under active management of the Higgins family until 1980, when it was chartered as a non-profit corporation managed by an independent board of trustees. Despite a strong base of visitors from New England and across the world during the next few decades, the Museum management could not build a sufficiently strong endowment. They struggled to keep the building open, but when the trustees and incorporators voted to donate the core collection to the Worcester Art Museum and auction off the remainder, the iconic castle building, the first steel and glass building in the United States, was closed on December 31, 2013.

**80 William Street.** The magnificent house that John Woodman Higgins had built for his wife was listed on the National Register of Historic Places. After several changes of ownership, it passed into the hands of Becker College which used it as the president's house, and later as the home of its Massachusetts Digital Games Institute.

**Breaknolle.** The summer retreat of the Higgins family remained in the hands of the family who purchased it from the estate of John Woodman Higgins. On a visit there in 2012, the author found that the new owners had left intact on the closet door in the upstairs master bedroom all the old measurements for the height of each grandchild put there by Grandfather Higgins more than 50 years earlier. Today it is owned by a businessman who reveres the memory and the legacy of John Woodman Higgins.

## CLASSMATES AND FRIENDS:

**The Milton Academy Class of 1958** continues to meet on important anniversaries, and in 2013 showed up for their 55th annual reunion. Most of them have been highly successful in whatever career they chose.

**John B. Scholz.** Mark's roommate became an acclaimed architect and now lives in Camden, Maine. Fascinated with Mark's story, he orchestrated a large email chain among Mark's Milton Academy classmates, and spent a day with the authors in Cambridge, Massachusetts sharing his personal recollections and listening with considerable relief to their findings.

**Randal L. Whitman.** Mark's chess partner married a classmate of Lisa's and became a linguistics scholar. He set aside that marriage and that career and eventually became a physician practicing pediatric medicine in Philadelphia. He now lives in retirement in Pennsylvania.

**Neil Goodwin.** Neil built a career as a film maker and a writer. His company Peace River Films has produced documentaries since 1972 on subjects ranging from wildlife to people, history, culture and science. He directed the Public Broadcasting Service movie based on Rachel Carson's book *Silent Spring*. He lives in Cambridge, Massachusetts.

**John Bart Gerald.** The last classmate to see Mark alive spent a brief time at the Protestant mission in Lambaréné before he came down with malaria. He spent weeks in bed unable to work. He became involved with a native girl and fathered a daughter he would meet many years later. Two years later, safely back at his parents' home in Manhattan, Bart wrote a largely autobiographical novel entitled *A Thousand Thousand Mornings* based on his brief experience in Africa. The lives of the two main characters loosely resemble Mark and Bart. He became involved in the American civil rights and anti-war movements of the 1960s before becoming suspicious of police and FBI in the United States. He moved to Ottawa, Canada, where he established a small writing business. He said he considers his notes from this period proprietary and shared little with the authors of this book.

## THE HOSPITAL STAFF AT LAMBARÉNÉ:

**Albert Schweitzer.** The great humanitarian was deeply troubled by Mark's death, and never forgave himself for his inability to dissuade Mark from going through the Congo. In 1962, he asked Ali Silver to write a letter to Mark's aunt Mary Louise thanking her for a cash gift that would allow the clinic to purchase prosthetic devices for patients who had endured amputations. Schweitzer added a post-script in his own hand-writing: "The memory of Mark Higgins is always in our hearts. I begged him not to go to the Congo. I wish I could have prevented him from leaving. He did not want to listen to me."

Schweitzer died quietly on September 4, 1965, in his cabin at the jungle clinic he had built in Lambaréné. He was buried in a simple grave next to his wife. The world mourned his loss. He was 90 years old.

**Lambros Passialis.** In a serendipitous miracle of symmetry, Lambros Passialis used the reward money he had been given for finding Mark -- who himself had used his experience working for Schweitzer as the reason for trying to find *him* -- to journey to Lambaréné in March 1961, where he finally met Albert Schweitzer. Lambros stayed and worked at the Schweitzer clinic for nine months and over the succeeding years remained in close contact with *le grand docteur*, corresponding with him at great length. He arranged for an award-winning biography of Schweitzer to be published in Greece. He was reunited with his sisters, traveled widely, and re-established his business career in Rwanda, Greece and in Katanga.

**Sonja Miller Poteau.** The nurse whose marriage Schweitzer had arranged moved back to Alsace with her husband Robert in the summer of 1959. They returned to Lambaréné in 1960 so Schweitzer could baptize their first-born child. In 1989 Sonja became the director of the Schweitzer Museum and Archives at Gunsbach, France, a position she held until she retired in 2009.

**Ali Silver.** The Dutch nurse who tended to lepers and served as the secretary to Albert Schweitzer devoted the rest of her life to the cause of preserving Schweitzer's memory. In 1967 she established the Schweitzer Museum and Archives at Gunsbach, France, which has since grown into a research and conference center. She compiled and

*Albert Schweitzer welcomed Lambros Passialis to Lambaréné in 1961. They shared a friendship bound by their knowledge about the final days of Mark Higgins.*

organized 10,000 letters written by Schweitzer and approximately 70,000 sent to him, as well as many of his hand-written books, sermons and manuscripts. She died in 1987 and was buried near Albert Schweitzer at Lambaréné.

**Mathilde Kottman.** The strict, humorless woman who Schweitzer had hired as his first nurse in 1923, and who became his faithful secretary, left Gabon in poor health in 1966 and returned to Europe where she went into a gradual decline. She died April 7, 1974, at the age of 77 years and was buried near Albert Schweitzer at Lambaréné.

**Siegfried Neukirch.** The cycling handyman remained at Lambaréné until Schweitzer's death in 1965. He left as he had arrived, by bicycle, and continued his tour throughout Africa. He returned to Europe and married, and he has enjoyed a life of adventure and travel all over the world, preaching the Schweitzer philosophy. He lives in Freiburg, Germany, and participates in reunions of the Schweitzer organization.

**Frederick Franck.** The dentist and his wife Claske Berndes spent several summers in Lambaréné from 1958 to 1961. They remained deeply influenced by Albert Schweitzer. Dr. Franck continued sketching and sculpting. Years later, his work appeared in the Museum of Modern Art, the Whitney Museum of American Art, the Fogg Art Museum, the Tokyo National Museum, the Cathedral of St. John the Divine in New York, and the Schweitzer Institute at Quinnipiac University in Hamden, Conn. The couple turned a six-acre property adjacent to their home in Warwick, N.Y., into a public sculpture garden named Pacem in Terris. They dedicated the park to Albert Schweitzer, Pope John XXIII and the Buddhist teacher D.T. Suzuki. Dr. Franck died at home on June 5, 2006. He was 97 years old.

**Olga Deterding.** After the Shell Oil heiress and socialite left Lambaréné, she lived in Tahiti for six months. From 1966 to 1969, she was engaged to the British TV broadcaster Alan Whicker. Subject to mood swings, she suffered from bulimia and an addiction to tranquillizers. She attempted suicide in Whicker's flat, before suddenly leaving him. Later she became involved with Jonathan Routh, co-host of the British version of *Candid Camera*; their affair lasted for several years. When the equally unconventional actress Jennifer Paterson became a close friend, Olga suggested that they might live together and become "the most famous lesbian couple in London." In the 1970s she attempted to buy *The Observer* newspaper, then struggling to survive. She died in a London nightclub on New Year's Eve in 1978 while choking on a steak sandwich. She was 51.

**David C. Miller.** The cardiology research project in which Mark participated at Lambaréné had at least one more beneficial result: David Miller found the work at Lambaréné so rewarding that he stayed there and in 1971 married Albert Schweitzer's daughter Rhena. He died of lymphoma in 1997, at his home in Lavonia, Georgia. He was 80.

**Fergus Pope.** When Doctor Pope got involved in one too many political discussions with Gabonese officials, he was summoned to Libreville, where he was told to pack and depart the country. He served a pediatric residency at Mayo Clinic before moving to Appalachia in 1969, where he created a network of county health departments and family planning, primary care, prenatal, and postnatal clinics, staffed by trained physician's assistants. At UNC Chapel Hill he completed residencies in pediatric and adult psychiatry. When he retired from medicine he developed Celo Farm, the family homestead where animals, nature, and man lived in harmony, echoing the Schweitzer ethic of reverence for life. He died in 2013 of complications from Parkinson's disease at age 83.

**Francis Catchpool.** After leaving the Schweitzer clinic, Catchpool married Adriana Calles Eller in 1960. Catchpool accepted an offer from Linus Pauling to work at the California Institute of Technology, developing a theory of anesthesia, among other medical research pursuits. He later returned to Africa and was involved in the Schweitzer Foundation and Aid to Biafran Children, and also served as project director for the Schweitzer Foundation in Oaxaca, Mexico, aiding Indian children. Catchpool in later years became a family practitioner in Sausalito, California, and a professor at the University of California, San Francisco. He died at age 81 in 2006.

**Adriana Calles Eller.** She and Frank Catchpool had a son, Chris, in 1961. They later divorced. In 1974 she married San Francisco trial lawyer Thomas Williams, who shared her passion for art, Mexican culture and travel. Adriana wrote several expert books on the life of Miguel Covarrubias, a prominent Mexican painter and caricaturist, ethnologist and art historian and his wife Rosa Covarrubias. She lives in northern California not far from her son.

suading the editors of the *Washington Daily News*, his company's flagship paper, to include Mark Higgins prominently in their Christmas 1960 tributes. The hard-charging writer died of cirrhosis of the liver at a London hospital in 1965 at age 50.

**Sylvia Kallio.** The Italian countess who enjoyed her long talks with Mark at Lambaréné and again at Brazzaville, divorced the Finnish sculptor Kalervo Kallio and moved to Washington D.C., where she taught French in public schools for 15 years. She died of complications from Parkinson's disease in 2001 at age 94.

**Norman Cousins.** The close friend of Carter Higgins and head of the United World Federalists and co-founder of the National Committee for a Sane Nuclear Policy whose nod of approval paved the way for Mark to go to work in Lambaréné remained editor of the *Saturday Review* until 1972. He died in Los Angeles at age 75 in 1990.

**The Albert Schweitzer Hospital.** Within three weeks after Schweitzer's death, the famous clinic in Lambaréné was electrified. For a while, it was managed by people Schweitzer designated. Modernized and now operated by the Schweitzer Foundation headquartered in Gunsbach, France, it serves thousands of patients today as a free community clinic. The original hospital buildings have been preserved as a museum and visitors are welcome. The somewhat splintered Schweitzer movement around the world is active in several countries.

Each year since 1979, The Albert Schweitzer Fellowship in the United States selects four third-year medical students to spend three months working as Fellows at the Albert Schweitzer Hospital in Lambaréné, Gabon on clinical rotations. Medical Fellows work as junior physicians in pediatrics or medicine rotations, supervised by hospital medical staff. Many Fellows have found their three months to be among the most valuable of their professional training, and several have reported that their lives and career plans have been changed in major ways by their experiences in Lambaréné. Upon returning, Fellows join a network of more than 3,000 Lambaréné and U.S. Schweitzer Fellows – the Fellows for Life network – who are dedicated to maintaining service in their personal and professional lives.

The Albert Schweitzer Institute at Quinnipiac University in Hamden, Connecticut, under the direction of David T. Ives, has committed itself to introducing Schweitzer's philosophy of reverence for life to a broad audience "in order to bring about a more civil and ethical human society characterized by respect, responsibility, compassion and service. The institute endeavors to keep Schweitzer's work and philosophies alive for people throughout the world and for future generations who strive to serve humanity and alleviate suffering."

## IN AFRICA:

**Patrice Lumumba.** Twelve weeks after he helped Congo win its independence from Belgium, and was sworn in as the country's first Prime Minister, the charismatic Lumumba was deposed in a coup largely because he opposed the Belgian-backed secession of the mineral-rich Katanga province. Lumumba was subsequently imprisoned and then executed by firing squad under the command of secessionists in Katanga. The United Nations, which he had asked to come to the Congo, did not intervene to save him. Controversy surrounds the circumstances of his death, with some people saying that Western powers and intelligence agencies aided Belgian and Katangan interests in his capture and death. After he was executed on January 17, 1961, his body was buried, then disinterred, dismembered and placed in a vat of acid. He was 35 years old.

**Frank Carlucci.** The man who was the political officer at the U.S. Embassy in Leopoldville in 1960 held several other diplomatic posts before returning to Washington and working closely with his former Princeton roommate Donald Rumsfeld. He became Undersecretary of Health, Education and Welfare during the Nixon administration; ambassador to Portugal under President Ford; Deputy Director of the Central Intelligence Agency under President Carter; Deputy Secretary of Defense, National Security Advisor and then Secretary of Defense in the Reagan Administration. He was chairman of the Carlyle Group, a global asset management firm, from 1992–2003 and chairman emeritus until 2005. He now sits on numerous corporate boards and resides in Virginia.

**William Canup.** The American consul in Elisabethville who was the intermediary between Carter Higgins and the then-anonymous Lambros Passialis returned to Washington, DC and the State Department where he rose to become Assistant Under Secretary for African Affairs. After retiring from the State Department, he worked with the DC Council of Governments, Georgetown University and AARP's Program Division. He moved to Santa Fe, New Mexico in 1998 and was appointed to the New Mexico Governor's Council on Indian Affairs where he served for three years. He died of Alzheimer's Disease at age 88 in 2009.

**Rev. Jack Mendelssohn.** The Unitarian Universalist minister who visited with Mark at the American embassy in Leopoldville went on to have a distinguished ministerial career. Disregarding his personal safety, he performed numerous acts of goodwill, such as accompanying the Rev. Jesse Jackson to Syria and to Cuba to negotiate the release of American citizens held by those countries. He died of prostate cancer at age 94 at his home in Maynard, Massachusetts, in 2012.

**Pierre Camerman.** The captain of the *ITB Inspecteur Mahieu* who transported Mark up the Congo River faced immediate challenges. No sooner had he embarked a large number of terrified passengers at Port-Franqui than rebellious militia tried to commandeer his boat. They demanded that he turn over all of his passengers. Gunfire and fighting erupted at the pier. Camerman was able to get the boat underway and also stopped several times to search for people known to be hiding in the bush. He steered straight for Brazzaville and delivered his passengers to safety. He returned to Belgium as the Congo descended into chaos in late 1960, as did many other OTRACO employees, happy to have escaped with just the clothes on his back. Camerman completed his career as captain of a tanker in Belgium. His daughter Alfonsine contributes to a website which preserves the memory and the work of many Belgians who worked in their former colony.

**Celestin Kumbusa.** The militiaman believed to be Mark's assassin was implicated a year later in the slaughter of 13 Italian airmen who were flying a mission into Kindu re-supplying the Malaysian contingent of the United Nations peacekeeping forces in the region in late 1961. Kumbusa was identified as Mark's killer by Lambros Passialis, who had taken refuge in Usumbura, then part of Rwanda-Burundi. Passialis never stopped searching for clues about the rebellion that dislocated his family, disrupted his life in Kasongo and resulted in Mark's death. Kasongo was a small place, and people knew one another. Passialis confided the name of Mark's murderer to

Albert Schweitzer in a letter dated January 31, 1962, which the authors retrieved from the archives at Gunsbach.

**Dag Hammarskjöld.** The Swedish diplomat, economist, author and Secretary-General of the United Nations continued his efforts at mediation in the Congo dispute. He was on his way to negotiate a cease-fire between UN forces and Katangese troops but was killed when his plane crashed under mysterious circumstances in northern Rhodesia on September 18, 1961. He was 55 years old.

**Rene Wadlow.** After trying to establish a secondary school in Gabon, the first scholar under Carter Higgins sponsorship built a career studying African issues and peace initiatives. He was a professor at University of Geneva and founding secretary of the European Association of Development Research and Training Institutes (EADI). Today he serves as editor of the online journal of world politics Transnational Perspectives and the representative to the United Nations, Geneva, of the Association of World Citizens.

**Gabon.** The Gabonese Republic gained full independence from France on August 17, 1960 and elected Leon Mba its first president. Today Gabon has an ostensibly multi-party system and a democratic constitution that allows for a transparent electoral process, although the country's two presidents since 1967 have been a father and son. Low population density, petroleum, and foreign investment have helped make Gabon one of the most prosperous countries in Sub-Saharan Africa, with the third highest gross domestic product per capita. In recent years Gabon has slowly begun preparing its extensive system of national parks to help make the country a popular destination for eco-tourists.

**The Democratic Republic of the Congo.** Africa's second-largest and potentially richest country has endured a series of wars since gaining independence from Belgium. Indeed, the troubles of the Congo represent the most horrific tragedies of the African independence movement. Since 1998 alone, more than five and a half million people have died as a direct result of combat in the Congo.

After Independence and the power struggle that ensued after Lumumba's assassination, Joseph Mobutu took an iron grip on the Congo, changed the name of the country to Zaire, changed the names of the principal cities to African names and assiduously courted outside powers for favor. Sport fans recall the "The Rumble in the Jungle," the historic boxing match he promoted in 1974 in Kinshasa, the capital city formerly known as Leopoldville. In that contest, the undefeated heavyweight champion of the world George Foreman fought against former world champion and challenger Muhammad Ali. It was called "the greatest sporting event of the 20th century." Ali knocked out Foreman in the eighth round.

Mobuto ruled for 32 years, aligning himself with the West and presiding over a kleptocracy in which he pocketed about $5 billion of the country's treasure for his personal use before he was chased out of power by Laurent-Desire Kabila. Zaire, since renamed the Democratic Republic of the Congo, by that time was falling to new depths of poverty and depravity and internecine warfare. Today the U.S. State Department strongly discourages American citizens from visiting there. Excerpts of the current State Department Advisory on travel within the DRC:

> Armed groups, bandits, and elements of the Congolese military remain security concerns in eastern and northeastern DRC. These armed groups, primarily located in the North Kivu, South Kivu, and Orientale provinces, as well as the northern part of Katanga province, and the eastern part of Maniema province, are known to pillage, steal vehicles, kidnap, rape, kill, and carry out military or paramilitary operations in which civilians are indiscriminately targeted.

> Travelers are frequently detained and questioned by poorly disciplined security forces at numerous official and unofficial roadblocks and border crossings throughout the country. Requests for bribes in such instances are extremely common, and security forces have occasionally injured or killed people who refused to pay. In the past year, several U.S. citizens were illegally detained by government forces, or were robbed of their valuables while being searched. Very poor infrastructure (road and air) makes the provision of consular services difficult outside of Kinshasa.

> There is no reliable public transportation system in the DRC. Overcrowded vans and taxis, which often do not meet western safety standards, serve as public transportation in Kinshasa. Few independent taxis are available, operating largely out of the big hotels, and most do not

*meet safety standards. You should avoid all travel by public transportation, and hire private transport from a reliable source.*

*The DRC has few viable roads or railways, but does have several major waterways. Boat transport is widely used; however, the vessels are often overloaded and/or badly maintained, and accidents are commonplace and often fatal.*

The Congo that Mark Higgins nearly traversed and in particular the eastern province where he was killed remains among the most dangerous places on the face of the earth.

## IN AMERICA:

**The Peace Corps.** Since 1961, the volunteer organization created by Sargent Shriver and President Kennedy has attracted more than 215,000 volunteers who have served in 139 countries. Nearly half of them have served in Africa. The genesis for the idea of creating the Peace Corps has never been completely resolved and of course may be attributable to more than one event. Kennedy himself originated the aphorism that "victory has a hundred fathers."

Mark's voluntarism and commitment to service was one impetus to make the Peace Corps idea a reality. Given the timing and the circumstances of the 1960 presidential campaign and the national publicity around the death of Mark Higgins, it is fair to suggest that his story of selfless service influenced John F. Kennedy and, at least in part, contributed to the paternity of the Peace Corps.

This is a most fitting legacy.

# Fifteen
# Personal Reflections

Because Mark was nine years older and was away at school during most of my girlhood, I only had a few opportunities to interact with him. Most of these occasions were at our beloved Brooks Pond or at formal family dinners or gatherings. The passage of years has blurred many specific memories, but one event stands out.

Sunday dinners with the grandparents were usually attended only by my immediate family. One Easter Sunday, when I was nine years old, I had been chosen as the official greeter at my grandparents' home at 80 William Street in Worcester, Massachusetts. This privilege came with a responsibility. This was a special day because Uncle Carter and Aunt Mary were bringing over my cousins.

In recent months we hadn't seen much of that branch of the Higgins family. Dick had gone off to college. Mark had been somewhere after high school and Lisa was living with her mother and stepfather in Manhattan.

When the doorbell rang, I properly welcomed Carter and Mary, shaking their hands and curtseying. I greeted my cousin Lisa, my playmate and mentor, and shook hands with my cousin Dick whom I admired.

Then Mark entered the foyer. I looked up at him, way up. As our eyes met, time stood still. My awareness of short physical distance between us blurred. I was floating. A different level of recognition was taking place.

Regaining my composure, I put out my hand to shake his. Mark's hand felt so large, enveloping mine with sureness and security. I secretly wished then that I would have big hands when I grew up. Today, whenever someone remarks about my large hands, I think back to that moment.

I have often wondered why we may have felt such closeness. A few shared physical traits bonded us: blue eyes, blond curly hair, large frames, and bad knees requiring surgery. Perhaps we both understood what it meant being the middle sibling. Mark was sandwiched between his older artistic brother and pretty younger sister. I was in between my sister Lee who was talented in the arts, and my cute younger sister Jody who required so much care because of her juvenile diabetes. During my early elementary school years, I spent a lot of time contemplating where I fit in and how to get the attention and approval of my parents. I decided that doing well in school would be the proper credential.

But that moment in the foyer with Mark resonated with me then, and it has stayed with me. It was as if he and I had become kindred spirits.

A few months after that gathering, Mark's stepmother Mary, my mother and I accompanied Mark to Boston's Logan airport. He was heading off to Africa for an assignment with Albert Schweitzer. Uncle Carter had said goodbye to his son earlier because he had to be in Pittsburgh to attend the national convention of the United World Federalists, which was beginning the day Mark left. At the airport that afternoon, I remember feeling both excited and confused about Africa and about the old doctor about whom I knew little. Most of all, it was sad saying goodbye to Mark. I wondered when I would see him again.

After he left, I began reading about Albert Schweitzer. I collected books that he had written. Discovering how famous he was and what he had accomplished filled me with pride that Mark was working for him. It intrigued me that Schweitzer believed his patients would heal better if they brought what was familiar to them in his clinic: family members, goats and chickens. The main lesson was that he revered the right of all living things to live: he wouldn't even kill a mosquito.

I began looking at the world differently, incorporating Schweitzer's thinking into my everyday life. For me, the philosophy easily extends to people, to all living things and to our environment. That's one reason I became an environmental educator.

Mark's time with Doctor Schweitzer in Africa was periodically highlighted by letters he sent to various family members. There was always excitement as newly arrived letters circulated among the adults, but I as a child, was excluded from that inner circle. I eavesdropped on the adult conversations to learn more.

The exceptions were the three letters Mark wrote just to me. He wrote them on very thin blue aerogram paper, folded in thirds with the flaps glued over the edges. Despite the pleading by my mother to let us open the mail together, I would hug each letter and scurry up the stairs to open it in the privacy of my own room.

In the first letter, Mark told me about the garden where he had been working. He said how hot it was and that he was assigned to clearing the garden which had become overgrown with weeds. Then, to his surprise, he spotted a hippo in the garden. Imagine that!

The next letter described Ooka, a chimpanzee that seemed to be more of a pet than a wild animal. Mark described how Ooka liked to visit him in his room and play with the straps of his rucksack and the laces on his shoe. I loved these animal stories.

When I got his third letter, I expected to hear of the next animal adventure. As I cut open the edges of the airmail paper, out slid a small photo with serrated edges. There was Mark in a white shirt, looking proud, although somewhat stiff, with a newly grown goatee. I carefully wedged that treasured snapshot under the edge of the mirror frame on my bureau.

Then I laid down on my bed to read about his next animal encounter. But instead of an animal story, this note spoke of a world totally foreign to me. He was writing about his work with Africans who had a disease called leprosy. These natives were only allowed to live in a village apart from other people. Some thought the disease was contagious. Victims were often scarred and sometimes deformed by the disease. I found all this very disturbing.

But then Mark described how he was helping them by constructing some buildings and by telling stories and singing songs to the children and making them laugh. That sounded like the Mark I knew. He was sharing his talents to help these outcasts. Mark was making a difference. I was so proud of my cousin. I wanted to be like him when I grew up.

Toward the end of the school year, I heard from members of our family that Mark was leaving Albert Schweitzer's hospital and that he was going to travel across Africa and go to Israel. After that he would return home, and I was looking forward to hearing about his adventures.

Months went by. None of us heard anything. There was unease in the air. The newspaper said there was fighting in the part of Africa where Mark was going. My grandparents, my father, Aunt Mary Louise and Uncle Carter began reaching out to people who knew Mark's travel plans. They wrote to Albert Schweitzer as well as to the State Department in Washington, to Senator Prescott Bush and other people to help ascertain his whereabouts.

Then one day, my father called me to his side and told me that Mark had been found. I felt a joyous relief. But my father paused. The pained look on my father's face told me there was more. Something was seriously wrong.

He was found near a river bank.

He was dead.

I felt the worst kind of hollow pain. We all did. We had never imagined that Mark wouldn't come back.

———

Shortly after Mark died, his stepmother destroyed almost all his personal belongings, letters and records. Neither of my sisters and none of our cousins were told much about Mark's experiences overseas, or about the circumstances of his death. We grew up being told that Mark had died of exposure along an African riverbank, that he had spent several days in a small Congolese village teaching native children to read and write, that he had found military clothing to replace his own tattered outfit, that he wanted to visit Israel before coming home that fall, and that he was about to enter the Massachusetts Institute of Technology. We had also been told that before going to Africa, Mark had contacted a mysterious stomach ailment which caused him to miss a whole year after high school. Some of that made sense, and some didn't. Most of Mark's story was unknown, and I always wanted to know the truth.

Decades went by. I finished school and college, got married and raised a family and went through a divorce. I began my career as an educator.

Other family members died off, one by one. People remembered Mark, but almost never spoke of him.

I never forgot.

For all those years, Mark's death troubled me. Since 1960 there had been a hole in my heart. So many questions remained unanswered. I knew so few details about his work at the jungle clinic and his travels eastwards.

Whenever I tried to find out more, the subject was changed. Papers were hidden away. It was a closed subject, as if there was a painful mysterious secret.

One night in 1974, when I was about 25, I spent the night as a guest of my aunt Mary Louise in Manchester, Massachusetts. She had set up a couch for me in her den. Shelves full of books lined the wall, interspersed with a few cartons. One shoe box, I noticed, was labeled "Mark."

Late at night, after she had gone to bed, I eagerly but anxiously opened it. I was trembling, not knowing what I would find inside. As I started leafing through the papers, a long typewritten letter dated January 20, 1961, caught my attention. A note at the top said it was "translated from French." I scanned through the letter quickly, nervously, hardly reading but looking for key words. It seemed to be a description of the Congolese town of Kasongo and the writer's family life. Mark's name appeared more and more frequently, page by page.

Just then, Aunt Mary Louise burst into the room. She shouted "You have no right to see this!" She slapped my hand, snatched the entire box from me, and left the den. That incident deepened the mystery. What was in there? What had really happened? What was I not allowed to know?

———— ❧ ————

Much later, when I set out to learn what happened to Mark and why, my journey became more than a search for answers about what happened to one young man. It became an examination of a family's legacy, a story about self-discovery, a search for peace, a reaffirmation of reverence for life, and about the meaning of death. It became a story about the struggle faced by the emerging nations of Africa in 1960 as they broke away from their colonial powers. And it led to the unraveling of a decades-old cover-up, a narrative concocted and perpetuated by his father. It led eventually to a whole new perception of who my cousin was.

Fifty years after his death, with time to spend on research, and with the active support and encouragement of my husband Bill, who came into my life at just the right time and shared my curiosity about this story, we decided to try to make this a project. We had to find out what influenced Mark's youth and schooling, what happened after his high school senior year, what his activities were at the hospital, where his travels took him and how he had really died. We knew it would take a lot of digging. Many primary contacts were already long gone.

There was so much we did not know.

From the minute we started on this journey of discovery, we encountered truly fascinating characters. We developed a whole new perspective on my cousin. I was about to learn a lot more than what may have been hidden in that carton.

A few years ago, Albert Schweitzer's daughter Rhena was scheduled to lecture at Quinnipiac University in Hamden, Connecticut, sponsored by the Albert Schweitzer Institute. I thought maybe she could tell me something. On the day of the event, carrying a photo and obituary of Mark, I hurried to get a front row seat. However, my spirits sank when the organizers announced that Rhena Schweitzer had taken ill and could not attend. Instead, Schweitzer's archivist, a woman named Sonja Miller Poteau, would speak. It turned out that she had been at the hospital when Mark had been there.

When Sonja came down off the stage and we came face to face, I held up Mark's picture and obituary. She radiated a big warm smile and said, "Oh, Mark Higgins! He was at my wedding at the hospital! The photo of my wedding party that shows Mark hangs in my living room in Gunsbach." I was beside myself: this woman knew Mark in Africa! Months later Sonja sent me a copy of her wedding photo, and there stood Mark in a handsome suit with the doctors and nurses in the jungle!

Other pieces of the puzzle trickled in.

I sought family members who might have known about Mark. Most had already passed on. At first, Mark's sister Lisa was reticent to return to a time of such extreme pain and sadness. Finally, she let me interview her. The hours she spent sharing memories of her youth became a new bonding experience between us.

Lisa, it turned out, had become the ultimate but unwitting archivist for papers about her brother. The provenance for the family records was strong, but there had been some occasions when it was all nearly lost. A year after her father Carter Higgins died, her stepmother Mary Bechhold Einstein committed suicide. Carter's papers passed to our grandmother Clara Carter Higgins; when she died, our aunt Mary Louise recovered files pertaining to family history and to Mark in particular. When she moved to smaller quarters, her son Philip delivered a big canvas bag full of papers, letters and photos to Lisa. A week later, Philip died.

Among these treasured documents were typed and handwritten notes from Mark; handwritten notes from Dr. Schweitzer to my grandmother, my aunt, and my father, and transcripts of other personal correspondence.

Lisa entrusted to me that bag and several other boxes and a portfolio of papers, scrapbooks and letters. I found a blue notebook, and I had a premonition that it held the letter that I had begun reading in my aunt's den so long ago. When I opened the notebook I found a few obituaries, condolence notes, as well as letters from people who had known Mark at Albert Schweitzer's hospital, official letters from the UN Forces, the American Presbyterian Mission, the U.S. embassy in Leopoldville, Senator Prescott Bush and more.

I also found the letter that I had both dreaded and ached to read. It was an emotional and detailed account of the details of Mark's death, written anonymously. Who would have written this? Would we ever be able to figure this out?

Inside these notes and letters, we began to see vivid aspects of Mark's personality and his activities at Albert Schweitzer's hospital. I saw how personable and well respected he was and how readily he had been accepted by the tribal patients. Imagining him there, singing and laughing with the leper children, comforted me.

Bill and I used these initial official documents and personal notes to trace Mark's journey through Africa. We knew that he had been seen on a bike in Brazzaville, that he purchased a boat ticket, that he attended a reception at the U.S. embassy on July 4, that he had been seen near the religious mission in Luluabourg, and that he was traveling by *commercant*. Every clue led to more questions and more research.

Several years after Aunt Mary Louise died in 2007, and 26 years after my father's death, a metal file cabinet full of my father's papers was delivered to me. I found a handwritten letter from Albert Schweitzer to my father dated April 4, 1965.

In this letter Schweitzer thanks the family for wishing him a happy 90th birthday and mentions that he often thinks of Mark. He added that Lambros Passialis, who found Mark, was just then visiting the hospital. At the time, Bill and I were trying to figure out who had written the anonymous letter; we pieced this together and realized that it was Lambros Passialis. Here was a major revelation. It helped to explain why Mark was headed toward Kasongo. It revealed that the reward money Carter had sent to Passialis had in fact allowed him to realize his dream of visiting Albert Schweitzer.

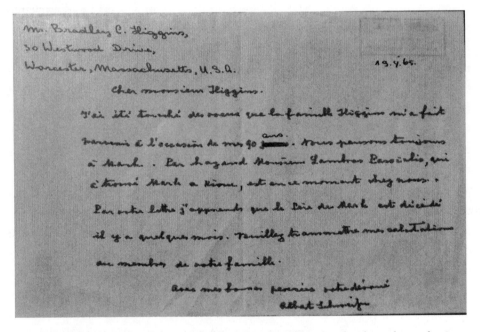

*The letter Albert Schweitzer wrote a few months before his death to the author's father identified the man who found Mark and provided a clue about identifying the militiaman who killed Mark.*

Knowing his name led us to purchase from the Schweitzer archives in Gunsbach, France, more than 90 pages of letters that Passialis had written to Schweitzer. One of these letters contained another surprise: Passialis had learned the name of the young militiaman who had killed Mark.

I visited Milton Academy to access yearbook archives and discovered a few things about Mark's achievements there. I reviewed the names listed under Mark's dormitory and yearbook photos. Research turned up one man, Phil Kinnicutt, a neighbor and classmate of Mark's. He agreed to send out an email to Mark's entire class. Very soon, these adult men in their 70s were recalling affectionate, hilarious stories about their years with Mark. They had all missed him as they went through their lives and often wondered what had really happened between the day he left school and the day they read about him in *Time* and *LIFE* magazines.

I was overwhelmed at the respect, warmth and continuing curiosity amongst class members regarding one of their own who had disappeared seemingly without explanation.

A few Milton alumni seemed to have a deeper connection, so I emailed them personally. John Scholz, who roomed with Mark, and Randal Whitman, another housemate, shepherded this process along. Scholz had stories to tell which warranted a personal meeting. Bill and I spent a whole day listening to his and Mark's prep school pranks, their visits to Brooks Pond, and their jointly supportive relationship, but also of John's continued ache for not knowing how Mark's story ended.

We shared what we had discovered: facts about Mark's role at Albert Schweitzer's hospital, how Mark had traveled eastwards and about his death. John was amazed to learn of Mark's responsibilities at the jungle clinic and, though much saddened by Mark's death, astonished at how far he had succeeded in traveling through Africa.

Equipped with the staff and visitor logs from the Schweitzer archives, we tracked down individuals who might provide primary information.

We researched the names of people in the staff log during the time Mark worked at the Schweitzer hospital. Most had passed away, but there were a few exceptions.

One was Siegfried Neukirch. Through his book about his incredible adventure bicycling from Canada to Gabon we were able to find and contact him. Via phone from Germany, he described Mark's last night before leaving Lambaréné and later sent us a picture of a staff party at the clinic.

Gene Schoenfeld was another. By phone from California, Gene told us how he and Mark would slip out of the Lambaréné compound late at night and observe the rituals of local tribes. These experiences became an important part of Mark's personal search for authenticity in himself as well as in peoples still adhering to their indigenous lifestyles. Sharing in them built Mark's confidence in relating to tribal peoples. I empathized since I also longed for authentic experiences devoid of pretense and privilege. Mark was doing what I wished I had had the courage to do.

We communicated with Adriana Calles Eller, who had married Frank Catchpool. She added more recollections to those that she had shared in writing with the family in the weeks after Mark's death.

Other people added color to Mark's journey. We talked with Patricia Getz-Gentle, the niece of Mark's stepmother Mary, who was a frequent guest of the Higgins family, and had been rumored to be a girlfriend of Mark. We talked with people who participated in the cardiology research project. We corresponded with Alfonsine Camerman, the daughter of the boat captain who took Mark up the Congo and Kasai Rivers.

James Fernandez was not listed in the Schweitzer visitor log, but we found an article he had written in 1963 for the academic journal *Massachusetts Review* based on his 1960 visit to Lambaréné. We found a Chicago phone number for James and Renate Fernandez. I called and left a message explaining that I was writing a book about my cousin Mark Higgins and wondered whether they recalled the person referred to in that article so long ago. Three months later, Renate called. She said that hearing my message gave her "goose bumps" and that she and her husband indeed had specific fond memories of Mark. In a long phone interview, she and Jim surprised us with amazing, warm and descriptive details of their conversations with Mark 53 years earlier.

When I met Renate in person, she shared stories about her and her husband's anthropological work. As she looked through the few pictures I had of Mark, she stopped and pointed to one saying "There! It's in the glow of his eyes and that slight smile. Yes, yes." Tears came to her eyes. "In Mark," she said, "there was a deepness, a sincere need to know people purely, untouched by colonization, and, hence his need to go into the jungle to meet tribes more untouched by western civilization than what he had experienced at Schweitzer's. Mark was a sincere soul, doing what he had to do despite perhaps knowing that he might die. It's not that he put himself in harm's way, but rather that he probably knew it didn't matter. He needed to do what he needed to do. He understood the 'ripple effect' of his beliefs and efforts and he knew that death may increase the ripple effect."

Renate told me that I was a part of that ripple effect as well. She understood why I had to write this book. She said she could see Mark in my eyes. She said we were soul mates.

As Renate and I departed, we shared a long warm hug. It was inconceivable to me that I was hugging someone who had hugged Mark in Africa more than half a century earlier.

Alexander Doman, Mark's half-brother, once told me: "I know Mark passing at his age of only 20 reflects the depth and maturation of a soul who is very, very deep. He had learned all that he needed in his short life. His life was in service of those in need. Few people understood that. That is why he was so close to Dr. Schweitzer. You, as Mark's twin soul, are also on a very important journey and are a most 'advanced' soul. Follow the path."

Recently I attended a spiritual workshop given by Roland Comtois, a medium. I was one of 45 people in the room. At one point, Roland singled me out and told me that he saw me as a "healer." He told me that he was getting a message from someone I knew, a man who had been shot and had died. He told me that the person on the "other side" was telling me to persevere on my project, to keep writing the book.

And so I did.

All of us can learn from the example of Mark Higgins. I challenge parents, students, career counselors, environmentalists, journalists, religious leaders and diplomats to find their own interpretation of Mark's experience.

Fundamentally, there is a need for re-examining the timeless philosophy of Reverence for Life. Schweitzer's phrase encompasses all relationships: how each of us treats our families, our neighbors, and our loved ones; the way nations engage one another in resolving differences; the way we regard treatment of animals and other life forms; the way we regard the precious gift that is earth itself and all of the environmental considerations that have emerged in the wake of new awareness.

Similarly, although his name is hardly recognized by succeeding generations, everyone can still learn a great deal from the life and example of Albert Schweitzer. The year 2015 is the centennial of Schweitzer's philosophical declamation about reverence for life.

Many people believe that the environmental awareness movement was sparked by Rachel Carson's seminal 1962 book *Silent Spring*, which arose from her admiration for the philosophy of Albert Schweitzer. Indeed, she dedicated that book to Schweitzer. Carson focused public attention on the problem of pesticide and other chemical pollution, and her work led to such landmark legislation as the U.S. Clean Water Act and the banning of DDT in many countries. It was completely in league with Schweitzer's public protests against atmospheric weapons testing.

The personal definition of reverence for life varies from one individual to another. It extends to our appreciation and understanding of the animal kingdom. Marine biologists continue gaining insight into the close relationships that whales and dolphins form within family groups. Researchers have become fascinated with the family relationships of mammals such as bonobos and elephants, and with the interdependent role played by migratory birds as they fly from one continent to another. Reverence for life extends to all these creatures great and small, and attests to their role in our mutual well-being.

More importantly, reverence for life touches the way we regard human life. In an era when it is no longer significant national news that four young people will be shot dead on any given weekend on the streets of one of our major U.S. cities, when there are random shootings in and around schools, there is deep longing for the restoration of a concept such as Reverence for Life. How can that simple concept be re-introduced into our consciousness, into our families and our neighborhood dialogues, and into the deliberations between nations?

~ ~

Discovering Mark's experiences and recreating his journey have provided enormous satisfaction, lots of joy, many surprises and a path toward healing and closure.

In May of 2014, Bill and I traveled with my adult children Emily Lutringer and Eric Lutringer to the Albert Schweitzer Hospital, which still serves as a free, walk-in clinic in Lambaréné. Over a two-week period, we traveled to and through many of the same villages Mark visited when he participated in the cardiology study, and we came away with new respect for his courage and his stamina. I was proud to discover what Mark had done and how he had done it.

Much of the old Hospital remained. Some of the original buildings were still being used. Schweitzer's room and *la grande pharmacie* were preserved as a museum. There was even the iconic pelican and antelope in a fenced-in area and chickens freely meandering around the grounds. We ate in the old dining room. Although it was configured differently, I paused, closed my eyes and imagined hearing the hubbub of newly arriving guests, the chatter of staff as well as Schweitzer's meal prayers and after-dinner piano playing. During our visit, there were a few people from Europe and the United States, but with the man himself long gone, the prayers and music have ceased. I was unable to eat until I spoke out loud a prayer expressing gratitude for and a blessing of Mark's journey as well as our own. With dreamlike amazement, I had returned to and discovered a part of myself that had been side-tracked during 54 years of the twists and turns of life.

I looked forward to visiting the still existent leper village. I sat on the

*The author re-enacts Mark's telling the story of "L'enfant de l'éléphant" while visiting the leper village in 2014.*

steps of the structure housing the bell, very much feeling Mark's presence. Walking past rows of huts and acknowledging with a smile or a nod a few patients, many old, some deformed and a few with sad eyes, I sat on an exposed root of a huge tree, then moved to another and then another. Once poised upon the third, I immediately felt a tingling yet comforting sensation. About ten children, perhaps aged two through fourteen, were sitting on a stone wall and standing nearby, all curiously looking at me. I suddenly stood up. Without consciously knowing what I was going to do, I spontaneously acted out the story of how the elephant got his trunk. The kids listened, laughed along, and chimed in with words to fill in my broken French. They knew the story! I felt such camaraderie with these youngsters, and, I also felt Mark was there with me.

A poignant and serendipitous moment occurred when I felt a calling to explore behind some old buildings. As I did that, I questioned those I saw. I called out looking for the oldest people around: *"Une vieille personne?"* Eventually an old man approached me. He told me that he was 90 years old and had worked there for Albert Schweitzer in the kitchen with his family.

*The author visits at Lambarene with Joseph Ndolo, who worked at the Schweitzer clinic when Mark was there in 1959-1960.*

I showed him a picture of Mark. At first there was no sign of recognition. Then I mentioned that Mark and Siegfried Neukirch had become good friends there. I knew that Siegfried had visited the hospital in 2013; perhaps my mentioning Siegfried would trigger this man's memory. Old Joseph Ndolo then looked again at Mark's photo and exclaimed, *"Oui, Oui, Je le connais. Mark Higgins!"* I explained who I was, about Mark's brief life and my journey. *"Venez, venez,"* he said, tugging on my arm and encouraging me to walk up to the main road. He pointed out the room where Mark had lived. He pointed out where Siegfried had lived and where the truck had been parked. What joy and closure I felt! As we left Lambaréné, I wondered who else may have been living in those old buildings. Three months later I received word that old Joseph had passed away.

———

We went to Africa to learn about Mark. At the same time, we were adding to our own lives.

Mark went to Africa to learn about himself. He went to Africa to find a reason to live. He found himself in the very nature of the journey. In the process, he gained an understanding of life and appreciation for diverse cultures and gratitude for the opportunity to serve.

He became his own man.

Spiritually, Mark still lives, inspiring people with his story, and sharing the message that each of us must have reverence for all living things because they are exactly that: living.

An exchange of notes in 2014:

*For me, as Mark's sister, reading about his death has brought a lot of closure. I had only known about what happened in a mythic sense, kind of the way Time Magazine described it. Now I see the context, the route, the planning, the logic of the trip, and the death itself which, though horrible, was not as horrible as imagining him being hacked to death alive.*

- Lisa Higgins Null

*I am so glad that it has been enlightening and healing for you, and has provided some closure. You and I can bond through this journey; it has been one of discovery about Mark but also self-discovery. I guess I have begun to compensate for his horrible death by the lives he had touched and being in awe about the long and arduous trek that we think we have recreated across much of the continent.*

- Clarinda Higgins

*That's how life is at its best.*

- Lisa

*Dear Lisa,*
*Your healing helps my healing.*

- Cousin Rin

# Acknowledgements

This project could only happen with a substantial amount of help. Starting to write this story five decades after the fact, it's not surprising that we missed the opportunity of talking with many important sources. Fortunately, many others were still alive, and eager to reflect on my cousin Mark Higgins. He made an impression on a lot of people.

Mark's sister Lisa Higgins Null opened her heart and reached back for many memories that she had tucked away for years. Whenever we sought an explanation of who was who, or a character description, Lisa gave us the complete answer.

When they learned of our query, the generous and wonderful people who staffed or visited Albert Schweitzer's jungle hospital in Lambaréné let their memories float back to 1959 and 1960. Among those who shared their recollections and stories with us via email and sometimes in long phone conversations were Adriana Calles Eller Williams, Siegfried Neukirch, Eugene Schoenfeld, the anthropologists James and Renate Fernandez, and others.

The tributes that poured in to Mark's family after his death include letters from doctors Steven S. Spencer, Frank Catchpool and others with whom Mark worked at Lambaréné.

A remarkable collection of exceptionally intelligent, successful and generous individuals wrote books or lectured about their experiences with *le grand docteur* in Gabon. Many of them are now deceased. The bibliography cites their works, which in many cases reference Mark or put the period of his service in context.

Librarians and researchers, as is their nature, were universally helpful. We called upon resources at the Getty Research Institute in Los Angeles and the Northwestern University Library, the Oregon State University Special Collections and Archives Research Center, the Special Collections Research Center at Syracuse University, the Library of Congress in Washington D.C., and the Presbyterian Historical Society Archives in Philadelphia.

Contemporary news accounts placed the events in Mark's story in context with what was happening as he crossed Africa. We have relied upon and cited accounts appearing in *The New York Times*, *The Saturday Review*, *Time* and *Life* magazines and the wire services of the Associated Press, United Press International and Reuters. Independent accounts appeared in the *Cleveland Press*, *Worcester Telegram*, the Scripps Howard newspapers, and others.

Jason K. Stearns, a current expert on the Democratic Republic of the Congo, took time from his doctoral studies at Yale to share advice about traveling in the Congo as we considered whether to visit Kasongo, the town where Mark was killed.

Special thanks go to Cyrille Mvele and Heather Arrowood in Gabon who run the wonderful environmental preservation group *Organisation Ecotouristique du Lac Oguemoué* in the lakes region south of Lambaréné. They went out of their way to make us feel welcome in Gabon and to take us by boat to several of the remote villages that Mark visited in the course of the cardiology study.

In Belgium, special thanks go to Eddy Hoedt, the historian for the Belgian Army's 3rd Parachute Battalion, for his work researching and sharing details about the Para-Commandos' operations in the Kasongo region in July 1960.

In Gunsbach, France, Sonja Miller Poteau and other record-keepers at the *Archives Centrales Schweitzer* in Gunsbach, France, generously provided us with lists of staff and the log book of the important people who visited there at the same time Mark was in Africa. In some cases we were able to purchase from the archive copies of original correspondence received by Dr. Schweitzer.

It's nearly impossible to express the emotions that the author felt as she listened to the reminiscences of friends and classmates who remembered her cousin. The wonderful things they said about him have brought Mark closer to us. It turns out that they were also searching for an answer: what happened to this bright young man, and what would have become of him?

# Appendix

After he learned that his son's body had been recovered, Carter Higgins sent $2,000 to be given to the person responsible for the report. The American consulate told him that the person wished to remain anonymous. Carter wrote his letter in French.

Lambros Passialis, who provided information to the U.S. consulate in Elisabethville and then to Albert Schweitzer about Mark's last days, typed an anonymous response to Carter Higgins on February 18, 1961. Passialis was writing from Elisabethville, to which he had fled as a refugee from the violence in the Congo. Carter received the letter on March 20, 1961.

This is the exchange of letters between the two men, translated from the original French.

*Oakham Road, North Brookfield, Mass. U.S.A.*
*January 6, 1961*
*Dear unknown friend:*

*I understand you are from Kasongo where my son Mark was. Your news is the saddest possible, but it is better knowing this, without forever having that doubt in my life. Thank you from the bottom of my heart.*

*Now his body is not far from here, and his spirit remains with me. He pursued this job, his goals in life. He learned a lot at the Schweitzer hospital in Gabon. The Africans called him "Doctor" Mark (or Dr. Long-Long because he was so tall) because he was providing care for them at same time that he was making them laugh.*

*He sought a better understanding of blacks and also that Africans would come to know Americans better. There are millions here wanting to love Africans, but understand so little that it will require years of effort before that happens. Maybe others, black and white, will suffer and die before the time when we will understand one another. What is past is gone, and I hope that my son has made a contribution.*

*Both Americans and Africans seek freedom. You seek the right to work, to believe, to earn a living with your friends, and for us it is the same. Here I run a factory that produces things made of steel and aluminum etc. We make and sell what we want. It's good for us and for our customers too.*

*I wish you success with your shop. I have found that getting people what they want takes hard work. Your success can be good for you and the city also because others will need your goods. Good luck to you.*

*There are bad Americans, and some who do misdeeds. But Mark was good. He described the need for education, books that might attract men for other necessities of life. In his heart, he had love for your people.*

*I understand that you are a Christian. Please say a prayer with me for him. And pray also for the friendship between the peoples of the new country and the countries younger than America.*

*I remain in your debt because of your help, my friend, and I send you my best wishes even as we communicate in a language that is strange to me.*

*Sincerely yours.*

*Carter C. Higgins*

—◦—

*Elisabethville,*
*Ex-Belgian Congo*

*Dear Sir and Benefactor,*

*I was pleased to receive your letter dated January 6th, which touched me deeply, and I apologize for this somewhat delayed answer. At the same time I am glad to tell you I received the money. The $2,000 you sent me is equivalent to 100,000 Congolese francs. I received this money in the presence of Monsieur William Canup, United States Consul in Elisabethville.*

*In your letter you call me "cher ami inconnu." You are right to do so. Actually, I asked Monsieur Canup to keep me anonymous and not to reveal who I was to anyone except you. This was just a precautionary step. Otherwise I could face reprisals from the Terrorists. This would involve not only my own safety, but also my family's safety.*

*Since you thought well of writing to me, I think I ought to tell you about myself. So, I hope I will not be an unknown person to you any more.*

*As you know, I am here as a refugee fleeing the terrible events which have bathed the place I live in blood. I come from Kasongo in the Province of Kivu, in the extreme northeast of the former Belgian Congo. The capital of the province is Bukavu, a city of 180,000 natives and 6,000 Europeans. They call Kivu "the country of the volcanoes" or "African Switzerland." These names reflect the number of volcanoes and lakes scattered through it. The biggest is Ruwensori which is an extinct volcano. Twenty-two thousand feet high, its peaks are snow covered although it is on the Equator. Its mate is perhaps Kilimanjaro, located across the area in the former German colony of Tanganyika Territory. (Ernest Hemingway made this mountain famous in his story, "The Snows of Kilimanjaro," which was made into a film starring Gregory Peck and Ava Gardner.)*

*For its part, Ruwensori is also celebrated in the book "Rachel Cade," written by the American Charles Mercer. Part of the action of this novel deals with climbing this mountain. The heroine is a young American missionary girl. Hollywood may make a film and the actor Peter Finch has been mentioned for the principal role but I do not know who will be the feminine lead. I know Peter Finch fairly well as he came to the Congo in 1957 with Audrey Hepburn to make "A Nun's Story." This time the heroine was a Belgian Catholic novice, Gabrielle Van Der Mal, a follower of Dr. Schweitzer. This film was taken from the well-known story of Kathryn Mulme, and was a best seller in 1956. I helped in the making of this film when I was still in Stanleyville in Oriental Province.*

*Kasongo is in the south of Kivu. My family lives there. We are two sisters and one brother, all my relatives. Our father was European and our mother African. I was born in Kasongo on July 11, 1929. My father moved from Greece when he was a young boy and arrived in the Congo in 1908 at the age of 32. He died in 1945, when I was still in school. Our mother died in 1947.*

*My brother lost his reason because of sleeping sickness which he caught when he was four years old. At that time, in 1930, they did not have the good treatments we have today. To take care of him, we had to wait for the itinerant doctor to come, who came by every six months. In the meantime we had to put him in the care of a native nurse without experience. My brother who was treated with Atoxyl seemed to be cured, but twelve years afterward in 1942, the sickness recurred again with great seriousness, causing the total loss of his reason. Our brother still lives with us in a special room. We prefer to keep him with us rather than put him in a nursing home where he would not be well taken care of. By agreement, my sisters vowed not to get married, but to devote themselves body and soul to my brother. This has gone on for 18 years. We live in the same atmosphere as that described in the book "The Snake Pit" by Mary Jane Ward.*

*Kasongo is an old town. It was formerly an important center for the slave trade. The market where they sold human flesh is still there. It is on the Congo River. In 1952 they built a new town 15 kilometers away, away from the river on firm ground. They named this village Kasongo-Poste, or simple Kasongo. Then the old town of Kasongo, where I live, became Kasongo-Rive because it is on the river. The new town was built at a higher elevation and all the regional activities are centered there: civil and military administration, higher schooling, hospitals, P.T.T. and T.S.F., the home of the archbishop, etc.*

*More than half of the population of Kasongo-Rive moved out to the new city of Kasongo, but we preferred not to leave our beloved town. Kasongo-Rive is actually a partly abandoned town. The only importance they still hang onto is the airport. They didn't know how to build this at Kasongo because the ground is not as flat as Kasongo-Rive. All the travelers who come, first come to Kasongo-Rive before going to Kasongo where there is a guest house for tourists. Your son, Mark, did this too.*

*Now let me tell you how I met Mark, your mourned-for son, and how he met his death.*

*One day last July, I went to Kasongo for some business matters. When these were over I went to the native village to visit my mother's family. There I learned that a young white man was living nearby and being sheltered by a black man. The black people received him in friendship because he was very polite to them. So I went to see him out of curiosity and to say "bon jour." I found that he was seated at a table. Around him were scattered many sheets of paper (without doubt he was making notes). When he saw me he greeted me cordially and offered me a chair. Seeing that he was busy I asked to be excused and took leave of him, not wanting to disturb him. It is unfortunate that he agreed to let me go because he would obviously have liked to talk with me. On the other hand I was under pressure to return to Kasongo-Rive before dark, especially as it looked like rain, but nevertheless I promised to visit him when he came through Kasongo-Rive to take the plane to Bukavu. After this we said goodbye. Alas, I will never see him again.*

The day after my interview with Mark terrible riots broke out both in Kasongo and Kasongo-Rive. These riots were followed by pillaging. I don't have the courage to tell you the awful cruelties we suffered through. At the root of all our troubles were Congolese soldiers. This large mutiny was stirred up by Patrice Lumumba, the Prime Minister, in order to chase the Europeans out of the country. The rebel soldiers started off by killing their Belgian officers, and then went after the European civilians. If we were spared, it was thanks to the providential arrival of Belgian Para-Commandos, who hurried to protect us. Your son, Mark, found himself left alone in the native village while the fight was raging between the Para-Commandos and the mutineers. At the beginning of the riots all the Europeans took refuge in a large public building where the Belgian parachute troops had their headquarters. Your son did not have the time to join them and take refuge in this shelter.

Many of the natives left their village following the rioters, like hyenas following lions, looking for booty. Mark was left alone in the village, numb with fear. There a rioter noticed him. This person went away for a minute and then came back with his comrades. Suddenly Mark was surrounded by a dozen rebels, one of whom kept him covered with his gun. The house where he was staying was encircled.

They took Mark for a Belgian spy or a Para-Commando, or a spy disguised as a civilian. Actually none of the black people could explain his long presence in the middle of the native village during the fighting. Mark did not have any illusions about what might happen to him. He asked their forgiveness and protested his innocence. He showed them his passport to prove that he was not a Belgian but an American. He even asked that they tie him hand and foot rather than killing him. It did no good. (You could not expect any sympathy from these people who were drugged with hemp and drunk with blood!). Then one of the rioters pointed his gun at Mark who was sitting down. To protect himself, instinctively, Mark raised his arm in front of him. The mutineer fired point-blank and Mark fell, killed outright. The slug went through his hand into his chest. Then the savages finished him off with machete blows, badly mutilating his face and limbs.

The Negro who sheltered Mark escaped into the brush. The rioters forgot *the body in the house; they didn't even give him the honor of a tomb. The body stayed in the house until it began to decompose so that there was a noticeable odor for several meters round about. The villagers then felt that they were obliged to do something and put it in a quickly dug hole behind an inn. As for me, I didn't learn about the assassination until two days afterward. Then I went to look around discreetly, not without risk, in the spot where it had occurred. One of the natives was suspicious of my interest and threatened me with the same sort of fate as that of the white man. Then I had to save myself in a hurry. When I got home I talked about it with my sisters. We decided to write the United States Consul at Leopoldville. As Lumumba had set up censorship on all correspondence with white people, we then decided it would not be wise to write. In the meantime my family left Kasongo-Rive to seek refuge in Usumbura (Rwanda-Urundi) Territory of the United Nations under Belgian protection. So I was left alone at Kasongo-Rive, but the situation became too dangerous for me because they were looking for me. I took advantage of the departure of a convoy of Asiatic and European refugees which was going to Kongolo (in what is now the Republic of Katanga) with hope of meeting again in Rwanda-Urundi. I had to take the train for Rwanda to Congoville and pick up a steamer on Lake Tanganyika for Usumbura, but the Baluba Tribesmen cut off the railroad so that I was blocked at Kongolo. Then I decided to go to Elisabethville. During the month of August, and up until now, I have been cut off from my family. I have no news of them. There is no communication. All of the public services are gone to pieces. This is what "independence" is! At this time there are new troubles in Kivu. A certain Kashamura decided to take those over. He began by confiscating under threat of arms 10,000,000 francs (about $200,000) from the Central Bank.*

*When I reached Elisabethville, I decided to tell Mr. Canup, United States Consul, about it (with a small delay for which I apologize) and to put myself in his discretion to keep me anonymous. Mr. Canup gave me every assurance.*

*Thanks to my reports, the UNO troops stationed in the region started investigations and found the body. (Mr. Canup tells me the body was sent to America by plane).*

*I thank you most deeply for your gift. I do ask you to remember that in* doing some service for you, I acted without any selfish interest as a Christian, and without counting on any reward. You treated me very generously but the true award a thousand times more important than money is to know in my heart that I did something good and useful. Money isn't everything. Surely it is necessary to live, but money cannot bring the joy we have when we have done something good.

From Monsieur Canup I learned that Mark had come to Lambaréné and Dr. Schweitzer. When I saw Mark, I took him for another of those tourists who visit us, and no more. If I had known that he came from Dr. Schweitzer, I would have done everything possible to get him to stay with me at Kasongo-Rive. For more than seven years I have been an admirer of Dr. Schweitzer. I have been corresponding with him for a long time. Wherever I wandered (across the Congo, Kasongo, Elisabethville) I have never failed to send him greetings on his birthday, for the New Year, etc.

You see the person I met did not mean much to me, but I did not know that he was a brother in the family that we had chosen for ourselves, that of Dr. Schweitzer. That is the way that Fate plays around with human beings, having thrown us together only when we are not permitted to really recognize each other. Customarily, when I see a foreigner I give him my name. But that day I don't know what held me back. (The designs of Providence cannot be fathomed). It is possible that Mark would have heard them speak of me at Dr. Schweitzer's. At the time when he was supposed to be at Lambaréné (January 1960), I sent Dr. Schweitzer for his 85th birthday present a nicely done, hand-painted portrait. It was a portrait of him. This gift pleased him very much, or so his letter said.

The day when I talked with Mark, when I got home I mentioned this to my sisters. And my older sister said that a young Englishman dropped by two days earlier when I was away from the house. He expressed interest in the oranges in our garden and my sister gave him some. After that he went on his way to Kasongo. Here is another trick of Fate: when Mark went by our house I was away. As my sisters do not express themselves well in French, they could not get into a conversation with a foreigner.

I have said that Mark was going to come to Kasongo-Rive to take the plane for Bukavu. On account of the troubles the service company shut down all its traffic with the interior of the province. That is why Mark didn't *come to Kasongo-Rive. I have also said that he promised to visit me when he did come to Kasongo-Rive. When he asked me how to find my house, the Negro who was his host broke in and said he knew where it was. Thus we left each other.*

*Mark is dead, a victim of devotion and love just like our Lord, Jesus Christ. As you said in your letter, "He made a contribution." And God will return it to him a hundred-fold. Wasn't it some poet who said that those who die young are loved by the gods? As you say, what is past is finished.*

*As a result of these unhappy events, we lost all our possessions. We were ruined a hundred percent. Thanks to your gift we are going to try to make up for the loss. But we must work hard as you told me in your letter. I have faith in succeeding. The money which Providence has sent to me in a mysterious fashion (when I didn't expect it) must have been a divine blessing, and I feel that your money will be the key to open for me other unexpected opportunities for material well-being. It is blessed money.*

*To start with, I want to realize a dream which I have had in my heart for three years: to make a pilgrimage to Lambaréné and Dr. Schweitzer.*

*I confess to an endless admiration for Dr. Schweitzer. His spirit animates me. Because of him I am living and breathing you might say. He is my master and my patron saint. In fact he is a living saint for me. Thanks to him I found a reason for living. The faith I have in him nourishes me daily.*

*Now I shall tell you how I discovered Schweitzer. I heard stories of him when I was 18 years old, in 1948. To me he was simply an old missionary, one of many white people coming into Africa. He was someone who did not particularly impress himself on my attention, as people like him, old colonials of the old period; you could find hundreds in the Belgian Congo. So I put Schweitzer in that same grouping. It was due to a providential coincidence again that I can pretend to have discovered Schweitzer. In 1954 I was in Oriental Province at Basoko, a town founded by the explorer Stanley, and located on the Congo River. One day I got aboard a boat to get across the river. The sun was hot as lead. In the boat there was a little Negro boy who was holding an old issue of Readers Digest, very dirty and badly torn up. As reading is not the least of my vices, I asked him to see this magazine. He asked me for a franc to buy candy. I gave that to him generously. Opening the front of the issue, I saw there was something about Dr. Schweitzer, a sub-*

*ject which didn't have any novelty for me. I quickly skipped the pages about him, and plunged into other articles of general interest. When I had exhausted everything else in the magazine, I was going to throw it in the water. Then suddenly I told myself that it was rather stupid to throw it in the water when I still hadn't read all of it. There were still about three pages about Schweitzer. I began to read the magazine; it was not about Dr. Schweitzer's life but a brief resume of his thinking. It was an article done by Fulton Oursler, the well-known author of the life of Jesus. The title of the article was "Notre Tache Seconde."*

After reading the article a light appeared in my spirit. I had just found my way to Damascus. Certain eternal truths that I had sensed, obscured in my subconscious, began to take shape. Ever since that day Schweitzer has been for me something else than a doctor, something else than a missionary or Colonial. Ever since that day I have tried to get together everything that I could connect with this prophet of modern times (books, newspaper articles, magazines, etc.). In this way I have built a "Bibliotechque Schweitzer" which unfortunately was completely destroyed during the riots.

This pilgrimage of which I am going to take to Lambaréné is one of the great dreams of my life. In times when everything is done by machine, and when human values have been debased to a catastrophic degree, there has to be a Lambaréné to set beside Hiroshima. It is a sad thing to feel that scientific progress is reaching toward evil, and not toward good. Will Schweitzer's message be understood before it is too late? And is this not the same Schweitzer who has said that even if Jesus came back to earth, we would not believe in him?

The men I admire the most besides Schweitzer are: Tolstoy, Saint-Exupery, and Gandhi. But the only man who has made a sacrifice out of his life, who really wanted to live his belief rather than talk about it, is Schweitzer. He is the man I choose as my master, as he himself has chosen Goethe or Bach.

Although I am only 31, I have read many, many books. I like American literature. The first book read was "Babbitt" by Sinclair Lewis. A book that affected me greatly was "Uncle Tom's Cabin" by Harriet Beecher Stowe. I have warm memories of "Forever Amber" by Kathleen Winsor, and "Gone with the Wind" by Margaret Mitchell. My preferred authors are Richard

Wright, Upton Sinclair, Thornton Wilder, Erskine Caldwell and Frank Slaughter. I like the latter particularly because in his book he brings out the spirit of devotion and sacrifice. As a general rule American literature is not mature enough; it is rather childish.

Among Europeans my preferences are: Charles Dickens, A.J. Cronin, and Thackery. That is because they realize true human values.

As for the politicians I like Abraham Lincoln who really accomplished something. I hate Roosevelt because he let everything go at Yalta (and now we have to pay for the consequences). I like Kennedy because he is a Roman Catholic as I am. I like Cardinal Spellman not just because he is Catholic, but because of his book "The Risen Soldier." I hate Joe Louis. I hate Woodrow Wilson because he was a man who ran away from his responsibilities (having promoted the League of Nations, he didn't want America to be a member). Among American women I like Harriet Beecher Stowe, Anne Lindberg, and Eleanor Roosevelt (she has to make up for her husband's mistakes).

Mr. Higgins, you asked me to say a prayer with you for Mark. I assure you that I pray for him constantly. Note that I am basically a Roman Catholic (in spite of my admiration for Albert Schweitzer). Mark had perhaps a different religion from mine, but he was probably a Christian as I am. It is the same Christ who died for the redemption of all of us. The first thing that I did was to have a Mass said for Mark's soul. I still, and will continue to, pray for him. I firmly believe also that he in Heaven will intervene for me so that I do not run off the narrow Christian road.

Mr. Higgins, please excuse me for calling you "mister" when I should perhaps say "papa." How many children have you?

If it is not inconvenient for you, I wish you would send me a little photograph of him. I want to fix Mark in my memory. I will send you a little picture of me. Perhaps someday we will meet each other. The proverb says only mountains will never move to meet each other.

If you wish to answer me, write in English. I have an English friend who will translate for me. I see that you have made great effort to write to me in French. I am writing to you in French and hope that you can understand me. I could write to you in English; however, it would be as you wish. Only I do not want to make it difficult for you.

*I even wrote Dr. Schweitzer to tell him about Mark's terrible death. The doctor has not answered me yet. I hope for an answer in several days.*

*I know that you have great sorrow. I do not ask you to forget it, but to overcome it. Perhaps in the love that you have for your dear son, you will find the necessary courage to overcome this grief. There is in this life one part for joy and one part for suffering.*

*I thank you very deeply for your gift.*

Passialis added a handwritten post-script:

*Mark had to die. But Providence wanted him to find death in Kasongo where he would find someone to assist him. May God's will be done.*

# Bibliography

**Books:**

Anderson, Erica, *The World of Albert Schweitzer*, Harper & Brothers, New York, 1955

---, *The Schweitzer Album*, Harper & Row, New York, 1965

Berman, Dr. Edgar, *In Africa With Schweitzer*, New Horizon Press, Far Hills, New Jersey, 1986

Brabazon, James, *Albert Schweitzer: A Biography*, Syracuse University Press, 2000

Braceland, Francis J., *The Institute of Living: The Hartford Retreat*; The Institute of Living, Hartford, Conn., 1972

Butcher, Tim, *Blood River: The Terrifying Journey through The World's Most Dangerous Country*; Grove Press, New York, 2008

Cousins, Norman, *Albert Schweitzer's Mission: Healing and Peace*, W. W. Norton & Company, New York and London, 1985

Cousins, Norman, *Dr. Schweitzer of Lambaréné*, Harper and Brothers, New York, 1960

Devlin, Larry, *Chief of Station, Congo: Fighting the Cold War in a Hot Zone*; Perseus Books Group, New York, 2007

Fernandez, James W., *The Sound of Bells in a Christian Country: in Quest of the Historical Schweitzer,* in The Massachusetts Review, Vol. 5, No. 3, Spring 1964

Fisher, James T., *Dr. America: The Lives of Thomas A. Dooley*, University of Massachusetts Press, Amherst, 1997

Franck, Frederick, *My Days With Albert Schweitzer: A Lambaréné Landscape*, Henry Holt And Company New York, 1992

Galvez, William, *Che in Africa*, Ocean Press, Melbourne and New York, 1999

Goldwyn, Robert M., *The Goldwyn Diary of November and December 1960 at the Albert Schweitzer Hospital, Lambaréné, Gabon*

Gerald, John Bart, *A Thousand Thousand Mornings*, (fiction) The Viking Press, New York, 1963

Helmreich, Jonathan E., *United States Relations with Belgium and The Congo, 1940-1960*; University of Delaware Press, 1998

Jilek-Aall, Louise, *Working With Dr. Schweitzer: Sharing his Reverence for Life;* Hancock House Publishers, Surrey, British Columbia, 1990

Johnson, Robert Craig, *Heart of Darkness: the Tragedy of the Congo, 1960-67,* manuscript online, 1997

Kalb, Madeleine G., *The Congo Cables: The Cold War in Africa-From Eisenhower to Kennedy;* Macmillan Publishing Co, Inc., New York, 1982

Kingsolver, Barbara, *The Poisonwood Bible,* (fiction) Harper Collins, 1998

Longnecker, J. Hershey, *Memories of Congo: Tales of adventure and work in the heart of Africa* (www.jesuscares4.us/memories/MemoriesofCongo.htm)

McKnight, Gerald, *Verdict on Schweitzer: The Man Behind the Legend of Lambaréné,* The John Day Company, New York, 1964

Mendelsohn, Jack, *God, Allah and Ju Ju: Religion in Africa Today,* Beacon Press, Boston, 1962

Meredith, Martin, *The Fate Of Africa: From the Hopes of Freedom to the Heart of Despair, A History of Fifty Years of Independence,* Public Affairs, New York, 2005

Mercer, Charles, *Rachel Cade,* (fiction) G. P. Putnam's Sons, New York, 1956

Miller, David C., Spencer, Steven S., and White, Paul D., *Survey of Cardiovascular Disease among Africans in the Vicinity of the Albert Schweitzer Hospital in 1960,* in The American Journal of Cardiology, September 1962, pp. 432-446

Monahan, James, *Before I Sleep ... The Last Days of Tom Dooley,* Farrar, Straus and Company, 1961

Munz, Jo and Walter, *Albert Schweitzer's Lambaréné: A Legacy of Humanity for Our World Today,* Translated and Edited by Patti M. Marxsen, Penobscot Press, 2010

Neukirch, Siegfried, *My Journey to Albert Schweitzer: An Autobiography,* Trafford Publishing, Bloomington Indiana, Third Edition, 2010

Ostergaard-Christensen, L., *At Work with Albert Schweitzer,* The Beacon Press, Boston, 1962.

Pauling, Linus, correspondence with Frank Catchpool, Special Collections & Archives, Oregon State University, 1959

Pauling, Ava Helen, *Lambaréné, Africa travel diary. July 1959.* Oregon State University Library Special Collections

Prunier, Gerard, *Africa's World War,* Oxford University Press, 2009

Schweitzer, Albert, *On the Edge of the Primeval Forest,* A. & C. Black, Ltd., London, 1921

---, *Out of My Life and Thought*, Henry Holt and Company, Inc., 1933, New York

Shipp, Joseph C., M.D., *Medicine with Dr. Schweitzer*

Stearns, Jason, *Dancing in the Glory of Monsters*, Public Affairs Press, 2011

Tayler, Jeffrey, *Facing the Congo*, Three Rivers Press, New York, 2000

Verhaegen, Benoit, *Rebellions Au Congo* Volume II, Centre de Recherche et d'Information Socio-Politiques, Brussels, 1966

Vogel, Michelle, *Gene Tierney, A Biography*, McFarland & Company, Inc., Jefferson North Carolina and London, 2005

Waldron, D'Lynn, *The Secret In The Heart Of Darkness: The Sabotaged Independence of The Belgian Congo*; online manuscript, 2001

Wofford, Harris L., *Of Kennedys and Kings: Making Sense of the Sixties*, Farrar Straus Giroux, New York, 1980

## Interviews, emails and institutional archives:

Catchpool, Frank, letter to Linus Pauling, 1959, from Pauling archives

Fernandez, James and Renate, personal and phone interviews

Gerald, John Bart, Milton classmate emails

Gentle, Patricia Getz, interviews and emails

The Getty Research Institute, Special Collections, Los Angeles

Knowles, Alison, widow of Dick Higgins, phone interview

Neukirch, Siegfried, phone interview from Germany

Null, Elisabeth Higgins, numerous personal interviews and numerous emails

Presbyterian Historical Society Archives, Philadelphia, Pennsylvania

Scholz, John, Milton classmate emails and personal interviews

Schoenfeld, Eugene, phone interview

Syracuse University Libraries, Special Collections Research Center

Whitman, Randal L.; Milton classmate emails

## Periodicals:

*The Independent*, London, July 28, 2006

*Fine Art Connoisseur*, Arthur D. Hitner, November-December 2008, "A Regionalist Masterpiece Deconstructed"

*Life* Magazine, Oct. 31, 1960

*The New York Times*, various citations

*Time Magazine,* Oct. 31, 1960

*Victoria Advocate,* Mar. 18, 1960, "Dr. Schweitzer's Hospital Never Lacking in Patients," by Robert C. Ruark

*Worcester Telegraph & Gazette,* Mar. 3, 2010, "Deep Roots in Worcester"

*Washington Daily News,* Dec. 24, 1960

# Index

# Credits

Cover and p. 93- photo, Rev. Hal Bruce Dallke

p. vi - Africa map graphic designed by Peter Barnaba and Diler Haji

p. 3 and 13 - photos, Erica Anderson Collection, Special Collections Research Center, Syracuse University Libraries

p. 31 - photo, Sonja Miller Poteau

P. 40 - photo, Adriana Calles Eller Williams

p. 43 - photo, Higgins Armory Museum

p. 61 and 63 - photos, Milton Academy Yearbook, 1958

p. 81 and 196 - photos, Siegfried Neukirch

p. 140-141-143-144 - photos, Alfonsine Camerman

Appendix - exchange of correspondence between Carter Higgins and Lambros Passialis, © Archives Centrales Schweitzer Gunsbach

Photo on back cover - Eric Lutringer

For more information visit:

**www.oakhampress-againstthecurrent.com**

# THE AUTHORS

Clarinda Higgins holds a bachelor's degree in Eastern Studies from Smith College and a master's degree in education. She taught elementary school for 11 years and has worked as an environmental educator since 1986. She was recognized with the Gold Award by the National Science Teachers Association. She has served as curator for a historical society, authored numerous articles on shellfishing, serves as a board member of a conservation association and holds leadership positions in various civic and non-profit organizations. She has traveled widely in third-world countries seeking authentic experiences and understanding. In working on this book she led a four-person two-week expedition through western Gabon.

William G. Armstrong Jr., her husband, holds a degree in political science and journalism from Kent State University. He is a former writer for the Associated Press, assistant dean of a business school, and worked for more than two decades as a senior public relations executive in New York. He served as a U.S. Navy public affairs officer for 30 years, retiring with the rank of Captain. He has written several specialty books, including *Business, Media and the Law: The Troubled Confluence* (NYU Press) and *Just Wind: Tales of Two Pilots Under Pressure* (iUniverse), edited a bi-monthly magazine and written numerous columns, speeches and tidbits. He is a director of The Albert Schweitzer Fellowship.

∞∞